CONGREGATIONS IN

There are more than 300,000 religious congreg⟨…⟩ ⟨…⟩ States; these communities have more members and generate m⟨…⟩ ⟨…⟩cipation than any other set of voluntary organizations in American society. This picture of dynamism belies recent, prevailing scholarship that perceives a decline in traditional religious authority, in Americans' commitment to organized religion, and in religious institutions' level of public engagement. Penny Edgell Becker, in this pioneering comparative study of local congregations, argues that the case for decline – in community, in commitment, in public engagement – does not stand up to closer scrutiny.

Congregations in Conflict: Cultural Models of Local Religious Life examines the nature of American congregations as institutions, looking in particular at how they deal with conflict within their ranks, to gain insight into religious culture, or the moral order of local religious life. In detailed and well documented case studies of conflict in twenty-three congregations – including Protestant churches, Catholic parishes, and Jewish synagogues – Becker examines such factors as organizational processes, the extent and types of ties between church members, their shared understandings about mission and identity, and level of public commitment. From these factors, the author develops four models of local religious cultures, each of which emphasizes different aspects of the mission imperatives that broadly characterize American religion – to reproduce a historic faith, to provide a caring community of believers, and to witness. Contrary to many academic accounts of general trends in American religion, at the local level Becker finds vital "public religion": congregations that provide caring and support for members, service to the local community, and important arenas for moral debate and public activism.

Penny Edgell Becker is Assistant Professor of Sociology at Cornell University. She is co-editor of *Contemporary American Religion: An Ethnographic Reader* (1997), is a contributing author of *Sacred Companies: Organized Aspects of Religion and Religious Aspects of Organization* (1997), and has published in the journals *Religion and American Culture* and *Social Problems*.

CONGREGATIONS IN CONFLICT

Cultural Models of Local Religious Life

PENNY EDGELL BECKER
Cornell University

CAMBRIDGE
UNIVERSITY PRESS

PUBLISHED BY THE PRESS SYNDICATE OF THE UNIVERSITY OF CAMBRIDGE
The Pitt Building, Trumpington Street, Cambridge, United Kingdom

CAMBRIDGE UNIVERSITY PRESS
The Edinburgh Building, Cambridge CB2 2RU, UK   http://www.cup.cam.ac.uk
40 West 20th Street, New York, NY 10011-4211, USA   http://www.cup.org
10 Stamford Road, Oakleigh, Melbourne 3166, Australia

First published 1999

Printed in the United States of America

Typeface Garamond 3 11/13 pt. *System* Macintosh [BTS]

*A catalog record for this book is available from
the British Library.*

Library of Congress Cataloging-in-Publication Data is available.
ISBN 0 521 59444 8 hardback
0 521 59462 6 paperback

To my parents, June and Tom Edgell, and my husband, David Edgell Becker,
for all that matters

CONTENTS

TABLES

ACKNOWLEDGMENTS

Formally acknowledging support and help is one of my favorite scholarly conventions. It belies the romantic image of the lone scholar and reminds us that research is a social process, done in the shaping context of specific communities and networks.

My deepest thanks go to those people in Oak Park, River Forest, and Forest Park, Illinois, who cooperated so generously in this research, sharing their time and their stories with me, an outsider.

This research was supported in part by a dissertation fellowship from the Louisville Institute for the Study of Protestantism in American Culture, funded by the Lilly Endowment. I was able to extend my field-work and take part in an enjoyable period of collaborative research while employed as a research assistant for the Congregations in Changing Communities Project, directed by Nancy Ammerman at Emory University and funded by the Lilly Endowment through the Institute for the Study of Economic Culture at Boston University.

The personal and intellectual debts that accrue over several years of work are too numerous to count. I have always felt that personal debts are best repaid in kind, but I do want to thank publicly my husband, David, for all of the practical ways he showed his love and support, like proof-reading the manuscript, and all of the less instrumental but equally important ways.

The encouragement of good friends made the long process of research and writing less lonely; thanks to Shoshanah Feher, Nancy Eiesland, Elfriede Wedam, Bonnie Lindstrom, and Anne Mini, all fellow travelers through graduate school and beyond.

Many colleagues took the time to give me helpful feedback on all or part of the manuscript, including Dan Olson, Rhys Williams, Charles Bidwell, Steve Tipton, Fred Kniss, Christian Smith, Heather Haveman,

David Strang, Sid Tarrow, Larry Moore, Robert Wuthnow, and Nancy Ammerman. Steve Warner, Elisabeth Clemens, and Kevin Christiano generously took the time to give me detailed comments on the entire manuscript. Ed Laumann reminded me early in the research to think not only about what tears groups apart but also about what brings them together. Grant Blank, Steve Ellingson, Harriet Morgan, Dick Flory, and Pamela Quiroz were all members of a faithful dissertation study group and supportive friends who suffered through many iterations of these ideas, including the most clumsy early ones. My sincere thanks to all of these people for helping me to achieve some critical distance and pushing me to answer inconvenient questions. Presenting at the Culture and Society Workshop at the University of Chicago has greatly enhanced this project and many others.

Some have served in the important role of mentor over the years. First thanks to Bob Wuthnow, who encouraged a love of ideas and research at a critical turning point in my life, providing an important example of scholarly excellence and commitment. To Martin Riesebrodt and Martin Marty, my appreciation for the constructive critique, goodwill, and encouragement that you have brought to all of our interactions. To Nancy Ammerman and Phyllis Moen, my deepest respect and gratitude for everything. Finally and most of all, to Wendy Griswold: My heartfelt thanks for your unfailing integrity, for your support and encouragement through early years of "finding my voice," for your infectious love of ideas, and for your deep commitment to excellence. Working with you was always exciting and challenging.

May I someday be half as gracious and knowledgeable as those who have helped along the way. To them goes the credit for many of the work's strengths; any oversights are mine alone.

Penny Becker
Ithaca, NY
November 1998

I

"WHO WE ARE" AND
"HOW WE DO THINGS HERE":
LOCAL UNDERSTANDINGS OF MISSION
AND IDENTITY

Martha immediately took me back to her kitchen and fixed me a cup of coffee. It was late August 1991, and I had spent the spring and summer doing research on Oak Park and its two neighboring villages, River Forest and Forest Park. I had been reading both local papers, spending time at the libraries and the historical society office, and I had a list of local restaurants where the managers did not mind if I spent hours when they were not busy, drinking coffee and taking up table space with my notes. The ice cream shop on Chicago Avenue had become a favorite. I had interviewed community leaders and informants, including one reporter on the local paper who grew up in Oak Park and spent most of one summer afternoon in the bagel shop at the center of town, chain-smoking and telling me about the community's history and politics.

I had just begun interviewing members of Martha's church, Hope Episcopal, the first congregation out of twenty-three in which I would conduct interviews. I would find out that many of the people I interviewed preferred talking in the kitchen, and this was particularly true of women like Martha.[1] In her sixties, Martha is a retired widow who has lived in Oak Park for over thirty years. She has been both a homemaker and a professional woman, and for many years an active member and leader in Hope Episcopal Church. She is thin and tall, and her straight dark hair, bobbed short, has a little gray. She is energetic and friendly. Once I was settled with a cup of coffee, she took a seat next to me at the kitchen table and asked me all about my research and my plans for the future. She seemed to be both practical and fun, and I found myself liking her more and more as we talked, relaxing in the big, sunny kitchen.

Her church had been going through a difficult time, and as the interview unfolded, she told me about it, growing more serious as she went along. Eventually, I would get eight different versions of this conflict from the people I interviewed in this church, although most agreed on a few basics. The conflict began after the new pastor came a couple of years ago. Several incidents would be mentioned in different combinations: conflicts over a moveable altar, over how a

I

funeral was conducted, over ministry to AIDS-stricken members, over finances, over administrative procedures.

Martha told me easily, clearly, about the course of events. She could talk in some detail about who was on which side, but she was unable to say why there had been no resolution, why the conflict kept cropping up again. She said, "We don't have the tools, we don't have the skills, to deal with conflict constructively." But this struck me as odd; if any group would have the skills to handle conflict, it should be this congregation full of highly educated people in business, management, the professions, people with what sociologists call "human capital," who might well have had specific training in management, even in mediation, that ought to help resolve things here.[2]

When I asked Martha if she could tell me what the cause of the conflict was, she paused. Then she told me about a meeting she had gone to several weeks ago, the annual evaluation meeting for the rector.[3] She has gone to the church for many years and thought she knew the place very well. But as several people got up to talk about the church and the problems it had been having, she had a sudden and upsetting realization, thinking to herself, "I wasn't going to the same church they were."

At the time, I was not sure quite what she meant. But as I talked to more people in this church, I would come to understand that, while the trouble began when the new pastor came, it was essentially a fight between two groups of lay leaders and core members. One group seemed to take for granted that their church is primarily about having a place to worship, about long-term friendships and family-like attachments, about people who know you and your family and could be counted on for help in times of crisis. Most of these people valued a traditional approach to doctrine and ritual practice. Many of them would tell me that the new pastor was himself the problem, saying with disapproval that his style did not fit with the congregation, that he would sometimes be uncaring and flippant, telling jokes during the sermon, and saying radical things just to provoke a reaction. These members were particularly upset about the moveable altar and the last-minute changes to the format of the funeral service. Many were long-term members, but there were quite a few newcomers in this group, as well.

For others, including Martha, the church is primarily about providing leadership in the community, about interpreting doctrine and ritual tradition in light of contemporary social reality and current members' needs, about taking a stand on issues like AIDS and gay and lesbian rights. For this group, the church is about service and witnessing to the community about the virtue of tolerance and the importance of diversity. This group was intrigued when the pastor experimented with the moveable altar, and they enjoyed the challenging and thought-provoking things that he said. They liked his jokes. Some of these people were long-term members, but many were newcomers, having joined in the last two to three years.

These two groups were not cleanly divided by length of membership, although more of the newcomers liked the pastor than did not. Ideology was not the divide between them; in interviews, they all self-identified as liberal or moderate and had similar views about ideologically salient issues like abortion and the role of homosexuals in the church. The new pastor has been more sympathetic with the views of the second group, and his arrival triggered a series of conflicts, opportunities for people to articulate, and thus to define and sharpen, their different underlying assumptions about "who we are" and "how we do things here."

Martha told me that she thought that part of the problem was a kind of Episcopalian rigidity that made compromise difficult. But fieldwork in twenty-two other congregations belonging to fifteen different denominations (Protestant, Catholic, and Jewish), as well as general experience in community organizations, convinced me that what was going on in Martha's church is not unique to Episcopalians. Faced with conflict that seemed to grow more acrimonious with no end in sight, many members, including those not so strongly committed to either group, would decide to leave, some attending other Episcopalian churches in the area.[4] Eventually, this conflict would reduce the Sunday attendance at Hope Episcopal from about 250 to under 100, and in 1995, when I followed up, the church, with a new pastor, was only just beginning to recover its attendance, along with some sense of optimism about the future.

From Conflict to Local Culture

In the process of understanding the patterns of conflict in the congregations in and around Oak Park, my interview with Martha was something to which I kept returning. There are various ways to interpret conflict, and as I learned more about Hope Episcopal, I kept trying to fit Martha's story, and the stories the other members told, into these preexisting interpretive frameworks, to see which one was the best fit. Was this really a conflict over ideas and symbols – the moveable altar, the proper way to conduct a service? Or was it really about power, perhaps a struggle between the pastor and the lay members over authority and control? Or was it at heart a fight between old-timers and newcomers and the accompanying generational transition in congregational leadership? All of these frameworks captured some partial truth about the conflict at Hope Episcopal, but each one left important things out, too.

The situation became even more complicated when I went beyond Hope Episcopal to consider conflicts in the twenty-three different congregations I had studied. Two Catholic parishes, two synagogues, and nineteen Protestant congregations from a wide range of denominations, these congregations were chosen to achieve some scope for comparison along dimensions identified in previous studies as relevant for conflict – size, polity type, and a liberal or conservative religious orientation. "Small" congregations are roughly 150 members or less, with an administrative structure revolving around the pastor and a small group of lay leaders, while large congregations have more than 150 members and a more formal administrative structure with more boards and committees (Rothauge 1990). I divide polity into "congregational" and "hierarchical," with the latter containing both presbyterian and episcopal polities as described by Moberg (1962). Congregations were labeled "liberal" or "conservative" depending on how the pastor and the majority of the lay people I spoke to (roughly ten per congregation) characterized the congregation's religious orientation (see Table 4 in Chapter 2). Over eighteen months, from late 1991 to early 1993, I conducted over 230 interviews plus participant-observation of services and the review of congregational documents like sermons, annual reports, newsletters, minutes of meetings, bulletins, and histories. Chapter 2 and Appendix A contain a much longer discussion of why size, polity, and religious orientation were the relevant dimensions and how the congregations were chosen and the fieldwork conducted.

How to make sense of conflicts in such a diverse group of congregations? In going through interviews and fieldnotes, I found that I kept returning to Martha's description of the rector's evaluation meeting, running up against someone for whom Hope Episcopal was "a different church." As May (1980) points out in her excellent study of divorce in the United States at the turn of the century, conflict can be the result of a violation of shared expectations, or conflict can result from the clash of two fundamentally different sets of expectations for behavior. The former is *within-frame* conflict and can be resolved by routine kinds of processes that enforce compliance with agreed-upon expectations. The latter is *between-frame* conflict, which is more difficult to resolve because the divergent expectations include different ideas about appropriate decision-making processes.[5] Between-frame conflicts in small groups are often fundamentally about identity, an attempt to forge an answer to the questions, "Who are we?" and "How do we do things here?"[6]

When I realized this, I began to think of conflicts like the one at Hope Episcopal, and several of the other congregations, as identity conflicts. Doing so enabled me to integrate the insights from various perspectives on conflict. Identity conflicts involve both power and symbols; they can be understood as conflicts over the power to symbolize different under-

4

standings of the congregation's identity and to institutionalize these understandings in very concrete ways, including the liturgy, the programs, the ways of making decisions, and the norms of interaction that, taken together, form the overall tenor of congregational life. This is why they are initiated by those with the most commitment to the congregation – the pastor and the most involved lay leaders. There was no need to choose between an explanation of conflict based on symbols and one based on power or a struggle for control, because both were caught up in actual conflict events as they unfolded in these congregations.

But not all of the conflicts I encountered were as severe as the one at Hope Episcopal. In most congregations, the conflicts were less intractable; they involved smaller groups of people, they did not cause the same kind of widespread emotional upheaval, and they were more routinely resolved. How could those smaller conflicts be related to identity? Martha's story, I realized, is about two groups of people whose different visions of mission and identity for the church include very different ideas about religious authority and member commitment. Most other explanations for conflict look at factors like the size of the group and its formal structure to explain variations in authority and commitment, which are in turn linked to variations in group processes like conflict and decision making.[7] Martha's story, along with similar ones that kept emerging from interviews with other members, led me to realize that, instead of using underlying variables like size and organizational structure as a proxy for authority and commitment, as previous studies have tended to do, I could study local culture as an expression of the locally negotiated understandings about appropriate styles of authority and commitment (cf. Coser 1956). If different local understandings of mission and identity explain why severe conflicts take the form that they do, then perhaps, I began to think, those local understandings also hold the key to interpreting the regularities and patterns in more normal or within-frame conflicts.[8]

Throughout the course of the fieldwork, then, the interpretive focus changed, and this became a comparative study of local religious cultures and how they are constitutive of but also constituted by organizational structures, like size and polity, and practices, like conflict and decision making. This change is a move away from thinking about a set of underlying variables that have a uniform effect on the organizations within a social space and toward specifying a limited set of organizational types, shaped by historical and institutional factors, within which the relationships between things like size, polity, authority, and decision making may be differently structured.[9] It is also a shift away from a methodology of "freezing" social process and making the analytical choice to designate conflict as an outcome toward looking at both the processes by which conflicts are made and the effects that conflicts in turn have on local identity and local practices. This shift was greatly influenced by my reading of Giddens (1984) on the importance of studying the processes by which actors in specific contexts reproduce or change social structure through their interactions.

This change in focus allowed me to better carry out some of my initial goals, including the goal of generating a better understanding of conflict in local religious organizations, especially the kind of serious conflict that Martha described in her church. A better understanding, I thought, should improve on existing studies in very specific ways. It should go beyond a laundry list of the possible causes of conflict. It should emphasize organizations and organizational processes over latent or potential conflicts in individual attitudes. It ought to analyze a congregation's whole pattern of conflict, including what issues people fight over, how they frame those issues, typical processes by which conflict plays out and is resolved, how serious or divisive conflicts are, and what effect they have on the congregation in the long run.[10]

Chapter 2 describes in more detail why the three factors identified in previous studies – size, polity, and cultural orientation – did not allow me to develop that better explanation of conflict that I had been seeking. While having some effect on the kinds of issues that caused conflict and the frequency of conflict, they did not allow me to explain why some issues are understood differently in different congregations, or why and where different kinds of moral arguments are used. They did not allow me to understand differences in conflict processes, including the role of the pastor, typical kinds of decision-routines, or favored kinds of solutions. They did not help me to understand why four of the twenty-three congregations exhibited a particularly severe set of conflicts that resulted, in three cases, in the exit of a large group of members.

In addition to changing the way in which I approached the original goals of the study, this change in focus also raised some entirely new issues, as I became interested in understanding more about these local religious cultures than just their relationship to conflict. I became interested in the content of the religious cultures themselves. There are over 300,000 congregations in the United States that provide members with a place of worship and fellowship.[11] Which ones foster the habits of caring and civic tolerance that Putnam and others find to be necessary for vital demo-cratic communities?[12] Which ones foster a more publicly engaged form of religion, and which ones are more privatized? Conflict, initially the sole focus, became a window into these larger questions of the shared and diver-gent expectations about legitimate goals and ways of doing things, or what might be called the moral order of local religious life.[13]

This is a particularly important set of questions in the sociology of reli-gion right now, because one influential branch of recent scholarship has developed a dominant narrative of religious change in the United States over the last forty to fifty years. While various terms have been used – pri-vatization, voluntarism, increasing individualism – several scholars have concluded that the civic capacity of American religion has declined in the last half of this century. They point variously to more individualism in religious discourse, to more switching among congregations over the indi-vidual member's life-course, to the declining legitimacy of pastoral author-ity, and to declining denominational loyalty. They interpret these trends as an indication that American religion has become less publicly engaged and that the very basis for any commitment to organized religion is being eroded. There has been very little comparative study of congregations, however, to assess whether trends in individual religiosity as reported in surveys or perceived changes in religious authority by denominational leaders have actually resulted in congregations that are less engaged in their local communities or in local religious cultures that are more priva-tized and inwardly focused.

This book is structured around a central argument: that congregations develop distinct cultures that comprise local understandings of identity and mission and that can be understood analytically as bundles of core tasks and legitimate ways of doing things. The primary thesis is that these local religious cultures are not completely idiosyncratic, but that they come in patterns shaped by the larger institutional environment that limits their range of variation. I call these patterns *congregational models*. In twenty-three congregations, I did not find twenty-three different congre-gational models; rather, I found four basic types: *house of worship, family, community*, and *leader* models. A few congregations, like Martha's, had two well-defined groups of people who operated from the assumptions of dif-ferent models; in most congregations, however, a single dominant model structured the public culture.

The secondary thesis is that the narrative of religious decline and increasing individualism has missed something important by failing to look seriously at local religious cultures. The four congregational models I found in this community do, in various ways, stress tolerance and foster caring relationships. They promote engagement with local civic life, ranging from compassionate outreach to the poor to activism on social and political issues. This suggests that an analysis of changes in religious discourse and individual religiosity needs to be supplemented by an analysis of the organizations and the institutional forms that shape religious participation, if we want to develop a better understanding of how social changes affect the relationship between religion and public life in the United States at the level of the local community.

In addition, I want to suggest that an institutional approach is useful in studying local culture, or the culture of individual groups and organizations. Congregational models are a specific example, within the institutional field of American religion, of a more general phenomenon, what Paul DiMaggio (1991) has called the *institutional model* of the group or organization. Rooted in an understanding of local culture as a negotiated order built up over time and through interaction, this analysis nevertheless brings a different lens – an institutional lens – to bear on the study of local culture, something that has previously been examined through a lens that foregrounds particular, idiosyncratic detail.[14]

Local Culture Through an Institutional Lens

In any field there are usually one or two paradigmatic studies that set the terms for the development of future work. A paradigmatic study of local culture that has influenced anthropology, history, sociology, and cultural studies is Clifford Geertz's (1973) description of the Balinese cockfight. Geertz describes the cockfight as a complicated social drama, a ritualized performance where every man knows and re-creates his place in the taken-for-granted order of Balinese society. And he evokes it beautifully. When you read Geertz's description, you can almost picture yourself there, straining with the others to get a view of the fifty-foot ring, seeing the fighting roosters tear each other apart – and running away when the authorities break it up.

In American sociology, the book *With the Boys*, Gary Alan Fine's (1987) study of how Little League teams build a unique social identity through the members' interactions, kept local culture on the intellectual agenda of cultural and organizational analysis for a new generation of scholars. In contrast to the cockfight, Little League may seem tame; no blood and feathers here. But the reader of Fine's study gets the same sense of watching as the members come to define themselves and be understood by others as a certain kind of team. They do this not only through the sport itself, but through all of the behind-the-scenes interactions that build up common understandings of "who we are" and "how we do things here" – local culture.

Local culture has often been studied this way.[15] In effect, anthropologists and sociologists have answered the question, "why study local culture?" by examining it as the *locus of social processes through which common understandings of group or organizational identity are built up and maintained over time.* These accounts are by definition descriptive, and the plausibility of the account is often judged by aesthetic criteria. Is the description "thick," or rich or elegant or compelling?[16] Is there internal consistency? Fine captures the emphasis on the particular and the idiosyncratic that are the hallmarks of this approach when he coins the term "idioculture," defining it as

> a system of knowledge, beliefs, behaviors, and customs shared by members of an interacting group to which members can refer, and that serve as the basis for further interaction. . . . This approach stresses the localized nature of culture, implying that it . . . can be a particularistic development of any group (1987:125).

There have been more studies that document the extent of such uniqueness than ones that specify its limits.

Surely the members of the Little League teams that Fine studied were free to come up with their own local culture that was negotiated, idiosyncratic, and particular. But how far could they go in defining their own identity? Their understanding of their own team might incorporate a range of attitudes toward winning and losing. But if they decided that baseball itself were not worth playing, how long would they remain a Little League team? Can one imagine a Little League team in which members understand their *primary objective* to be making money, housing the homeless, kayaking, or robbing liquor stores, instead of playing baseball?

The twenty-three congregations I studied all have strong idiocultures. These are comprised in part of narratives about formative events, leaders, and founding families. But they also have more unexpected elements. For example, when I asked the pastor of one UCC[17] church about what brings his congregation together, he laughed, and then he told me about their "donut program." They make and sell donuts at the weekly farmers' market. Everyone I talked to in this congregation spoke about "our donuts." Sometimes they smiled or even laughed, but they mentioned this spontaneously and spoke of it as something special. No other congregation does anything like this, they repeatedly told me. Besides, getting up in the middle of the night to make donuts and then stand in the cold morning air to sell them breeds a certain camaraderie.

Donuts are a part of this church's idioculture. In other congregations, the idioculture includes stained glass windows designed by an important artist or stories of the heyday in the 1950s when the Sunday School had over 1,000 people. Two congregations had stories of near-death, when the congregation almost shut its doors due to lack of members, and resurrection, to a present with several hundred members and an impressive annual budget. In short, each of these twenty-three congregations exhibits the richness and variety that one would expect in the culture of living communities, and the idea of idioculture is a useful one to employ in understanding some things about them.

It is no wonder, then, that the emerging field of congregational studies has concentrated on this idiosyncratic approach to local religious culture. Local congregations are places where individuals come together to form, interpret, and enact their religious commitments. The congregations where people find what they need to meet a variety of needs, and that people join for a variety of reasons, are not simple aggregations of individual preferences; nor are they straightforward reproductions of larger religious traditions. In congregations individual commitments and larger traditions are combined in ongoing, creative ways. A large and growing body of work develops this view, showing congregations to be crucibles where individual ideas, beliefs, and commitments interact with religious traditions, changing both and forming robust local cultures.[18] Fine (1984) gives this view of organizational culture the label "negotiated order," a term that evokes both the regularities of group life and the processes that reproduce it.

But if the idea of idioculture is helpful in understanding some things about congregations or other organizations, I argue that it is only partial. There are other things we might want to know about the culture of a group or organization that are not captured well by the emphasis on rich idiosyncrasy that has developed in the typical approach to local cultures. The emphasis on the particular and the idiosyncratic provides only one analytical lens through which to view local culture. Like any lens, it captures some things clearly in the foreground and makes other features appear more remote or indistinct. In short, while it is possible to identify the particular within the culture of a group or organization, it is also possible to identify patterns that are common across similar groups and organizations, bundles of cultural elements – ideas, symbols, programs, habits, ritual practices – grouped together in recurring ways.

I argue that the bundles of understandings about mission and identity in local cultures make a difference in what sociologists call organizational process and outcomes, or, in more common language, how decisions are made, how conflicts arise and are resolved, how goals are set and programs developed. In doing so, I am making use of a set of ideas from an approach to organizational theory known as the *new institutionalism*. Institutional analysis can provide another, different kind of analytical lens through which to view local culture.[19] This lens allows us to identify features that the local cultures of similar groups and organizations have in common – art museums, congregations, families, or Little League teams. Taking some insights from institutional analysis can help us understand things about local culture that an idiographic approach cannot.

In sociology, the new institutionalists have developed a comparative approach to studying culture in organizations that has the potential to span levels of analysis from individual behavior to society. Institutional analysis also has the potential to shed light on two issues at the heart of this study – what the local cultures of organizations within the same institutional field have in common, and how culture influences organizational process, including conflict. To date, there have been few studies that develop this potential. For example, how institutions shape conflict within organizations has remained virtually unexplored, despite other work that suggests that conflict is governed by just such taken-for-granted notions of "who we are" and "how we do things here" that institutional analysis is ideally suited to examine.[20] There are several reasons for this. Much of the "new" institutionalism gives primacy to a supraorganizational approach. When analysis is done at the organizational level, a major focus has been on the legitimating or ceremonial role of institutional culture vis-à-vis powerful outsiders, not on how institutions shape internal processes.[21]

Nevertheless, there has been some work that addresses how institutions shape an entire bundle of ideas about organizational goals and legitimate means of achieving them and so lead to different patterns of behavior in organizations. DiMaggio (1991) identifies two different institutional models of the art museum, one more elite and the other more democratic. Galaskiewicz (1985, 1991) analyzes two different corporate roles in an urban grants economy. Fligstein's (1990) work on "conceptions of control" identifies different bundles of ideas about the nature and purpose of the organization arising in the sales and marketing operations of large corporate firms.

All three authors take an explicitly institutional approach to the culture of the organization, and all three find common patterns among the organizations within a given institutional field that shape and delimit the ways in which people think about the organization's goals and legitimate means of achieving them. An art museum may have an idioculture, but its director is not free to institutionalize a completely idiosyncratic view of the museum's purpose and how to carry it out. If she attempted this, the museum would lose legitimacy. More importantly, it would lose public attendance and outside funding (see Alexander 1996).

The congregational models that I analyze are like DiMaggio's models of the art museum. They are not completely idiosyncratic; they are shaped by common expectations in their institutional environment about what a congregation might and should be like. However, they are not some simple or straightforward imprinting of a larger denominational culture or religious tradition. Congregational models are, in effect, the constitutive rules for the formation of local religious cultures; they are legitimate bundles of core goals or tasks and the means of achieving them (cf. Sewell 1992). In *With the Boys*, Fine points out that local cultures are built up over time out of elements – jokes, stories, rituals, donuts – that are available, triggered, functional, and appropriate.[22] In his later work, Fine (1996a, 1996b) moves toward an analysis that links the formations of idiocultures to features of the larger institutional environment, including occupational rhetorics and discourses about the nature and purposes of work. I will argue that congregational models in particular, and institutional models in general, are the sets of rules within a given institutional field that determine which bundles of elements go together and, therefore, which ones are available, functional, and appropriate, yielding a stable number of organizational types.

House of Worship, Family, Community, Leader

When I studied these twenty-three congregations, I only found one place known for its donuts. But I did not find twenty-three different approaches to mission, nor did I find twenty-three different sets of ideas about what local congregations in general ought to be like. Rather, I found four different bundles of ideas, ways of doing things, discourses, and taken-for-granted assumptions about "who we are" and "how we do things here." I found four different patterns of local culture, or congregational models. Nineteen of the twenty-three congregations had institutionalized one of these four models as a dominant model; congregations with the same model showed similar patterns of within-frame conflict. Four of the twenty-three congregations were in a period of transition from one model to another; each of these showed the same kind of serious, between-frame conflict that Hope Episcopal experienced.

It is possible to think of the congregation primarily as a provider of religious goods and services to individuals – worship, religious education, and rituals like weddings and funerals that mark important life events. I call this a *house of worship* model. Congregations that have adopted this understanding concentrate on the core tasks of worship and religious education. The primary goals are to provide an intimate and uplifting worship experience and to train members, especially children, in the denomination's heritage, doctrine, and rituals. These congregations make limited demands on member loyalty and time and assume a segmented form of attachment, where religious involvement remains relatively separate from other areas of members' lives. Decisions are made by clergy, paid staff, or committees. A good contemporary metaphor might be of a specialty religious store where you go for specific goods – a religious Crate and Barrel, say. A more historically sensitive metaphor would be that of a temple – a ritual center that may not be connected with nonreligious elements and activities in people's lives.

In some congregations, the dominant model is that of a *family*, a place where worship, religious education, and providing close-knit and supportive relationships for members are the core tasks. These are the three things that are done well, that people are proud of, and that are valued above all of the other activities of the congregation. Members of these congregations know and care about each others' lives. They are patriarchal, in the sense used by Riesebrodt (1993): Informal, personal connections and length of membership are more important bases of authority than are formal structures or positions, with the congregation being run by a small group of long-time lay leaders who are all good friends and belong to extended family networks.

One can also understand the congregation as a *community* of intimate ties and shared values. Such an understanding does place value on worship and religious education and on providing members with a feeling of belonging and family-like attachment. But it also deems it important that the policies and programs of the congregation express the values and commitments of the members regarding social issues. Figuring out how to interpret and apply shared values is the most important communal enterprise. Their chief form of witness is in living their values, institutionalizing them in local congregational life. If a house of worship is like a religious store and family congregations are like patriarchies, community congregations are like democracies, with more emphasis on formal and open decision-making routines that include all members.

It is also possible to think of the congregation primarily as a *leader*. Worship and education are important here, too. And so is expressing members' values. But leader congregations are different than community congregations in three respects. First, the values that they express spring more directly from the official tenets of their denomination or tradition and less from members' own interpretations and life experiences. Second, their view of witness is more activist, having less to do with living their values and more to do with changing the world beyond the congregation, engaging in political and social action beyond their own four walls. Third, intimacy is less valued here as a public good. Providing members with intimate connections or a feeling of belonging are low priorities in this understanding, although here too some individuals can find close friends by seeking them out. These congregations are participative, but they are more like branches of a social movement organization, with a strong mission, than like democracies, which have a more diffuse mission.

Congregational models are historically bounded "models of" and "models for" a congregation, in the form of a set of core tasks. But the core tasks of the different models are not local or idiosyncratic ideas. They are religious imperatives broadly institutionalized in the field of American congregational religion – *religious reproduction* through worship and education, *building religious community* within the congregation, and *witness* to outsiders. These imperatives have appeared in different combinations in different historical periods, according to Holifield's (1994) discussion of the history of congregational forms. The four congregational models found in this community define ways in which these twenty-three congregations approach these core religious-institutional tasks today, in this community (see Table 1).

Table 1. *The core tasks of the four congregational models*

Core Task	Congregational Model			
	House of Worship	Family	Community	Leader
Religious reproduction	Worship Religious education	Worship Religious education	Worship Religious education	Worship Religious education
Religious community	Intimacy is possible/ individual choice	Provide close, family-like attachments for most/all members	Provide close, family-like attachments for most/all members Community of values	Intimacy is possible/ individual choice Community of values
Religious witness	Presence in community is witness	Presence in community is witness (live our values)	Express members' values in policies and programs (live our values) Be a leader in community, denomination, or beyond (change the world)	Adopt pastor's or denomination's policies and

Not surprisingly, all four models emphasize religious reproduction. They all place importance on education, which reproduces the religious tradition, and worship, which is the local, communal enactment of the relationship of the believer to the sacred.[23] Waugh (1994) calls the congregation an institution of education and worship at the center of a religious community's life, and worship and education are central to each of the four congregational models.[24]

Congregations are by definition local communities of believers, and it is common for case studies of congregational life to emphasize that they are places where members find intimate personal connections and participate as "whole persons." Warner (1994) calls fellowship the "master function" of congregational life and uses a family metaphor to describe the intimacy of attachment within congregations. But my study shows what others have suggested – that such an emphasis on fellowship and intimate connection, while common in congregational life, is not distributed uniformly; instead, it receives more emphasis in some traditions, and in some congregations, than in others.[25]

The models also orient the congregations to the religious imperative of witnessing to their faith and tradition. The range of responses to that imperative can be characterized as "worshipping together is our witness" (family and house of worship models), "living our values is our witness" (community and leader models), and "being a leader in the community is our witness" (leader model). These are local enactments of mission orientations that are broadly institutionalized in American religious organizations and are particularly close to the "sanctuary," "civic," and "activist" mission orientations used by Mock (1992).[26]

The term "model" implies that ideas about a congregation come in bundles and are institutionalized in ways that broadly affect congregational life. It also implies the idea of moral order. Because congregational models are ideas about core tasks of the congregation and legitimate means of achieving them, they are an "is" that implies an "ought." This is similar to Jepperson's (1991) idea of institutions as "packaged social technologies" with accompanying sets of rules for their enactment. Douglas (1986) probably has the best discussion of how institutions imply a set of moral obligations, patterned relationships, and legitimate behaviors that come to be valued for their own sake. In general, institutions link specific programs, goals, and ways of doing things to larger conceptions of the good.[27]

The idea of a model also implies that congregational models are to culture what formal polity is to structure. Like Sewell's (1992) idea of a schema as something that organizes both ideal and material resources, these models constrain and shape programming, the distribution of resources, and the development of idiocultures.[28]

To call the models "institutional" indicates that they are taken for granted and unarticulated unless challenged. This is a sense of the word that the new institutionalists sometimes deemphasize, because they fear that older institutional analysis, in its emphasis on the taken-for-granted, sometimes implied that organizational culture is functional, unitary, and consensual.[29] However, it is possible to identify a pattern that is dominant in the public culture of the congregation – in discourse, symbols, and patterns of member interaction – without implying that there is perfect consensus or a completely unitary culture. It is possible that there would be emergent or residual models preferred by a small number of congregants. Dominant institutional patterns may persist and have effect despite disagreement or even opposition.[30] And in this case, it was possible to distinguish between nineteen congregations where there was indeed one dominant model and four where the dominant consensus was being actively challenged, showing that the same approach can help us to understand both how culture works as a taken-for-granted ground of activity and how it works as a resource for conscious, strategic, and referential action.

Finally, congregational models are institutional in another sense, that of being "institutionalized." They are not just common understandings, but they are manifest in policies and programs, in taken-for-granted ways of doing things, in sermon topics, in the interaction of members with each other and with visitors, and in the forms of liturgy and ritual, all of which fit together to provide an overall sense of identity and tenor of congregational life. When I interviewed members, they did not tell me, "Well, I believe we're really a house of worship," and then list all of the characteristics described in Table 1. Instead, they would tell me what their congregation is good at and what they are not good at, what programs are valued and cherished and what ones are not. They would say that their witness is their believing presence in the community, or that their witness involves eradicating racism and sexism from the community. These things repeatedly fell into the same limited set of bundles that I, for analytical reasons, call "models" of congregational life.

The Significance of Congregational Models

In Chapter 2, I describe the process of discovering patterns in the local cultures of these twenty-three congregations – patterns in their discourse and practice that I argue constitute four distinct congregational models. This discovery fundamentally changed the way in which I thought about what it means to conduct a comparative analysis of organizations and organizational processes. Initially interested in how underlying or structural variables like size and polity might influence processes and outcomes, I came to discover that the standard variables that sociologists use to capture variations in commitment and loyalty, in authority, and in mission and identity are not always good proxies for these.

Part of the significance of congregational models is in their discovery and in the argument that they serve as an important mediating level of analysis in two ways. They mediate between "underlying variables" like size and polity (formal structure) and group processes, by institutionalizing patterns of authority and commitment that are related to, but not determined by, these structural features of the organization. They also mediate between larger cultural formations – traditions, ideologies, discourses – and social action at the local level. I agree with Nee and Ingram (1998) about the importance of developing analyses that can examine the link between institutional culture and agency at the local level as the next step in developing a multilevel understanding of the relationship between social forms and social action. For these reasons, an expanded analysis of institutional models may prove to be useful in general and in other institutional fields.

In the nineteen congregations that had institutionalized one dominant cultural model, there was conflict mainly over the content of the model or conflict about the implications of the model for any given decision. In each kind of congregation – house of worship, family, community, leader – conflict exhibited a different pattern, but in no case was it either unresolvable or threatening to the health of the congregation as an organization or a community. This within-frame conflict was often painful, but it was usually amenable to being resolved by some previously existing organizational routine. Chapters 3–6 examine patterns of conflict in each of the four types of congregations. Rather than using congregational models as underlying variables, I develop an analysis in Chapters 3–6 that shows that within-frame conflict is a process that is constituted by congregational models and through which the models themselves can be reconstituted.

Chapter 7 discusses the transitional congregations. In these congregations, the serious, between-frame conflict is a process by which opposing models are articulated and through which the current dominant model is challenged. These congregations had conflicts that were more emotional, involved larger percentages of the members, and were harder to contain. Provisional decisions or solutions would hold only for a time, until a new event triggered the old conflict all over again. These between-frame conflicts were not over how to interpret and apply some shared understanding of mission and identity to particular situations; rather, they were more fundamental conflicts over the very nature of the congregation's identity and core tasks – over which congregational model to have in place.

Chapter 8 examines the utility of developing an institutional lens for the comparative study of group and organizational cultures in other fields. This chapter develops the argument that understanding how culture is firmly rooted in things like norms, core tasks and goals, and decision-making routines as well as in the symbolic and ritual life of the organization is a key step in analyzing the link between local group processes and larger institutional formations. This chapter also explores why there is a stable variation in institutional models in the American religious field and suggests other institutional fields in which the analysis of the variation in institutional models at different organizational levels might be a useful approach to analyzing the link between culture and group process.

Chapter 9 focuses on what was learned about these congregations as *religious* organizations. Scholars who have studied postwar American religion have constructed a lament for the decline of religious authority and commitment. Wuthnow (1988) uses the term "restructuring", while Roof and McKinney (1987) talk about voluntarism and Bellah et al. (1985) talk about increasing individualism. Despite some real differences in individual accounts, these and other studies comprise a body of influential work that, taken together, constructs a metanarrative about the declining significance of denominational attachment, increasing rates of member switching, the growth of an individual-expressive or personalistic style of commitment, and growing divisions between liberals and conservatives. This metanarrative rhetorically links this institutional restructuring to various forms of decline – in community, in public religion, in social capital.

These authors tend to rely on case studies and analyses of religious discourse rather than on comparative studies of authority and commitment in historically located religious organizations. This leads to a linear narrative about disembodied trends – increasing privatization, voluntarism, and individualism, all driven by ongoing modernization. These authors assume that liberal or mainstream religious groups are more affected by modernization than are conservative groups, but that no group is immune from its corrosive effects. They share a pessimistic view about the viability of religious tradition and traditional religious authority in the contemporary United States. Bellah, in particular, questions whether the entire rationale for participation in religious organizations and perpetuating traditional faiths is not eroding in our society. And while they note that religious participation is robust, these scholars question the depth or character of contemporary spirituality and commitment or the ability of private devotion to motivate public religion.

This comparative study of local congregations makes it clear that increasing voluntarism and individualism do *not* lead to one single pattern of local participation, to one reaction to religious authority and tradition, or to one style of member commitment. In Chapter 9, I discuss how voluntarism means, at the local level, the freedom to negotiate and implement a *limited range of local religious cultures* that have different implications for understanding the effects of an individual-expressive style of commitment on the organization of local religious life. Chapter 9 explores those implications in more detail, suggesting ways in which we might want to rethink our analysis of American religion as a public space and the forms of community and civic involvement that it fosters. Here, I join others whose work has begun to challenge the linear narrative of change that has structured earlier work and argue that the case for decline – in community, in commitment, in public engagement – needs closer scrutiny.

Notes

1. "Martha" is a pseudonym, as are all names of individuals and congregations. The names of the communities are real. This choice was made to protect the confidentiality of those who, in many cases, discussed with me sensitive aspects of their own histories and their congregations' conflicts. Identifying the communities was done to address the concerns of a growing number of sociological researchers who feel that not doing so presents two serious problems. First, it prevents other scholars from making comparative or follow-up studies. It also collapses what might be important distinctive features of a community's history and politics into "underlying variables" like size and demographics. See Warner (1988) Demerath and Williams (1992), Ammerman (1997a), and Eiesland (1998) for examples and discussion. See also Burawoy et al. (1991) for a more general discussion of the extended case study method and its engagement with real communities.
2. This is not meant to be an elitist statement, but rather an institutional one. Management and the professions are institutional locations for storing and

spreading specific techniques of conflict resolution, as witnessed in the prevalence of articles like "Conflict Resolution Skills for Supervisors," "How to Cope with Conflict Between the People who Work for You," and "Effective Team Management" (conflict management is listed as the single most important team management skill), just a few of the many articles revealed by a quick search of *ABI Inform*, which indexes business and professional journals. Managers and professionals think and talk about how to manage conflict and develop institutional repertoires for managing conflict that are widespread in training programs. For Martha to say that the people in her church do not have the skills or tools to manage conflict, then, is an indication of just how intractable she perceived this situation to have become.

3. "Rector" is the term for the head pastor of an Episcopalian parish.

4. One of these other churches is also included in this study. The pastor there told me that an important part of his parish's ministry over the last year or so was to provide what he called a "healing place" and a "refuge" for people fleeing the conflict at Hope Episcopal, especially those who were looking for warmth and intimacy in congregational life and a traditional worship service, all of which his small congregation provided. This congregation is discussed at length in Chapter 4.

5. One of the few empirical studies of this that is also a comparative study of organizations is the work of Hannan, Baron, and colleagues at Stanford University on conflict in high-tech firms in the Bay Area. For a longer discussion of the conflict that ensued when managers tried to alter the basic model of the employment relationship in these firms, see Hannan et al. (1996).

6. Cf. Goffman (1974:428ff.).

7. Hirschman's (1970) work, for example, indicates that conflict is influenced by who is willing and able to voice dissent and who is likely to exit when dissatisfied. Both of these behaviors (voice and exit) are influenced by the distribution of authority in the group and by the loyalty or commitment of the members.

8. Along with Victor Turner's (1974) work, Lighthall's (1989) study of conflict and decision making in a secondary school, *Local Realities, Local Adaptations*, was a prompt in thinking about conflict in this way. So was Simmel (1955, 1971), who emphasizes that conflict flows out of patterns in group attachment and that between-frame conflict can be the most intractable.

9. Abbott (1992, 1997) argues that we need to move toward an understanding of the limited set of social types or forms that structure action and resources — both spatially and temporally — within a given field of activity. See also Mohr and Guerra-Pearson, who call for studies of how "organizational forms are both embedded within and constitutive of institutional space" (forthcoming) to understand the arrangement of both resources and practices within a given field.

10. For other reviews of the literature on conflict in religious organizations, see Becker et al. (1993), Starke and Dyck (1996), and Kniss (1997). For a recent review of the literature on organizational conflict, see Jehn (1997).

11. How many people belong to those 300,000 congregations? Measures of religious "belonging" fall roughly into three types: attendance figures, self-identification as a member, and official membership counts. There is a debate about weekly church attendance, with the lowest estimates between 30% and 40% of the American population (see Wuthnow 1988; Hadaway et al. 1993); Kosmin and Lachman claim that "80 million Americans attend worship services on any given weekend" (1993:1), which would be roughly 32% of the U.S. population. There is less debate about the number of people who identify themselves as belonging to a religious group; Kosmin and Lachman (1993) give that figure as somewhere around 90% of the American population, which is consistent with other sources. Official membership figures from denominational sources consistently come in somewhere between the two extremes and are close to Gallup poll estimates of membership at around 62% of the American population (cf. Watt 1991). By any measure, religious organizations encompass more Americans than any other single form of voluntary organization in the United States (Watt 1991).

12. Putnam is famous, of course, for his "bowling alone" thesis, which argues that the amount and the nature of civic participation is changing in the United States, indicating a long-term decline in social capital or the skills and habits necessary for effective interaction in the public sphere (*Current*, June 1995). A very intelligent debate of this thesis has taken place in the pages of *The American Prospect*, in an article by Putnam, "The Strange Disappearance of Civic America" (no. 24, Winter 1996) and in a series of rejoinders by Michael Schudson, Theda Skocpol, and Richard Valelly in the next issue (no. 25, March/April 1996), which includes a reply by Putnam. The criticisms of Putnam span his data, methods, and interpretation; my own view is that Putnam has data to show a restructuring or reconfiguration of civic participation, but the jury is still out on whether that leads to some overall decline in any meaningful sense. It may, however, lead to a worsening social division between cosmopolitans and parochials. See Hammond (1992) for an excellent discussion of the differences between a parochial and a cosmopolitan orientation to civic life and community involvement. Nicholas Lemann makes a similar point in a critique of Putnam published in the April 1996 *Atlantic Monthly*.

13. If Lighthall was an exemplar of looking at conflict as tied to local culture, Elaine Tyler May (1980) was an exemplar of thinking about conflict as a window into "moral order." Her study of divorce in the United States in the late nineteenth and early twentieth centuries uses data on the rhetoric of divorcing couples to analyze what she calls the shared and divergent expectations of what

the obligations of marriage entailed for both parties. This is similar to Wuthnow's (1987) understanding of the moral order as encompassing both a set of conceptual categories that organize relationships among groups and the social relations themselves that are shaped by obligations defined by the conceptual categories (*Meaning and Moral Order*, esp. Chapters 2, 3, 5).

14. I follow Fine's (1984) development of the idea of "negotiated order" in describing the culture of individual groups or organizations. The idea of applying different "lenses" to the analysis of organizations is taken from Martin (1992).
15. See, for just a few excellent examples, Geertz (1973), Kanter (1977), Sahlins (1985), Abu-Lughod (1986), Laitin (1986), Hopewell (1987), Jackall (1988), Lighthall (1989), Anderson (1991), Apter (1992), Kunda (1992), and Bell (1994).
16. "Thick" refers to Geertz's criterion for "thick description," the ethnographic method described in *The Interpretation of Cultures* (1973).
17. United Church of Christ.
18. This body of work consists of a wealth of case studies and a few more general, synthesizing or theoretical accounts. See, for example, Blau (1976), Swatos (1981), Caplow et al. (1983), Greenhouse (1986), Ammerman (1987), Furman (1987), Gremillion and Castelli (1987), Hopewell (1987), Neitz (1987), Wertheimer (1987), Warner (1988, 1994), Hammond (1988), Olson (1989), Prell (1989), Seidler and Meyer (1989), and Wind and Lewis (1994). These studies mostly emphasize the local, the particular, and the idiosyncratic. For example, Gremillion and Castelli (1987) note that the parish one belongs to is a better predictor of stands on theological and social issues than standard sociological variables like gender and age. The Notre Dame Study of Catholic Parish Life concluded that

> It may be more important that I am a member of Saint Francis parish than that I am a sixty-four-year-old woman. And I may think more like a forty-year-old man from Saint Francis parish than a sixty-four-year-old woman from Sacred Heart (Gremillion and Castelli 1987:46).

Bass finds that, in "every congregation, deliberate efforts to transmit tradition are evident" (1994:178). However, she also notes that congregations

> do not simply inherit tradition; they contribute to it. A living congregation does not leave a living tradition unaffected. . . . *Congregations enable great traditions to find expression in ever new historical forms, and thereby to be both perpetuated and changed* (Bass 1994:185, emphasis in original; cf. Flynt 1994).

Carroll and Roof (1993) find that local congregations are locations for eclecticism and creativity in matters ranging from governance to ritual practice.

19. For general introductions to institutionalist arguments and approaches, see Zucker (1988), Powell and DiMaggio (1991), Friedland and Alford (1991), and Brinton and Nee (1998).
20. Exceptions to this general neglect include Barley (1986), Douglas (1986), Brint and Karabel (1991), Orru et al. (1991), and Searing (1991); cf. Lighthall (1989). The review by Strang (1994) makes a similar point.
21. For example, see Meyer et al. (1983), Tolbert and Zucker (1983), Meyer et al. (1987), Meyer and Rowan (1991), Scott and Meyer (1991), and Searing (1991).
22. See Fine (1987:130ff.). Friedland and Alford (1991) urge the discovery of the institutional content of these aggregative rules for organizations in particular institutional fields.
23. Although all congregations consider worship and religious education to be core tasks, congregations with different models go about worship and education somewhat differently. How they do this will be examined in Chapters 3–6.
24. In the U.S. context, scholars agree that these are the primary institutional tasks of congregations. Bass notes that

> Whether religious traditions generally and necessarily require congregations for their sustenance may be open to debate, but within the North American context of religious voluntarism it is evident that congregations have provided ancient transnational traditions with indispensable means of extension into new historical settings (1994:187).

Cf. Blau (1976), Gremillion and Castelli (1987), Wertheimer (1987), Davidman (1991), Bass (1994), Holifield (1994), Warner (1994), and Waugh (1994).
25. See Bass (1994), Flynt (1994), and Nelson (1997) for studies that demonstrate that an emphasis on intimate interpersonal ties is not a feature of every congregation; cf. Hall (1988).
26. For discussions of different ways of classifying mission orientation, see Dudley (1983, 1988), Roozen et al. (1984), Carroll and Roof (1993), Dudley and Johnson (1993), and Gilkey (1994). All of these authors preserve a basic distinction between inwardly and outwardly oriented groups. It is common to acknowledge the difference between a "civic" orientation, which is concerned with the local community, and an "activist" orientation, which actively seeks to change the world. Some authors also make the distinction between those that see their primary mission as saving individual souls (an evangelistic orientation) and those that see the changing of societal institutions as their goal (see Dudley and Johnson 1983; Roozen et al. 1984).
27. Cf. Selznick (1949), Tipton (1982), and Wuthnow (1987).

28. Cf. Swidler (1986), Greenwood and Hinings (1988), DiMaggio (1991), and Sewell (1992). The core idea that all share is that culture and action are mutually constitutive in reality even if analytically separable. See Emirbayer and Mische (1998; cf. Archer 1988) for a much longer and more thorough discussion of the different ways of theorizing the link between culture, structure, and agency and for an excellent literature review. For a good example of cultural approaches to the study of religion, see the entire volume of *Sociology of Religion* for 1996, edited by Rhys Williams.

29. See DiMaggio (1991) and DiMaggio and Powell (1991) for a discussion of the differences between older and newer institutional approaches in sociology and organizational studies; cf. Selznick (1949). For similar discussions of institutionalist analysis in anthropology and political science, see Douglas (1986) and Searing (1991).

30. See, for example, Jepperson (1991), Powell (1991:190–191), Fligstein (1990), Martin (1992), and Eliasoph (1996).

2

THE CONGREGATIONS OF OAK PARK, RIVER FOREST, AND FOREST PARK

I had been to Oak Park before, to go to a movie or out for ice cream with a friend who had grown up there. Today I was going, for the first time, to do research. I was going to the public library, but I thought I would first drive through to get a feel for the place during the daytime.

Driving to Oak Park from Chicago, the urban feeling stayed with me. There was a lot of traffic for eleven in the morning, and people were speeding on the Eisenhower Expressway. I did not notice much change in the buildings lining the side of the expressway as I approached the exit for Austin Boulevard, on the eastern boundary of Oak Park. And when I exited onto Austin and drove north to the main east–west street, I was passing blocks of brick three-flats and a few city homes crammed together on tiny lots. Most of the people on the sidewalk were African American, but the people in the cars and on the smelly, old city buses were mixed, all ages and races. This is a major city thoroughfare, a commuter-way.

When I turned west on the main street, the city feel continued for a while. I did see fewer people on the sidewalks, but there were still large apartment blocks and small houses. Then I came to some car dealerships and eventually, on my right, I saw a large, dark stone building with a small tower set back from the street, with a small green lawn and a large parking lot. Bethlehem Congregational Church, the sign said. I learned later that another congregation also uses the building, renting the space until they can afford their own.

On the right came the high brick walls of the high school football stadium, and then I was in the center of town. There was still a lot of traffic, and the buildings were densely packed together, and there were about equal numbers of whites and African Americans on the sidewalks. But this corner of the main street and Oak Park Avenue seemed more like the downtown of a small community. The public library is here and just up the street, the post office. There are busy restaurants, small clothing boutiques, and the offices of the local newspaper. There is a park next to the library, and people were out eating an early sandwich or just sitting on the benches in the sunshine. The buildings here are two or three stories, retail below and professional offices or apartments above.

Oak Park, River Forest, Forest Park

I kept driving west and came to two huge churches across the street from each other; then I came to another one a block farther on. Each is big enough to be a cathedral in a small city or a large college chapel. One is Romanesque, the other two variations on Gothic, all with stained glass windows that stretch upward for two or three stories. Oak Park used to be called the "city of churches," and these large main-street churches attest to the time, about eighty years ago, when the Episcopalian, Presbyterian, and Congregational churches were the dominant public institutions in the growing village. The Presbyterians have since sold the large Romanesque building and merged with the Congregationalists across the street, whose Gothic building is big enough for both congregations now. The Presbyterian church was bought in the 1970s by a fundamentalist, independent Baptist church that has about 700 people attending on a Sunday morning and a mailing list of over 1500.

Just west of these churches is another group of businesses – a pancake house, a diner, and a few chains like the Gap and Chernin's shoes. The shops continue, off to the left, on a side street that is now a pedestrian way. But here, the street looks a little more tired. Some of the storefronts are empty, and some of them, like the store for balloons and party supplies, seem less substantial, more likely to come and go quickly. There is an old movie theater, with a big, old-fashioned, lighted sign. It is second-run now, although they keep one or two screens to show current art films.

I turned right and circled back to the library, but if I had kept driving across Harlem Avenue, I would have been in River Forest. Largely residential, it is very much like sections of north Oak Park. It has large houses, each one different, on big lots with old trees. During my research, when I was there during the daytime, the pedestrians I saw were children walking home from school, somebody out walking the dog, or occasionally a couple taking a stroll in the early evening. Forest Park, to the south of River Forest, is like south Oak Park. It has some nice detached houses on smaller lots, but there are also apartment buildings and a downtown street with diners, small shops, and heavy pedestrian traffic. There are several taverns, some of which date from the time when Oak Park was "dry" and people had to go to the next village for a drink. All three suburbs combine a lazy suburban feel in their residential sections with an urban density and large apartments and retail strips on the major commuter streets that form their borders. In late 1992, between all three communities, there were seventy-seven congregations.

Oak Park, River Forest, Forest Park

This is a comparative study of twenty-three congregations or "cases." But it is also a case study of the congregations in and around one community.

Twenty out of the twenty-three congregations are in the Village of Oak Park, an urban suburb nine miles from the center of Chicago. The other congregations are in River Forest and Forest Park, two communities that are immediately adjacent to Oak Park. (For more details on method, see Appendix A.)

Oak Park is a complicated community, trying to work through some challenges that are typical for collar suburbs of large cities, and some that are more particular to its own history. It is a community that encompasses more than one set of contradictions. In one sense it is an urban area, with good restaurants and an active arts community, with racial diversity, with gangs and drugs in the high school, and with large apartment blocks lining the major streets. When you walk around in the summer, especially on one of the commercial streets, it feels like a city: the sidewalks are crowded, the air is gritty, and the fumes from the cars make your eyes sting.

In other ways it has a very suburban feel (Hummon 1990). On the side streets, the houses have big front porches and backyards; moms (and some dads) walk the younger children to school. Local government is strong; people refer to the place as a "village" and support community organizations too numerous to count. The Frank Lloyd Wright home and studio are here, and the architecture tour draws people from all over the country. When I asked people what makes the village unique, they talked about the architecture, and about Petersen's Ice Cream, which they called the best ice cream anywhere, and about the fact that Ernest Hemingway grew up here.

It is relatively easy to give a facts-and-figures description of Oak Park. Out of a population of just over 50,000, seventy-seven percent are white, eighteen percent are black, and four percent are Hispanic. The median age is just over thirty-one, the median family income is just under $52,000, and the per-capita income is just over $21,000.[1] The community has excellent schools and village services and is a magnet for young professionals, the most common household type being a young married family with children. Oak Park was organized as a village in 1902 and has a tradition of strong local government.

The Oak Park of the 1950s and early 1960s was very different than the village of today. It was a white, politically and socially conservative community, a prosperous and largely Republican suburb, with many businessmen and -women and some professionals and their families. It was still the Oak Park that Hemingway, who was cosmopolitan but not particularly tolerant, had called a community of "broad streets and narrow minds."

In the late 1960s and early 1970s, Oak Park underwent a period of rapid racial transition. As African Americans began to move into the community, white flight began. But Oak Park is rather famous in some academic and policy circles for achieving racial integration. This happened because of the committed action of community leaders from a variety of institutions, who decided that they had too much invested in the community and cared about it too much to abandon it. And it grew out of a progressive tradition of local government. Community leaders believed in the legal process, and they believed that they could do more than passively watch as white flight occurred. The religious congregations, and especially some of the more vocal pastors, were actively involved.[2]

They began by working to pass an integrated housing ordinance and working one-on-one with local real estate agents. The goal was to have black families scattered throughout the village, not moving in block by block. Black families, when moving in, were referred by real estate agents to all-white blocks. They also passed an equity assurance program, to assuage fears about falling property values, and adopted a "diversity statement." Mostly, though, they did a lot of communicating. There were open meetings, community meetings, and meetings in churches and the high school. The village leadership tried to communicate two main things. First, they believed that welcoming black residents was the right thing to do. Second, by managing change intelligently they believed that they could stay in control of the process and achieve stable racial integration as an alternative to having whites abandon the community in droves. By 1972, housing prices had leveled off and white flight had all but stopped. And young professional families, black and white both, were more than willing to buy what houses were coming on the market, because by now Oak Park was becoming known as a success story.[3]

When Oak Park became an integrated community, that meant the physical presence of African Americans as community residents. It has also meant ongoing negotiation of racial matters. In the last five or six years, African American leaders have been more vocal in demanding not only the right to live in the village but also the right to have fair treatment and representation within its local institutions, even forming a local political party for this purpose. Focus groups conducted for the community's current self-study, "Vision 2000", saw some African American residents questioning the "dispersal principle" that figures prominently in the village's first formal statement on diversity, the one that guided the work with real estate agents in the early 1970s. As one African American resident asked, "What's wrong with all-black neighborhoods?"[4]

On the one hand, there is a broad consensus in the village that integration as a policy has worked, and most residents think of themselves as lucky, having worked hard and succeeded in making a very difficult change come about. However, most also acknowledge that racial diversity brings a continuing challenge for the community to progress in its interracial and interethnic relations. As Richard, a white fifty-one-year-old man working on his doctorate in theology, told me in June of 1992,

> We are just now getting past the stage of being polite to one another. I think tolerance and integration are very different. Up till now people have been tolerating each other, but now we are getting past that, and the polite smile, and really getting to know each other.

Richard was sounding a common theme in my interviews – that there was still plenty of racism in Oak Park, especially institutionalized racism in the high school, in politics, and in other civic institutions. But, like virtually everyone else I spoke to, he also felt hopeful about their ability to move toward a true integration of the community, not just of the houses and apartments.

The village's newfound reputation as a tolerant and progressive community has led to other forms of diversity. Oak Park now has an active and visible gay and lesbian population. The progressive reputation attracted many professionals who value tolerance and diversity for their own sake. Richard's story about his decision to move from an all-white and much more conservative suburb to Oak Park in 1975 was a typical account:

> I felt like I was in a snow storm, it was so white . . . knowing life isn't like that, I moved to Oak Park. I wanted my kids to grow up in an integrated community, seeing all kinds of different people, knowing all kinds of different people.

For Richard, moving to Oak Park was putting into daily practice his commitment to social justice, and his story was repeated in its main points by many people I talked to. But for others, the decision to move here was driven more by the availability of affordable housing and excellent public services, all within a short train ride to the central city. Between those seeking diversity and those seeking an affordable, convenient, and safe middle-class community, the 1990 census shows that Oak Park was transformed in the 1970s and 1980s to a community where young middle-class couples with children were the most common family type and where professionals, managers, and specialists make up just over fifty percent of the population.

While race remains an important issue in the public life of the village, it is not the only concern or even the dominant one. A recent proposal to extend health benefits to same-sex partners of village employees generated public controversy. The Oak Park of the present is one where individuals vary widely in their beliefs and attitudes toward social and political issues. It is a more diverse community than before, in many respects. In national elections, about one-half of the residents vote Republican and about one-half vote Democratic. Religious liberals and conservatives are both well represented. The Unitarian and Congregational churches are filled with community residents, but so are the Assemblies of God, the fundamentalist Baptist, and the Plymouth Brethren congregations. Conservative and Reform temples are across the street from one another.

The dominant style of local politics is a kind of aggressively progressive liberalism. And currently, the more conservative people feel quite alienated from the village government and its policies. As one woman, a self-identified conservative Baptist, reports:

> It's changed totally. It has become a humanistic, gay rights community, pushing all of the things we don't believe in. [pause] The administration is absolutely ineffective. [pause] They never do what the people want.

From granting benefits to gay partners of village employees to banning Christmas carols from school holiday pageants, the village's progressive and secular leadership has convinced many of the more traditional residents that it is out of touch with their concerns and values.

It is important to remember that, while professional couples with children are the most common household type in Oak Park, there is diversity along the dimensions of occupation and income as well. The renters who live in the large apartment blocks on the major streets are more likely to be single or to have lower paying semiprofessional jobs than are the dual-career families who have bought the big houses on the side streets. There are many working-class people living in the smaller houses on the south side of the village, as well. The public relations on the village, that it is an integrated community of progressive professionals, captures a large part of the truth, because it describes the group that provides the leadership and the values that govern most of the community's important organizations and civic institutions (cf. Lamont 1992). But this image also fails to do justice to the actual variation not only in the socioeconomic status but also in the political and social attitudes that exist in Oak Park.

If the growing pains of a diverse community are one major concern in the village, finances are the other issue that has people worried. Economic issues have taken on more importance in recent years, receiving a central place in the community's recent (1997) self-study. Property taxes are high and have risen especially rapidly in the last few years. Older residents and those with moderate incomes are finding the tax burden hard to bear. And like most of the built-up collar suburbs, Oak Park has lost some of its business and retail base to larger suburban malls and business parks located farther west. A law was passed to help local businesses rehabilitate their operations, and the village is trying to attract retailers to fill vacant space on the main shopping street. They have stopped the loss but have not attracted enough new businesses to increase the tax base significantly.

River Forest and Forest Park, the two communities to the immediate west of Oak Park, contain three of the twenty-three congregations that I studied. They are in many ways similar to Oak Park geographically and economically, and they share many joint community institutions. Forest Park is more like south Oak Park, demographically and economically, while River Forest is more similar to north Oak Park.

Forest Park is a village of 15,000 people that borders on the immediate west of the south half of Oak Park. Forest Park is 76.6 percent white, 13.0 percent black, 8.4 percent Asian or Pacific Islander, and 4.9 percent Hispanic. The largest single group is in the twenty-five to twenty-nine age range, and the median home price ranges between $75,000 and $99,999.[5] Forest Park underwent racial integration at the same time and for some of the same reasons as Oak Park, and it is also a stable community in terms of ethnic mix. Community leaders note that they, too, have taken the lead in promoting racial integration, and they point out that they have done it without the fanfare and widespread attention that Oak Park has received.

River Forest is also immediately west of Oak Park, directly north of Forest Park. It is a smaller community, as well, with 11,669 residents. It is ninety-five percent white and has a median family income of $78,889.[6] River Forest is wealthier than Forest Park but about as rich as northern Oak Park, although it is more racially homogeneous than northern Oak Park. River Forest has been less touched by racial changes, although having a joint high school with Oak Park means that it has shared in the concern over the ongoing incorporation of racial minorities into full participation in community institutions. It is also affected by some of the same economic and social concerns as the other two communities, particularly the economic pressures felt by all of the collar suburbs. Oak Park and River Forest have a joint Chamber of Commerce, and they have tried to work together to enlarge the business base of the two communities.

The congregations in and around Oak Park are as diverse as the community. There are three huge Protestant churches on the main street and several others just like them a block or so off the main street. There are also a few large Catholic churches scattered around the community; one, on the northern edge of the village, has a campus that takes up a city block, including a small convent, a rectory, and a school. The two synagogues, across from one another on a major cross-street, also have big buildings with classroom wings.

But there are many small neighborhood congregations with on-street parking and immaculate tiny lawns, and there are some congregations, including small evangelical groups and some black congregations from the West Side, that rent space in the Presbyterian, Congregational, and Methodist churches until they can afford their own. A few small congregations meet in members' homes, and there are a couple of storefront black congregations on Madison Street, in the south part of the village.

Choices

I chose to study congregations in and around Oak Park for several different reasons. One reason is pragmatic. In the early part of this century, Oak Park was known as a "community of churches." It now has both a large number and a large variety of congregations. As of late 1992, Oak Park, River Forest, and Forest Park together had a total of seventy-seven congregations.[7] And although Baumgartner's (1988) work indicates that middle-class persons and communities tend to suppress and avoid conflict, other work on religious organizations more specifically suggests that they can be locations for conflict over a wide range of issues and ideas, some of it quite intense, even within middle-class, professional communities (Warner 1988; Becker et al. 1993). Oak Park was a community in which I was able to develop good access to community leaders and to each of the congregations I wanted to study (see Appendix A).

33

Issues of access aside, I also chose Oak Park because it serves as a good exemplar of a specific kind of religiosity. It has self-aware and self-defined groups of religious liberals and conservatives. The middle-class professionals who make up the dominant group in the community tend to exhibit a voluntaristic and individual-expressive style of religious commitment, in both of the ways described by Hammond (1988, 1991, 1992). For most, religion is not based on an ascriptive identity; and even for those for whom it is, for example, the Jewish members of the two synagogues, the ascriptive identity is not taken for granted but is consciously affirmed. Moreover, none of these congregations serves as a subculture that encompasses most of its members' lives and primary ties, but is rather one association, and one set of connections, among many. And as a community confronting both the issues of racism and the presence of an active lesbian and gay community, it confronts daily the kinds of social issues that Glock (1993) and Hunter (1991) have identified as the most difficult for contemporary religious organizations in the United States.

As a case, then, Oak Park is a good exemplar of some important and defining dimensions of the institutional field of American congregational religion – individual-expressive commitment, well-defined groups of liberals and conservatives, and an engagement with social and moral issues that have been important and even defining ones for religious institutions in the United States. This enables the kind of theoretical generalization, as described by Snow and Anderson (1991), that was the overarching goal for this study.[8] The tri-village area of Oak Park, Forest Park, and River Forest can serve as fertile ground on which to investigate the dynamics of conflict and commitment within a very specific kind of contemporary congregation.

Of course, there are real limits to the ability of any community to serve as a good exemplar of such a large and complex institution as "American religion" or even "middle-class American religion." While some attempt has been made to incorporate Catholic parishes and synagogues as well as Protestant congregations, diversity on other dimensions was not achieved. Although some of the congregations in Oak Park are primarily ethnic or new immigrant congregations, none of those is included here. Hammond (1988) gives reason to think that the dynamics of commitment and authority, which are at the heart of this study, are different in such congregations. To use his terms, they tend to foster a communal-expressive, not an individual-expressive, style of religious commitment. There are no historic Black Church congregations in Oak Park, but if there were, these would have been excluded from the study for the same reason: I wanted to examine congregations with an individual-expressive style of commitment. So, to the degree to which African American religion is represented, it is in the participation of African Americans in traditionally white denominations and congregations.

The congregations in this study exemplify white middle-class religiosity and a set of religious institutions that are dominated by a white middle-class history and culture. They exemplify the voluntarism and the division between liberals and conservatives that have come to be understood as some of the most important institutional features of American religious life, features that are paradigmatic of contemporary white middle-class religion, but which are also, many believe, becoming more common features of American congregational religion more generally.

If this is in some sense a case study of the congregations in one community, it is also a small-scale, comparative case study of twenty-three local congregations. For this study, I collected data in two synagogues, two Catholic parishes, and nineteen Protestant congregations. There are both similarities and differences between parishes, Protestant churches, and synagogues. However, in the contemporary United States, all three traditions have a congregational form of organization; problems with divisions between liberals and conservatives; concern over race, sexuality, and lifestyle issues; and a voluntaristic style of commitment.[9] It is for these reasons that all three types of congregations are included in this study.

If the community was chosen for a mix of pragmatic and analytical reasons, the congregations to be studied were chosen specifically to vary on dimensions highlighted in previous studies as having some influence on internal congregational processes, including the causes and consequences of conflict. These dimensions are size, polity type, and a liberal or conservative cultural orientation. Other studies have suggested that these features affect the distribution of authority in a congregation or shape members' commitment, which are thought to influence the frequency and intensity of conflict. Appendix A contains a longer discussion of this literature, along with other notes on interviewing and data-gathering, and Table 2 shows the resulting mix of congregations.

Conflict

This began as a study in decision making and conflict. I wanted to understand the cultural or symbolic aspects of conflict – what kinds of issues do

Table 2. *Choosing the congregations*

	Liberal		Conservative	
	Small	Large	Small	Large
Congregational Polity	3	3	3	3
Hierarchical Polity	3	3	3	2*

* An attempt was made to find three congregations for this cell, but only two could be found in the tri-village area.

congregations fight about, and how do they interpret these issues? I also wanted to understand conflict processes: who participates, who wins and who loses, what typical kinds of decision-making routines are employed, when and why does conflict escalate, and how is it solved? And I wanted to understand the relationship between conflict and power implied in the forms of participation and resolution. Finally, I wanted to understand the impact of conflict on the larger life of the congregation. From the beginning of the study I thought that a good understanding of conflict must move toward identifying an entire pattern of conflict in each congregation, across all of these dimensions of conflict. It also meant understanding both the structural features, like formal polity (organization and governance structure), and the cultural features, like beliefs and symbols, that made a congregation prone to one conflict pattern over another.[10]

Earlier studies provided insights into the kinds of conflicts that I might encounter in these congregations. Some find that conflict can be a struggle over symbolic issues, often revolving around issues of worship and ritual. Symbolic conflicts may be prompted by some threat to the congregation's survival and can be accompanied by an emergent or nascent form of religious experience.[11] One comparative study, the pilot for this research, suggests that conflict over ideas and symbols may be common in all contemporary religious organizations.[12]

Another group of studies concentrates on "divides" within American religious organizations that may cause conflict at the local level. One is a division between clergy and laity, attributed variously to differences in education or political stance, clergy indifference to lay members' feelings of ownership, or different amounts of power.[13] A second division is between liberals and conservatives, although there is some debate over whether this would cause conflict at the local level.[14] Becker et al. (1993) also find a division between older and newer members underlying at least some conflicts. Such divisions may be latent until triggered by specific events, as discussed by Takayama (1980), Kniss (1997), and Eiesland (1998).[15]

Once the congregations were chosen, I gathered information about them in a variety of ways (see Appendix A). The most extensive way was through a series of structured interviews with eight to ten members and the head clergy-person in each congregation. This made for a total of 231 interviews – 203 with lay members and 28 with clergy. Just over one-half of the lay members were in leadership positions. The interview schedule, which appears in Appendix B, facilitated a three-part, structured discussion, ranging from forty-five minutes to an hour and a half, designed to illuminate the kinds of issues outlined above. First, I asked the respondents to describe their feelings about their present congregation and their history of religious involvement. Second, I asked them to characterize their congregation on a variety of dimensions – the membership, the programs and activities, the goals and plans, and the history and future trajectory. In the third and final part of the interview, I asked them to tell me about any conflicts in their congregation during the last five years.

The definition of conflict encompasses several elements. First, conflict is an intense form of sociation, or interaction. The opposite of conflict is not harmony but indifference or anonymity (Simmel 1971; see also Levine 1971). To engage in conflict assumes a degree of connectedness between the parties. Second, conflict involves two or more parties who perceive their interests to be incompatible and engage in action oriented to the defense of their interests, be they ideal or material. Persons or groups engaged in conflict are aware of their own interests and the interests of those with whom they are engaged in conflict; as Kriesberg notes, "a fundamental aspect of social conflicts is the awareness of the parties that an incompatibility exists" (1973:4). Conflict, then, is a pattern of interaction that is conscious, intermittent, and personal.[16]

This focus on manifest events, instead of latent divisions, also means that I am using conflict events as a kind of cultural object.[17] They have producers and an audience. They also are themselves comprised of a constructed and a negotiated set of meanings. A conflict over the church school budget may be understood by all parties as a simple administrative matter, to be resolved by vote. Or it may be understood as a referendum on how much the congregation can afford to reach out to a nearby poor, African American community by subsidizing school tuition. Or it may be seen as a struggle over control by two groups who have fundamentally different ideas about what the priorities of the local congregation ought to be. And these publicly negotiated meanings may be themselves the object of contention. More than once people told me that "they" (the other side) would want me to think that the conflict was about one thing (gender, outreach) while it was in fact "really" about something else. In some congregations, people were very aware that what was at stake was not only an outcome but a definition of the situation.[18]

Members and clergy reported a total of sixty-five conflict events.[19] I found conflict over some of the same issues as previous studies have found. There were conflicts over worship and ritual, although only one of these became anything like the conflict over the congregation's very identity that occurred at Hope Episcopal. There were conflicts over gender and sexuality issues and conflicts that people reported as being "about" the pastor. The most common kind of conflict, over administrative issues like money, staff, and personnel, is something that previous studies have not identified (see Table 3).

The divisions identified in previous studies have some presence in this community. There is some factionalization between older and newer

Table 3. *Conflict issues**

Staff/money/programs	37 conflicts in 16 congregations
Worship/ritual	13 conflicts in 9 congregations
Gender/sexuality	10 conflicts in 10 congregations
Pastor	9 conflicts in 8 congregations

* These add up to 69, not 65, because 4 of the conflicts – 2 over
inclusive language and 2 over ordaining women – were
double-coded as being about both "worship and ritual" and
"gender and sexuality."

members and between the pastor and laity, although a division between factions of liberals and conservatives within congregations motivates little internal conflict here.

This study also identifies other ways in which congregations can have differences in their overall style of conflict. One of these is the fact that similar issues can be framed, understood, and argued about very differently in different congregations. In some congregations, approving money to remodel the church or decisions about what staff to hire are understood as administrative matters and are resolved by some agreed-upon organizational routine. In other congregations, such issues are viewed as moral matters and are subject to a lengthy process of public debate to decide what to do.

Likewise, some of the conflicts over the pastor are understood as personal conflicts between the pastor and the lay leaders and talked about as differences in temperament or style. But the other conflicts surrounding the pastor have more to do with the pastor being supported by one faction of lay leaders and opposed by others. In some congregations, the pastor is the primary person who puts issues on the agenda, sometimes provoking conflict in the process. The pastor in these congregations also takes a strong lead once conflict is begun, trying to steer the congregation toward his or her desired outcome. In other congregations, the pastor never plays this role.

In some congregations, the process by which decisions are made is itself "up for grabs," and it is evaluated as a moral matter. Is the process open and inclusive, and does it arrive at a decision that reflects some true consensus of values, or at least one that represents the range of views of the congregation members on a particular topic? In other congregations, only the outcome is seen as being either moral or immoral. Sometimes the lay and clergy leadership in a congregation will regularly seek compromise solutions. But compromise is not the norm in every congregation, and in some congregations compromise solutions are never utilized. Some conflicts rage through a series of events. Organizational routines, like voting, are attempted but cannot contain or resolve the conflict. Eventually, in these congregations, a large group simply leaves.

In Chapter 1, I talked about the process of discovery that made me reject a certain way of understanding the conflict at Hope Episcopal and turn toward another kind of understanding. In reviewing the overall pattern of conflict in all twenty-three congregations, I had to undergo a similar process. This was because the three congregational features built into the study from the beginning – the congregation's size, polity, and liberal or conservative orientation – provided a partial, but not a robust, explanation of these differences in conflict. For example, neither size nor polity has any effect on the *issues* that congregations fight over, but cultural orientation does, at least in some issue areas. Liberal congregations were the only ones to fight about inclusive language and becoming "open and affirming" of lesbians and gay men, while conservative congregations had the only conflicts over premarital or extramarital sex. But these issues came into play in only seven out of sixty-five conflicts. There were no other differences in what liberal and conservative congregations fought over.

Polity and cultural orientation, together, do have an effect on the *amount* of conflict. Conservative congregations with a hierarchical polity have the least conflict, and liberal congregations with a congregational polity have the most. But this is mostly because two congregations – one Episcopalian and one Catholic – report "no conflict." When these two are excluded, this relationship disappears.

In short, I did find some things that were congruent with previous studies. I did find conflicts over symbols and rituals, over gender and sexuality, between clergy and laity, and between older and newer members, but none of these was the most common type of conflict, nor do they together account for all of the conflict found. The dimensions identified in previous studies – size, polity, liberal/conservative orientation – explained only a very limited amount about conflict in these twenty-three congregations. Which congregations fight over which issues is not explained by the factors in the literature, with one exception: Being liberal or conservative is linked to differences in conflict over sexuality issues, a small percentage of total conflicts (cf. Glock 1993). Size does not predict the amount of conflict, but polity and religious orientation may have some relationship to the amount of conflict.

Moreover, these dimensions do not adequately explain the other kinds of findings that emerged through the fieldwork. Specifically, they do not explain very much about conflict processes and outcomes. In some congregations similar issues are framed, understood, and argued about very differently; the pastor plays a different role in different kinds of congregations; and some congregations favor compromise more than others. These three dimensions also do not provide an adequate explanation for the four congregations undergoing a more severe, uncontainable form of conflict.

Liberal and conservative congregations are equally likely to frame conflicts as moral, to have a pastor who sets a strong agenda or one who does not, to favor compromise or never utilize it, or to have a kind of serious conflict that rages through a series of events and ends in the exit of large groups of people. Size and polity have some effect on these other features of conflict. All of the conflicts over the pastor that are framed as personal occur in small congregations. However, out of twelve small congregations, six had no conflicts over the pastor and none at all were framed in personal terms. Why do some small congregations have this kind of conflict while others do not? Four of the congregations that tend to view the process itself as moral and have lay people put things on the agenda are small, but two are large. Only one of the congregations that frames issues in personal terms and fights over the pastor has a congregational polity. Those that tend to frame issues as moral are more likely to have a congregational polity, but this general relationship does not hold in three congregations.

When size and polity are conceived of as "underlying dimensions" or variables and the conflicts are aggregated, it is possible to see some effect on conflict. However, when one focuses on congregations as cases[20] and asks if these dimensions allow one to predict or explain the overall pattern of conflict, including the kinds of issues that arise, the amount of conflict, and how conflict plays out once it has begun in any given congregation, the answer is that almost one-half of the congregations do not exhibit the expected pattern of conflict. Size and polity, together, cast some light on conflict in thirteen out of the twenty-three congregations. But that means that a little less than one-half of the congregations do not fit the pattern that one would predict using size and polity.

Looking for New Explanations

When I realized this, I began to consider alternative explanations. It is a convention to portray this process as rather neat and orderly, proceeding from well-defined theoretical propositions or one compelling moment of insight. In fact, it was a much longer and messier process of casting about, but it was not a random process. In addition to the studies of conflict in religious organizations that provided the initial guidance for choosing the congregations, there is the work of scholars like Simmel (1955, 1971), Coser (1956), Kriesberg (1973), and Hirschman (1970), who look at conflict as something that flows out of certain patterns of group life and group culture. In particular, these scholars focus on theoretical questions of boundaries, loyalty, and commitment.[21]

The insights of these scholars also helped to make sense of some observations from the fieldwork that had been noted at the time but that did not seem to fit with the initial focus of the analysis – observations like Martha's comment, reported in the vignette in Chapter 1, about realizing that some of her friends and neighbors "weren't going to the same church" that she was, and the fact that, in some groups, conflicts over finances or governance quickly became argued in moral terms while in others they were never mentioned at all.

These scholars ask such questions as, how are the people in the group attached to one another, and how do they interact with one another? How do they think and talk about the group's identity and purpose? Hirschman (1970) talks about how members' loyalty to a group affects things like how easy it is for members to leave if they are dissatisfied. This in turn affects people's willingness to engage in behavior that leads to conflict, like voicing their dissatisfaction. An unwillingness to voice complaints can stem from a desire to suppress conflict before it is likely to endanger the group's survival or one's membership in it.

Coser (1956), drawing on Simmel (1955), says that groups that are emotionally important to people, where they participate as "whole persons," have different kinds of conflicts than issue-based groups, like social movement organizations, where people have a more remote and segmented attachment. The first moment of insight was when I realized that some of the congregations sounded a lot like Coser's (1956) description of a family or a family-like group while others seemed to be more concerned with social and political issues and values.

In addition, from the work of Coser (1956), Turner (1974), and Kurtz (1986), there is the insight that the authority structures of the group must be taken into account. In groups that are more ideological, more outward-oriented, and in which members expect the leaders to be the official carrier of the group's message to the outside world, those leaders are less prone to compromise. Once conflict has begun, the ability of the leader to take a strong and substantive stand has an impact on how the conflict plays out. It was clear to me that, in some congregations, the pastor plays a much stronger leadership role, although this did not break down along liberal/conservative lines, as I had expected.

It made sense that things like size and polity might be related to dimensions of group life like loyalty and authority. But it also made sense that these might not be perfect proxies for ideas about why the group is important or what its purpose is. As May (1980) argues, it is the violation of shared expectations, or the discovery of divergent expectations, that triggers conflict. Expectations are linked to, but not determined by, organizational structure. Coser (1956:97) notes, for example, that small groups might more easily develop norms and habits of intimacy, where members have a family-like attachment to each other, but that size and the ideas that people have about the nature and purpose of the group must be kept analytically distinct, because the two do not always covary (cf. Friedland and Alford 1991). So it made sense that looking at size and polity might allow one to predict the pattern of conflict in some congregations, but not in all congregations.

This work also provided the basis for beginning to think about why some congregations experienced severe, long-term conflict that did not seem amenable to resolution by any previously existing organizational routine and that leaders felt powerless to stop. If most routine conflict takes place within a consensual frame that shapes it, between-frame conflict is likely to have two characteristics that make it particularly prone to escalation. First, the legitimacy of the routines or the authorities that have in the past resolved conflict are likely to be called into question along with the rest of the frame (cf. Kurtz 1986). In addition, between-frame conflict is more likely to become an arena for political action or the overt deployment of power, which tends to raise the stakes with each round of conflict (cf. Pfeffer 1981).

Because I had asked people about more than conflict, I had some way of getting at their ideas about the nature and purpose of the congregation. I also asked people what the congregation did well, what was special about it, what they liked about it, and what they would change if they could. I asked them what the congregation meant in their life, and I heard in reply everything from short answers that indicated that it was the only large Episcopalian church nearby to long histories of religious searching.

In short, I began to think of congregations *as* congregations, as groups that have their own identities, and not just as straightforward aggregations of underlying dimensions. From this point of view, conflict is not a discrete outcome caused by underlying dimensions. Conflict is a group process that is shaped by members' understandings about the nature of authority and by their own commitment and that in most cases articulates and reinforces a public consensus on "how we do things here." But it is also a process through which, on occasion, groups with a different understanding about the appropriate goals and ways of doing things in congregational life can challenge the previous consensus in an attempt to bring about fundamental change.

Was there something about the identity of each congregation that might explain why it had a particular kind of conflict more than others did, on a variety of dimensions? It would make sense if this identity was related to, and yet not completely determined by, structural factors (size, polity) and cultural orientation. This fit not only with what people like Coser and Simmel had written about conflict, but it also fits Fine's (1984, 1987) and Turner's (1974) descriptions of what local culture is, what role it plays in group life, and how it comes to be in the first place.

Moreover, it fits in with a growing body of work in sociological theory and method that recognizes that, while variable-based approaches may be useful forms of explanation for some kinds of social phenomena, they can at other times obscure more than they clarify. Abbott (1997) has pointed out that seeing outcomes – like conflict events or the characteristics of such events – as variables that can be expressed as the product of one or two underlying dimensions only works with cases that are relatively evenly distributed in social space. But real social phenomena tend to be aggregated into "types" of cases because certain kinds of social forms and social processes tend to be institutionalized while others are not. With this kind of data, looking for patterns or clusters of cases that share some properties on multiple dimensions is a better way to begin an analysis (cf. Abbott 1988, 1992).

This implied that the variables (size, polity, liberal/conservative orientation) were not having some linear effect on conflict because conflicts do not occur randomly. Conflicts may cluster in certain ways because congregations, as organizations, occur in a limited number of discrete types. And perhaps how the variables (those specified in advance and others that had not been anticipated) cluster together to determine a type is what affects conflict patterns. So when I began my search for alternative explanations, I began to think about how to identify empirical types of congregations that might share bundles of features that are relevant to conflict – things like authority structure and norms of member commitment and the degree to which they favored intimacy or issue-based debate.

As a practical matter, all along I had been coding all of the interviews, fieldnotes, and written materials with several categories. One was an "Identity" category. In every place where members, clergy, or written materials talked about things that made the congregation unique, that it did particularly well, that people were proud of, or that were special and noteworthy about it, I coded whatever specific attributes were listed. Statements in interviews that began with "we" were triggers to look for identity statements. This yielded a large number of codes for all twenty-three congregations together, but when separated out by congregation it was usual for members of each congregation to have consensus around anywhere from five to ten items.

These items were all listed in the summaries that I had typed up for each congregation. My first step was simply to read through the case summaries again, concentrating on the identity section. As I read, it became clear that each congregation placed central value on worship and religious education, but that they varied on how much they valued the promotion of fellowship and intimacy among members; how much value they placed on the congregation as an arena for debating social, religious, and political issues that members found important; and how activist they were in the community. As I read through each case summary, I began to make up piles that differed on these three dimensions; whenever I encountered a congregation similar on these dimensions to one I had read before, I placed it on that pile; new types began their own piles.

When I was done, I had five sets of summaries, corresponding to the five groups of congregations introduced in Chapter 1: *houses of worship*, where worship and education are the only strong elements that were repeatedly mentioned in the kinds of "identity-statement" just listed; *family congregations*, where worship and education are important, but so is providing social interaction and fostering intimacy among members; *community congregations*, where worship, the spiritual growth of members, fostering close connections between members, and taking social stands on issues that members care about are important; *leaders*, which do not focus on intimacy or fellowship but care about taking stands on social issues and providing leadership in the community and in their denomination; and *mixed* or *transitional congregations*, where there was such a variety of responses to identity types of questions that no dominant pattern was discernible.

The first four are groups of congregations where there is a high degree of consensus about identity. The last one is a group of congregations where there are at least two groups with two different sets of ideas about congregational identity. I was reasonably certain not only that I had identified distinct types but that I was able to place most of the congregations within a single dominant type.

After I tentatively identified these five groups, I went back and reread each interview, fieldnote, and piece of documentation for each congregation within the group and systematically coded answers to the following questions (see Appendix B):

"What does being a member of this congregation mean to you?"
"What role does the congregation play in your life?"
"What brings this congregation together?"
"What are the pressing issues facing the congregation in the short term?"
"What does your congregation do well?"
"In what areas would you like to see your congregation improve?"
"What are the congregation's goals over the next five years or so?"

The answers fell into patterns that confirmed my earlier coding as revealed in the case summaries, with one exception. I was not certain whether the Assemblies of God church should be coded as a "community" model or placed in the "mixed" pile because some people seemed to respond to my question out of a "family" model while others seemed to fit a "community" model. With this congregation, I ended up doing more observations and reinterviewing the pastor before assigning it to the community model. (See Chapter 8 for a longer discussion.)

In the twenty interviews for the two house of worship congregations, only two people told me that the congregation was a place for warm and supportive relationships, while eighteen people spent a lot of time talking about the congregation providing a good atmosphere for worship. Eighteen out of twenty listed worship as the thing that they do well and that brings people together, and nothing else was mentioned consistently. In family congregations, ninety-five percent of the members, spread evenly throughout the six congregations, said that the congregation meant, for them, a location for close, supportive friendships and family-like attachments. Over ninety percent said that what their congregation does well is to provide a warm and caring atmosphere.

In community congregations, over eighty-five percent of the people interviewed said that they found the congregation to be a place of warm and supportive relationships, and over seventy percent also give a religious reason for belonging, mentioning a specific doctrine or belief that the congregation expresses that is important to them (things like, "it's Biblical" or "it's Christ-centered"). In each community congregation, both fellowship and religious beliefs were mentioned as part of what brings the congregation together, and in each one, over fifty percent specifically mentioned the congregation's tolerance and openness as something that the congregation does well. (This is true for liberal and conservative ones alike.) In leader congregations, over eighty-five percent attend for religious reasons, while only about thirty percent said that they find friendships and support there. Between one-half and three-fourths of the interviewees in each one said that outreach is something that they do well, and over one-half said that the congregation provides "leadership for the community."

As I read through the interviews and fieldnotes again, I also began to realize that there were other patterns within each type of congregation. In each one, the pastor and the lay leadership played different roles, not only during conflict but also in other routine decisions. There was a different tone to the social interaction before and after the worship service: Members interacted with one another differently and reacted to me, a stranger, differently, asking different kinds of questions of me. Congregations of some types had a strong sense of history and goals dominated by finances, while others had little sense of history and goals dominated by a language of spiritual growth. The chapters that follow outline the ways of doing things that make each type of congregation different.

These differences, I argue, are driven by the core tasks that have been institutionalized in the congregation. Congregations that are primarily about worship are different on many dimensions than those that also think that providing a family-like atmosphere is vital. Both family congregations and houses of worship are different than those congregations where engaging in social issues in some way is important, and different still are those where people think a major congregational responsibility is being a leader or engaging in activism. In addition, my rereading confirmed that in four congregations there were deep divisions that predated the specific conflicts that were causing so much concern. These are the congregations that were, during my fieldwork, in a period of transition from one congregational model to another.

The argument here needs to be specified. I am not saying that size and polity have no effect on conflict. Rather, I argue that they have an indirect effect that is mediated by congregational culture. Small congregations are more likely to think of themselves as families or communities and large ones as houses of worship or leaders. Congregations with a hierarchical polity are more likely to think of themselves as families or houses of worship, while those with congregational polity are more likely to think of themselves as a community of shared values or as a leader (see Table 4).

But, out of nineteen congregations that have institutionalized a dominant congregational model, there are six exceptions to these general rules of thumb. Also, an explanation focusing on the congregational model is the only one that can account for the conflict in the transitional congregations. None of them is growing, so the transition is not triggered by a change in size. And one-half are congregational and one-half hierarchical, so polity is not the explanation. A focus on structural variables and ideology, then, left me unable to understand the conflict pattern in ten out of

Table 4. *Congregational models and other congregational characteristics**

	Size (S/L)	Polity (C/H)	Liberal (L)/ Conservative (C)	Denomination
House of Worship	1S 1L	0C 2H	1L 1C	Catholic, UMC
Family	6S 0L	1C 5H	3L 3C	Episcopal, UMC, Nazarene, UCC, Pres. USA
Community	4S 2L	5C 1H	2L 4C	AOG, Baptist, Conservative Jewish, LCA, UCC, Plymouth Brethren
Leader	1S 4L	4C 1H	3L 2C	Baptist, UCC, Pres. USA, Reform Jewish, Disciples
Mixed	0S 4L	2C 2H	3L 1C	Catholic, MS Lutheran, Episcopal, Unit. Univ.

* For size, "S" indicates small and "L" indicates large; for polity, "C" indicates congregational and "H" indicates hierarchical. "Baptist" indicates independent Baptist congregations. Other abbreviations are specified in Appendix A.

twenty-three congregations, while a focus on congregational models allowed me to understand and explain conflict in all twenty-three.

With a refocus of the analysis to congregational models, there was a shift in what this study is a case of (cf. Ragin and Becker 1992). From a study of the underlying variables that influence conflict patterns in local congregations, this became a study of four different ways of imagining, and institutionalizing, religious communities at the local level – four different congregational models. These four models are bundles of core tasks and related ways of doing things that are defined culturally; they are related to structural variables, like size and polity, but they are not determined by them. They are related to conflict because they constitute and are constituted by factors that shape conflict in groups – the nature of the ties between members, the norms of commitment, and the structure of authority.

But whose local culture is it? As Griswold (1992) has noted, an important question is, who imagines the imagined community? (cf. Anderson 1991). Who has the power to determine the public culture, to institutionalize one preferred model? We tend to think of local cultures as somehow evolving "naturally," but Fine's (1984) idea of local culture as a negotiated order underscores the role of power in determining the dominant features of the public culture. In these congregations, the leadership was provided by a set of mostly white managers, businesspeople, and professionals, many of them Baby Boomers, but some of an older, World War II generation. The public culture here is a reflection of the individual-expressive religion that is paradigmatic of this group (Hammond 1992). The dimensions along which the congregational models vary reveal the divisions among this group of mostly white managers and professionals over religious questions. How publicly engaged should religious organizations be? How activist? It reveals the tendency to use the local congregation as a place to reconstitute family-like connections for a group that is highly mobile. It also reveals the moral seriousness and cultural exploration that Tipton (1982) and Roof (1993) have noted, as members attempt to construct congregations that embody the moral and civic values and concerns of white, middle-class professionals.

Notes

1. The demographic and economic information comes from the 1990 census.
2. Raymond (1972), Goodwin (1979), and Turner (1981) have discussions of this

process. Also, see Ammerman (1997a) for a short synopsis of the social changes affecting Oak Park in the recent past and a comparison with other communities undergoing demographic, economic, and cultural changes.

3. Several people I interviewed made the point that many whites did not leave because it was in their economic interest to stay, given the state of interest rates and property values in the area in the early 1970s. Clearly, for some, economics were more important than values in the decision to move to Oak Park or Forest Park.

4. "Race question still in Vision 2000's big picture," by Todd Shields, Oak Park *Oak Leaves*, February 12, 1997; http://www.pioneerlocal.com/homepage/op/ ophome.html [accessed 19 June 1997]. I was also able to get a copy of a draft of the village's "Vision 2000" report from the village government, which is based on a series of focus groups and open community meetings. Race and diversity, education, and economic development are the three most prominent themes in the "Vision 2000" report. Among the key questions the report identifies as emerging out of the focus groups and open meetings are the following: "Who defines diversity?", "What is the goal of diversity?", and "How do we rid ourselves of institutionalized discrimination?"

5. 1990 census.

6. 1990 census.

7. Based on phone books, community guides, the Community of Congregation's membership list, and a driving street survey.

8. Feagin et al. (1991) is a good sourcebook for those interested in more general questions about the role and usefulness of case studies in social research, and many articles contain discussions of problems of generalization and typicality. For a slightly different approach to the same questions, compare with Burawoy (1991), especially the introduction. Glaser and Strauss (1967) and Strauss (1995) talk more generally about the process of generalization and inference in qualitative research, and much of this discussion is particularly applicable to case study research, as is Lofland and Lofland (1995). See also Ragin and Becker (1992).

9. For a discussion of what congregations have in common as a form of organization, see Cantrell et al. (1983), Caplow et al. (1983), Hunter (1991), Carroll and Roof (1993), Glock (1993), and Warner (1993). For similarities and differences between synagogues and other kinds of congregations, see Blau (1976) and Wertheimer (1987). For Catholic parishes and the congregational form of organization, see Swatos (1981), Gremillion and Castelli (1987), and Seidler and Meyer (1989).

10. See Appendix A. Previous studies of conflict in religious organizations tended to provide a "laundry list" of causes of conflict or issues around which conflict might revolve. They were heavily reliant on surveys that identified conflict-

ing attitudes or beliefs in individuals or on case studies rather than on a comparative analysis of conflict events. For additional reviews of this literature see Kniss (1997) and Becker et al. (1993).

11. This literature includes case studies (LeFevre 1975; Greenhouse 1986; Furman 1987; Neitz 1987; Warner 1988; Prell 1989) as well as more general or synthetic accounts (Leas and Kittlaus 1973; Dudley 1983; Leas 1992).

12. Becker et al. (1993) contains a review of this literature and concludes that the voluntaristic nature of contemporary American religion means that members use the congregation as a forum for expressive struggles over identity and values; compare the discussion there with some case studies (Kurtz 1986; Kniss 1997); see also Leas (1992).

13. A variety of studies over the years have developed this argument; see Hadden (1969), Hoge (1976), Nelsen and Maguire (1980), Wood (1981), and White (1990).

14. See Roof (1978), Marty (1986), Roof and McKinney (1987), McKinney and Olson (1989), Hunter (1991), Glock (1993), and Ammerman (1994); cf. Wuthnow (1988).

15. None of these studies provides a guideline for choosing the congregations to study, because they do not indicate that conflict between factions or over identity should occur more in some kinds of congregations than in others.

16. Park and Burgess (1924); cf. Weber (1947) and Coser (1956).

17. See Griswold (1987) for a discussion on cultural objects, which she defines as "shared significance embodied in form." On considering events as cultural objects, see Sahlins (1985:xiv), who notes that "an event is not simply a phenomenal happening, even though as a phenomenon it has reasons and focus of its own, apart from any symbolic scheme. An event becomes such as it is interpreted."

18. Of course, understanding when latent divisions do not lead to overt conflict is also important, and I collected as much information about that as possible. When someone told me that the congregation had "no conflict," I would use probing questions like these: "During the last five years, what events or issues in the congregation have been the subject of disagreement? Have there been any events or issues that have resulted in prolonged or heated debate? Over which people have left the church (temple)? Which have caused hurt feelings or other problems?" Through this and through coding other parts of the interviews, I have some information from each congregation about latent factions – tensions between older and newer members, between clergy and laity, between those with children and those without, between those preferring a more informal worship style and those who want a more formal one, and, in a few cases, between liberals and conservatives.

19. Counting only conflicts mentioned by two or more respondents.

20. See Abbott (1992, 1997).

21. Other work has taken these theoretical ideas about the relationship between conflict, group culture, and patterns of interaction and applied it to settings as diverse as the Catholic Church (Kurtz 1986), the Mennonite community in the United States (Kniss 1997), middle-class suburban family life (Baumgartner 1988), and executives in major corporations (Jackall 1988; Morrill 1995). These studies, conducted in vastly different settings, illustrate how styles of participation in conflict are directly related to the normative pattern of relationships among individuals, including patterns of obligation among members and styles of commitment to the group. This work also discusses how and why conflict, in some circumstances, quickly becomes framed as either moral or personal, and it examines implications for understanding under what circumstances specific conflicts become larger struggles for power over group identity.

3

HOUSES OF WORSHIP

When I walked into the United Methodist congregation one Sunday morning, I was greeted by a man who looked to be in his mid-forties. His dark hair was cut short, and he wore a dark suit with a carnation boutonniere. He smiled at me, said, "Welcome! How are you this morning?" and shook my hand. I replied that I was fine, and he handed me a bulletin. He told me to sit anywhere and make myself at home. He asked, "Do you have any questions?" I said no, smiled, and went in to sit down.

It is a huge sanctuary, with gray, heavy stonework, dark wood, and a vaulted ceiling, with seating for about 500 on the main floor plus a large balcony. At one time several hundred people attended services each Sunday morning. Now there were just over a hundred people in the sanctuary, which was typical for a Sunday service. Many of them were older, but there were also younger couples, some with children.

The small congregation was spread out through the first twenty pews. Taking a seat at the back edge of where the people were, I had one-half of a twenty-foot pew to myself. Nobody sat by me or spoke to me as the service began. About fifteen minutes into the service, the time came for the passing of the peace, a ritual that is performed in many churches, Protestant and Catholic, every Sunday. It involves turning to the people seated close by and exchanging some form of greeting, usually "Peace" or "Peace be with you." In some congregations it is accomplished in a few moments, with no other activity, but in others the ritual also includes a handshake, an embrace, or walking to people seated in other parts of the sanctuary and greeting them, lasting several minutes in the most gregarious gatherings. In this church, people turned to one another in their pews, saying, "Peace." The couple in the other half of my pew, about fifteen feet to my right, looked at me and smiled. I smiled back. No one came over to speak to me, and I did not initiate contact.

At the end of the service, I was a bit surprised that the pastor did not stand at the doors of the sanctuary to greet people on their way out, a common end-of-service ritual in many churches and standard practice in other Methodist churches I have attended over the years. Most of the people left quickly, by the main and side doors, hurrying to their cars in the chilly fall weather. The usher who had greeted me was still at the back of the sanctuary, so I asked him how to find the fellowship hall. The bulletin had said that the coffee time would be held there.

He pointed out the adjoining fellowship hall, a cavernous room decorated with banners made with felt, the kind we used to make in Sunday School and Bible school classes when I was growing up in a Methodist church in Ohio: rainbows and Jesus as the Shepherd leading chunky white felt sheep. The pastor was standing at the entranceway to the fellowship hall; since I had not yet made an appointment to talk with him about my research, I introduced myself simply as a visitor. He shook my hand, said, "Welcome!", and pointed out the information table over to the side that had brochures and flyers about the congregation's various committees, programs, and mission activities.

There were perhaps thirty-five people standing scattered around the big room, some alone but most in small groups, drinking coffee in paper cups. To one side were two tables covered in white butcher-block paper, which had two big silver-colored coffee urns and store-bought cookies on paper plates. No one spoke to me, so I introduced myself to several people, including a young woman in her late twenties standing at the information table. When I asked her how long she had been coming here, she said that she had just been a few times. I said I had attended several congregations in the area, and I asked her what she particularly liked about this one. She hesitated, then said that she had always been a Methodist and that the pastor gave good sermons. And she liked Methodist mission activities. I stayed only fifteen minutes, and by the time I left, perhaps fifteen or twenty people were still there.

A couple of months later I attended the main Sunday morning Mass at the Catholic church in the north part of town and had an experience that was in many ways similar to my visit to the Methodist church. This was a much bigger congregation, filling up their large sanctuary for the ten o'clock service. Just like at the Methodist church, the only person who spoke to me unprompted was the official greeter at the back of the sanctuary, who smiled, said hello, and handed me a program. I found that it was easy to remain completely aloof. After the service I did speak to several people as they were slowly gathering up their things, ready to leave. Everyone was polite, but it was hard to strike up a sustained conversation. There was no coffee hour the Sunday I attended, and when I asked people about this, they said that they used to have one and it was something that they were thinking of starting up again.

In both congregations, I asked several people questions after the service, questions that I had found in the past were usually a good way to get people talking about their congregation. "How long have you been coming to this church? What do you like about it? Do you live in Oak Park?" In both churches, people would smile and answer politely, but they did not volunteer too much information; and apart from asking if I lived nearby, they did not evince much curiosity about me. At the coffee hour at the Methodist church, people told me that, if I really wanted to know about the church, I should talk to the pastor.

At the Catholic church, members and the priest reported no conflict. At the Methodist church, three small administrative conflicts were reported. One was when the pastor persuaded the older secretary who had been there for a long time to leave and hired a secretary who could put in more hours and who was familiar with the computer. The former secretary had been disappointed when the previous pastor had left, and she made this known.

The pastor said it was a matter of efficiency to hire someone with better skills. Some people felt that it was unfortunate to in effect fire the older secretary. They felt sorry for her. But this was never talked about as an interpersonal conflict, and it did not mobilize a group of older members against the pastor. Rather, it was discussed, at least publicly, as a staff issue, something within the pastor's appropriate purview. As one person said, "Of course he has the right to put his own team into place."

Initially I would wonder if the lack of reported conflict in both of these congregations stemmed from a reluctance to share unflattering information with an outsider. I also considered the possibility that they might have a good deal of what I would call conflict, but they might perceive it differently. Later, after more fieldwork in each church, I came to view the lack of conflict as genuine and as linked to the limited style of member commitment in these two congregations.

Who We Are

To call a congregation a "house of worship" might seem redundant. By definition, a congregation is a worshipping community. Of the twenty-three congregations in which I did fieldwork, all view worship as an important ritual in the life of the congregation. The only activity or program that receives as much attention and as many resources is religious education. All twenty-three congregations have some formal program of religious education for children, and the vast majority have one for adults as well, ranging from in-home Bible study or discussion groups to Sunday School classes to the Conservative temple's series of visiting speakers who lecture on topics from history to art to faith.

Worship and religious education are the keys to reproducing a religious tradition, teaching people the symbols, beliefs, and rituals that distinguish a particular religious heritage from others.[1] They are also the central activities that produce and reproduce religious participation and membership.

Worship is the most publicly available congregational activity, bringing in outsiders who may go on to become members. Worship and religious education are also central to internal reproduction, or the maintenance of the existing membership, by teaching the young the traditions of the faith and by renewing the faith of existing members. Worship is also the public venue in which the congregation's identity can by symbolized. Is the church a formal or informal place? To what extent do children participate in the service? What musical traditions are featured, and what metaphors are used in the service? The choices made regarding these kinds of issues, and many others, result in a worship style and experience that says something about the larger tradition, but also about the particular history and members of a congregation.

Worship here is understood broadly, reflecting the understanding of those I interviewed in these congregations. It includes the regularly repeated masses or services that occur each week, on Sunday or Saturday and perhaps other days, depending on the tradition and the size of the congregation. But it also includes the ritual life of the congregation more broadly. All congregations provide rituals like baptism, bar and bat mitzvahs, or some dedication ceremony for children. They provide weddings, funerals, and other religious rituals for important life events.

All congregations are worshipping communities, and all provide for the religious education of their members. A congregation would not survive as such without these activities. So what distinguishes a congregation as a "house of worship"?

In *some* congregations, worship and education are not only conducted, they are viewed as the primary and most important tasks of the local congregation, to the exclusion of other priorities. They are what members value most. They are what the congregation is known for in the community. All of the other activities that congregations sometimes engage in and value highly, from mission to fellowship to outreach, are either not done at all or are consistently deemphasized. *Houses of worship* concentrate on worship, religious education, and the rituals that mark life events. These activities are consistently valued above all other tasks; they are central to the congregation's public discourse and social identity.

In only two of the twenty-three congregations, the United Methodist and the Roman Catholic churches highlighted at the beginning of this chapter, did I find this sense that the only centrally important tasks are worship, religious education, and rituals like weddings, baptisms, and funerals. When I asked both members and clergy what their congregation does well or what brings the people there together, ninety percent in each congregation said "worship," and it is from this response that the term "house of worship" is drawn. If worship is of central importance, a part of that is making newcomers feel welcome, and about one-third of the people in each congregation said that they do a good job of being friendly and welcoming to newcomers on a Sunday morning, usually mentioning that they have greeters present at each worship service.

I asked members about what their congregations were like, but I also talked to them about their own feelings of loyalty and attachment. Across all twenty-three congregations, the responses to questions about loyalty and attachment revolved around several basic themes. Some people talked about religious reasons for belonging. Others spoke of the congregation as a place to make connections with other people, using words like friendship, family, support, fellowship, caring, or community to describe what the congregation meant to them. Still others used a language of service; for them, the congregation was a place to "give something back" to the community or to reach out to those in need. Some people talked about the congregation as a "community of values," a place to discuss social issues or morality or ethics with like-minded others. Some talked about the congregation as a venue for activism, that is, a place to work with others to effect change in their local community or beyond.

The two house of worship churches were distinctive in that people spoke primarily about religious reasons for belonging. When asked "What does being a member of this congregation mean to you? What role does it play in your life?", three-quarters immediately gave a religious answer, most often saying that the church is, for them, a place to worship and to express or explore their belief in God. About one-third told me that the congregation is a location of important friendships or is "a community of shared values." When I asked people about the activities that they value most, people talked about the religious education program or special worship services held at Christmas or Easter.

It is not that these congregations engage in no other activities besides worship and religious education. Both of them engage in compassionate outreach to the poor, usually by giving money to programs instituted by and carried out through ecumenical or denominational organizations. But when I asked members what they liked about the congregation, what it does well, or what brings the congregation together, nobody ever talked about outreach or compassionate ministry, just as they never gave any of the other reasons for belonging that were common in other congregations.

57

They never talked about leadership in the community, and they never said that the congregation gives them an important arena in which to discuss and debate important social and religious issues – all common responses in other congregations. Rather, they talked about how the ritual life, especially worship and religious education, helped them to develop their own faith.

A quote from one member of the Catholic congregation is a good illustration of the dominant orientation in that congregation, and it is typical of the responses that I received to questions about what the church means in people's lives:

> For me, church is spiritual. I come there for [pause] to listen to the Scriptures, to hear the homilies, to have inspiration – guidance – basically just a chance to reconnect to my religious convictions, and to pray.

Although this woman is a long-term member and was on the church council at the time of the interview, she has and seeks few friends there and could name no social issues on which the congregation had taken a corporate stand.

It may seem as though such an orientation is particularly Catholic or, at least, that it is exemplary of the strong Roman Catholic emphasis on personal devotion and the Mass as a ritual that fosters individual connection to the divine.[2] I did not expect to find this kind of discourse in the United Methodist (UMC) congregation. In the UMC heritage, the idea of *connectionalism* is of central importance, signifying not only a formal relationship of church administration and governance, but also a strong doctrinal tradition of linking personal salvation and piety to compassionate outreach and social action in the world. Connectionalism implies a strong preference for public over private religion. As the UMC *Book of Discipline* states:

> Scriptural holiness entails more than personal piety; love of God is always linked with love of neighbor, a passion for justice and renewal in the life of the world.[3]

Yet, at the United Methodist church, members spoke about their commitment to their church in language that sounded quite a bit like that of the members of the Catholic church. Carol, a black professional woman in her sixties, was typical for this UMC congregation. When I asked her, "What does this congregation mean in your life?" she told me:

Well I guess I joined because I've always been churched. I shouldn't say always, but for many, many years. . . . And I'm not comfortable unless I have that support. It means something to me. You know, I don't use the pastor as a sounding board. If I have personal problems, I don't usually go to him with them, you know. So that's not the way I use it. It's more internal, you know? I enjoy being in church on Sunday, I like to hear the message, I think the pastor here gives exceptionally good messages.

She goes on to say that the church is not, for her, about friendships with other people:

See, I'm not, I can't really say, I don't use the church as the center of my social life, at all; it's peripheral at best. It's just the feeling that I get, something that I want, and my husband shares that. We're . . . very faithful.

Worship is understood as having two main purposes in both of these congregations. The first is to promote the individual's spiritual development and renewal. In order for this to happen, members note that the service must be "done well." Both pastors are sensitive to this. In both congregations the head pastors told me that they make an effort to get regular feedback on the liturgy via surveys, retreats, and more informal means. This annual effort can be contrasted to the other twenty-one congregations, in which people reported engaging in this kind of assessment of the worship life only in times of major transition, such as the calling of a new pastor.

But what does it mean to do a service "well" in a house of worship? In both congregations, people indicated in recent member surveys that what they want most is a *feeling of intimacy* in the service. People use adjectives like "rich" and "meaningful" and "intimate" to describe what they want. This is not an interpersonal intimacy, not an intimacy with fellow worshippers. Rather, intimacy in this context specifically refers to music and ritual that promote a feeling of closeness to and connection with God. The feeling of intimacy and the desired connection is with the divine, not the human. Members of both congregations told me that they wanted "an emotional, mysterious, religious element" in the worship service. Members of the other twenty-one congregations almost never talked about worship using this language of mystery and transcendance.

Worship is also an important part of the public witness of these congregations. In both, the members and clergy take particular pride that their worship services are open to all of the members of the community. On the signboard of one congregation is the phrase "A Church Where All Are Welcome." The pastor told me a story of how a mixed-race couple saw that sign and then called up the Chamber of Commerce to ask about congregations where they might feel at home. The Chamber of Commerce recommended this church, and the couple are now members. The pastor explained to me that that is what a church is all about, being a place of worship where everyone in the community is welcome. In the Catholic church, members tell me that their very presence and activity are their witness to the community. This is particularly true of their five Masses on Sunday, but also of the school and all of the activities that keep their physical plant humming with activity almost every day of the week.

This is a different way of thinking about what worship is and what it does than I found in the other twenty-one congregations. In this view, worship is a kind of public activity that testifies to the presence of the believing community within the larger community. There is a religious-institutional basis for this view in the theology of many denominations. Occasionally, a pastor in one of the other twenty-one congregations would articulate this rationale to me. For example, one Episcopalian pastor, whose church has institutionalized a family model, told me that traditionally his denomination thinks of the church as meeting and worshipping on behalf of the local community. The Lutheran pastor in a community congregation told me that holding their summer services outdoors is part of their testimony to their vital and active presence in the neighborhood. And the Rabbi of the Conservative synagogue told me that their physical presence and ongoing viability as a congregation is a witness to their Jewish faith and the presence of a Jewish community within the larger secular (and gentile) one.

So the idea of worship as witness, the active and visible sign of the community of faith within the secular community, is relatively common, at least among the clergy. But only in the two house of worship congregations was the idea of worship as public witness articulated by pastors and lay leaders alike. Moreover, it is the only form of witness for which members and clergy see the congregation as responsible.

Members were prone to connect this idea of witness directly and explicitly to the length of time that the church has been present in the community. When the very presence of the congregation is a witness to the community, the length of time that the congregation has been around seems to take on a highlighted importance. A dominant theme in congregational literature is having a long history in the local community. Brochures and bulletins feature prominently the congregations' founding dates and carry such phrases as "we are a historic church." These congregations see themselves as long-term providers of religious services and resources to the community as a whole. In interviews, members talk of the same themes, emphasizing the stability and duration of the church's community presence.

How We Do Things Here

The centrality of worship and education to the congregational identity is linked to typical ways of doing things; it goes along with an overall congregational style. This style encompasses typical ways in which members interact with each other, ways of incorporating new members, the role of the pastor, and typical ways of making decisions.

The worship service in these congregations may effectively foster a feeling of intimacy between the individual and the divine, but it also effectively maintains a sense of distance between persons. It is easy to be anonymous. When I attended, both congregations had ushers who also served as official greeters, introducing themselves to me and smiling, handing me a bulletin, and telling me that they hoped I enjoyed the service. It is this kind of activity – having official greeters, following up with a mailing to people who fill out the guest cards – that is mentioned by the one-third of the respondents who feel that their congregation does a good job of welcoming new people. They refer to the fact that they have an official program in place for greeting new people and answering their questions.

Apart from this interaction, though, few people spoke to me, unless I initiated conversation. When I did ask a question (from "Where's the ladies' room?" to "Have you gone here long?"), I got a smile, a direct reply, and not much chitchat ("Down the hall on the right" or "Six years"). People were quite nice, but not very curious about a newcomer and not given to lingering or chatting with a stranger. Even during the passing of the peace, the most interactive part of the service, it was easy to remain apart. And when the service ended, most people left quickly, many by the side doors, speaking to no one and hurrying to their cars. One congregation did not have a coffee hour; and in the other very few people stayed and the coffee hour lasted for about twenty-five minutes.

In these two churches, it is left up to the visitor to make contacts, and remaining apart from fellow worshipers is a choice that will be respected. This is the case not only for visitors but also for members. As one woman commented about the Catholic parish, "If you don't have kids in the school, you can go for five years and not know anyone there." She was not complaining, because she was not looking for a closer set of attachments through the church. In the Methodist congregation, some long-term members reported that they had close friends in the congregation, but others did not. Those who did not had never felt pressured to become more friendly. They had not left the church looking for a friendlier one, and they reported that their lack of social connections in the congregation had not hindered their ability to serve in positions of lay leadership. Carol, quoted above as saying that the church is peripheral at best to her social life, had been the president of the Administrative Council in the past and was currently chairing the Pastor–Parish Relations Committee.

The optional nature of friendship here may not be surprising if one compares these two churches to other community, voluntary, or professional organizations, but it is surprising in congregations. Warner (1994) has written that fellowship is a "master function" of congregational life. And pastors in Oak Park, River Forest, and Forest Park were more likely than not to tell me that interpersonal closeness, fellowship, friendship, social connections, and emotional support are increasingly in demand; they are things that members expect the congregation to foster.

The pastor in the United Methodist congregation tried to foster more interpersonal intimacy in his congregation, out of his own sense that such intimacy meets important spiritual and personal needs. In one conversation, he talked to me at length about how the impersonality of modern life is both physically and emotionally isolating, wearing on the spirit. He asked me how often in the last week someone had given me a hug, other than my own husband, and, when I hesitated, he noted that for most people that kind of intimate, friendly contact is not part of daily life outside of their own families. He felt that the church should be a place where that isolation is broken through, where people have real, caring friendships and close contact. He said this was part of being the body of Christ and a necessary basis for forming the kinds of connections that foster spiritual growth as well as emotional healing.

So he was saddened to have found that kind of intimacy to be difficult, if not impossible, to foster in this congregation. He had been trying to move the congregation toward a different model, one that emphasizes the congregation as "a family" or "a sharing community," and one that is more willing to examine their stands on social issues like race or the roles of lesbians and gays in society and in the church. To him, intimacy is a precondition of that kind of conversation. The church he had envisioned this congregation becoming sounded to me like the congregations that will be discussed Chapter 5, "community" congregations that foster both interpersonal closeness and a sense of being a community of shared values.

As a first step toward this new model, the pastor had instituted a "Sharing of Joys and Concerns" time in the Sunday service. Preceding the formal prayers, members were to gather in a multilayered circle around the altar and speak to one another about particularly good things that were happening in their lives (joys) or ask for prayers about anything that had been troubling them (concerns). Then, during the formal prayer, the pastor would include the joys and concerns just mentioned by the members. This practice symbolizes the congregation as a caring community, involved in one another's lives, talking about their private joys and needs, and lifting one another up in prayer.

Some of the newer members were very happy to see the pastor initiate the "Joys and Concerns" time because they were dissatisfied with the current service, finding it too impersonal. Connie, a younger professional woman who recently joined the church, was one of these newer members who was initially excited about this change to the worship service. However, in our interview, she told me that it has not really worked, that people "have not gotten behind it." When I asked her to elaborate, she told me that, to her annoyance, people use the "Sharing of Joys and Concerns" time to "share trivial things" instead of revealing truly personal experiences or insights. Connie had complained about this to the pastor, hoping that he would encourage people to open up more during this time. But he had reminded her that not everyone is comfortable or has experience sharing intimate things in public.

And he is right. Saying that she thought that the new practice was a good idea, Carol nevertheless described her own response to the "Joys and Concerns" time this way:

> Some people do get up and say what's bothering them, if they had a death in the family or someone's ill, or they're starting a new job or they're moving away or their baby's sick, whatever is going on. Or there's a birthday, or something to celebrate. . . . It's just open. And

some people are able to do that better, more than others. I'm not really able to, too much. I might come up with once in a while a birthday or something. When my mother was very, very ill, I couldn't share that. I guess [pause] that was too personal for me. And yet there are people who do share very personal things.

The other people I interviewed, except for Connie, concurred. They said that they liked the "Joys and Concerns" time well enough, but expressed surprise that anyone would actually share intimate things out loud in the service. One older man gave a typical summing up when he said, "Usually, I sit back and watch." During the Sunday service that I attended, the "joys" expressed included two birthdays and children traveling back home from college for a visit, and the concerns included prayers for a sick aunt (no details given). Few people participated, and no one shared anything that caused them, or anyone else, emotional discomfort.

Of course, some members in these two congregations do have friends in the church. About one-third of the members I interviewed told me that they have some very good friends there. These are mostly older people who are long-term members and who have been actively involved in leadership over the years. But, in contrast to some other congregations, providing a close and caring set of relationships between people is not a congregational goal here. It is not mentioned by members, in mission statements or planning documents or promotional literature, as something that they want to do a better job at. Friendliness and forming close interpersonal connections are optional in these two congregations in a way that they are not, for example, in community or family congregations.

House of worship congregations do provide support for members in times of personal crisis, but they tend to do so via the church staff or specific, formal programs, as this woman on the Parish Council of the Catholic church told me:

I think we, probably, if you were to stand aside and look at the parish, you probably would say we do a good job in kind of being aware of what our needs are. We have a number of programs that people have instituted in order to reach out to others. We have a lot going on . . . we have people who are concerned about others in need, a variety of needs, bereavement needs, financial needs, whatever, and we've developed programs, we've started programs to begin to help, to reach out to them.

In the Methodist church, support in crisis is left to the pastor for the most part, and people reported that he is quite good at pastoral support and counseling. As with the welcoming of visitors and new members, the meeting of personal needs and the reaching out to members experiencing grief or hardship are handled efficiently and professionally in these congregations, through the paid staff or through formal programs.

This is in contrast to some of the other congregations in Oak Park. For example, in family and community congregations, lay members often mobilize spontaneously to help one another when illness or some other crisis strikes because "we're family." House of worship congregations see crisis support as a religious responsibility, and they have formal measures in place to meet it, just as they do with the responsibility to welcome newcomers to Sunday worship.

Some of the congregations in Oak Park are places for social activism, but the house of worship congregations are apolitical, in two senses. First, the congregation itself is likely not to adopt formal policies or statements on social or political issues. The Methodist congregation is proud to welcome all members, but it has no policy on race or integration. Although many individual members are concerned that the village continue its history of tolerance of lesbians and gays, the congregation has no policy of inclusiveness.

In the Catholic church there was recently an attempt by a few members to have the congregation take a strong and official anti-abortion stand. This is in a church where most people would probably identify as pro-life, according to the pastor and the lay leaders to whom I spoke. People did not disagree with the views of these ardently pro-life Catholics, nor did they resist their efforts. They were simply uninterested in taking any formal, corporate action, like changing their mission statement or adopting a congregational resolution condemning abortion and supporting the local crisis pregnancy center. A few of the more outspoken pro-life members left the congregation in frustration at their inability to mobilize their congregation to action.

More generally, these congregations offer no public forum for discussion of social issues. When I asked people at the Catholic church whether their congregation was liberal or conservative, or if there would be a consensus on such issues as abortion or homosexuality, I was told that such issues were not discussed from the pulpit; the pastor gave homilies on the Bible, not on contemporary society, as this man told me:

From the pulpit I think there's very little discussion of social issues. . . . The pastor tends to stay to the Reading of the Day and sticks to the message being put forth in it.

In fact, the priest and several members told me that, when they had had a series of open meetings to discuss women's roles in the Church, it was so poorly attended that they had decided that the congregation just was not interested in that kind of social/religious issue. Even people in sympathy with the general point were not interested in using the local church as a forum for discussion of these issues. One woman, who told me that she was sympathetic with the idea of women priests, told me,

But, I'm [pause] I'm not carrying any signs. . . . [And] there are no strong lobbying groups in the congregation, on any issue.

When leaders reflect on their congregations, they are aware that this lack of issue-based debate can be interpreted as apathy. A report from a January 1991 planning retreat in the Methodist congregation concluded that there is

a. some feeling that we don't communicate important activities with enough excitement and enthusiasm;
b. some feeling that we ought to create more excitement by the way we communicate, by the way we encourage participation, and by the way we follow up on things.

Among the suggestions generated by the retreat, as reported to the congregation, was this one:

We give ourselves permission and support each other in being more demonstrable about our enthusiasms.

The pastor and a couple of lay leaders told me that this refers, in particular, to exploring their congregation's stands on social issues like race and homosexuality, which mean a lot to a few people but are generally not talked about in the congregation. Yet eleven months later, in November, when I completed the bulk of the fieldwork in this congregation, there was no sense among members that this change had come about, and there was no widespread feeling that it was even desirable. It was also clear that the absence of issue-based debate, while disturbing to the pastor and some lay leaders, was viewed as appropriate by most members, and it did not keep them from feeling a real attachment to their congregation.

Another aspect of these two congregations that can lead some members to conclude in frustration that the majority of their fellows are apathetic is the tendency to delegate decisions to very limited numbers of people. Clergy, staff, and administrative committees make most of the decisions and run most of the programs, generally without widespread discussion or input. Normal organizational inertia is compounded in such a congregation. New programs are difficult to get off the ground, because they are not likely to be supported by a broad and enthusiastic lay constituency who feel that they have some voice in running congregational affairs.

In the Catholic church, one couple told me about their attempts to convince the pastor and Parish Council that they need more young adult and late youth activities and more parents involved in the school. Their experience serves as a good example of a kind of scenario that was mentioned to me by many lay leaders and both pastors in these two churches. The husband told me of the difficulty that he and his wife encountered in generating participation and support for any new program, even a limited one, to address youth needs. He expressed their frustration with the lack of response this way:

> I think that there needs to be more participation beyond the requirements. You know what I mean? It's like any club or organization; there are obligations beyond just showing up. And I just think, I think both the church and the school could be more aggressive or forceful in suggesting the . . . participation.

His wife concurs:

> I'm at a point right now where I just wish there were more people to step up and do things, you know? . . . I think there's a tremendous need to deal with the high-school-age-plus segment of the congregation. . . . After eighth grade, there's really no teen club, or anything like that.

But they were unable to get adults to volunteer as youth ministers or to help with starting a teen club.

The wife thought that this was a symptom of a more general problem, and when I asked her if there were one thing she would change about her congregation if she could, she replied immediately:

> I'd like to see more involvement by a wider group of people. . . . I would really like to see a wider group of people involved. Because I

think it would enhance everybody's life to have more people involved. And I don't know how you do that. I'm not sure how that happens.

As with the "Sharing of Joys and Concerns" time at the Methodist church, it is possible for a pastor or lay leader to start a formal program, but it is impossible to generate widespread participation.

Taken together, these two congregations have an overall style of doing things that is different than that of the other congregations in and around Oak Park. Both of these churches are good at fostering an intimate and religious worship experience, a one-on-one connection with the divine, and a feeling of mystery and transcendance, as reflected in my own interviews but also by the surveys that each congregation had recently done of its members. Both churches put a lot of resources into adult and children's religious education, usually using the denomination's own materials. They pay a great deal of attention to performing the rituals that mark members' important life transitions, and they meet members' needs during crisis times by having a ministry program in place for such occasions. They have elaborate, well-attended holiday services that members talk about even months later. These congregations are smoothly administered, using the formal decision-making routines and bodies that the denominational guidelines spell out. They view the worship service as their public face, an important witness, and have official greeters to take care of newcomers.

In comparison with most of the other congregations in the immediate community, it is also possible to characterize these two churches by what they are not and what they do not attempt. In these congregations, there is no real emphasis on closeness or intimacy among members, no idea that the congregation ought to take corporate stands on social issues, and no value placed on leadership in the larger community or denomination. All of the additional things that a congregation could become – a close-knit community, a place where members express their own preferences and values, a player in village affairs, a leader in the denomination – these congregations have not become, despite demands from small groups of members who would like to see their congregations expand their mission in one or more of these areas.

What is found in these two churches is a focus on a very specific interpretation of the religious functions of the congregation, revolving around corporate worship and religious education, around ritual and the believer's relationship to the divine, and around members' spiritual growth. And despite the urging of pastors inspired by seminary training that emphasizes outreach[4] and a few lay leaders who have had prior experiences with more socially intimate or activist congregations, these churches will not enlarge their set of core tasks. They remain primarily religious centers that provide worship, religious knowledge, and the ritual markers of life's transitions – baptisms, weddings, and funerals.

As such, the religious values that these congregations embody have mostly to do with the private aspects of religion, in two ways. First, they foster experiences of transcendance and mystery rather than social activism or evangelism. Second, they provide the ritual basis of personal piety through the Sunday worship, through the rituals that mark major life events and transitions, and through the programs that make sure that the church's presence is felt in the lives of members when a personal crisis strikes, whether that be the loss of a loved one, a serious illness, or the loss of a job. Some of the older members do talk about the congregation as an outlet for service, mentioning the outreach programs run by the denomination and by ecumenical organizations that the congregation supports, as well as the programs that they have in place to assist their own members in crisis.

It is important to remember that, while a few members become frustrated by this and interpret it as apathy, and while some religious leaders rail against this kind of "religious sanctuary" idea of the local church, most of the members of these two churches do not in fact feel that they have an apathetic orientation (cf. Marty 1994). Some of them are engaged in community affairs and issue-based activism through other organizations, and they find their faith both relevant to and sustaining of their efforts in these other arenas. They report that the local church is an important part of their lives and that belonging to it gives them a place to express and strengthen their religious faith.

Conflict in Houses of Worship

Both of these congregations were remarkable, when compared to the other congregations that I studied, in their lack of reported conflict. There is very little that members and clergy call "conflict" in these congregations. The Catholic church reported no conflict at all, by the definition employed here – at least two people reporting an incident or an issue that they describe as "a conflict." The Methodist congregation had three conflicts over money and personnel. These conflicts were framed as administrative and had a narrow scope of participation, being resolved in a committee or by the pastor. A typical conflict was whether to raise the pastor's salary. This was confined to a subcommittee of the main administrative board, the Pastor–Parish Relations Committee. The committee voted not to raise the salary, and the issue was resolved, and even those who had disagreed accepted the decision as having been made by the proper authority and following the right procedure.

However, not everyone is pleased with the lack of conflict in these two churches. This state of affairs bothers a few lay leaders. Connie, the same woman at the UMC church who wanted a more intimate sharing during the "Joys and Concerns" time, told me that she wishes the church had more conflict. In this wish she is joined by a few lay leaders in each congregation who feel that things are tranquil because potentially controversial issues are not raised or debated by the congregation. In particular, Connie was concerned that her congregation avoided any discussion of racial problems or poverty in the village and had not assessed their stand toward welcoming openly lesbian and gay members. She felt that the UMC heritage, with its emphasis on linking personal piety to social reform and social activism, ought to speak to these issues and that the local church was the appropriate forum at least for some debate and discussion of them.

The UMC pastor tends to share this view of the congregation as unwilling to confront "issues." He attributes this in good part to the congregation's history. In the late 1960s, the congregation experienced an ongoing and divisive battle between factions he describes as "liberal" and "conservative." The pastor at the time was very active in the Civil Rights movement and wanted the congregation to take a vocal stand on racial justice. The congregation was split apart into liberal and conservative camps, and many people left. The current pastor thinks that the memory of this incident still dampens the congregation's willingness to engage in overt conflict.

However, the unwillingness to engage in issue-based debate or provide a public forum for discussion of issues like racism or homosexuality is broadly shared by old-timers and newcomers alike, by those who still remember the earlier conflict and those who know little about it. And this reticence is viewed more positively than negatively by most people in lay leadership and, they report, by most members.

It is not only issue-based debate that is avoided here. There is also little of the kind of interpersonal conflict that tears apart congregations that emphasize close interpersonal relationships among members, especially family congregations. When the new pastor came to the United Methodist congregation several years ago, he almost immediately instituted some changes. He persuaded the secretary to leave and hired a new secretary. Later he made changes in the janitorial staff. In a family congregation, it seems likely that this kind of action on the part of a new pastor might have sparked an emotional, congregation-wide conflict. But in this congregation, the pastor's actions had legitimacy, sparking little public debate.

In the Catholic parish, members report that differences do arise. While not described as conflict, there are ongoing concerns about differences between the north and south parts of the parish. The north part is over the village border, in the neighboring urban community. It is largely African American and gradually becoming more so. Members worry about what to do to attract more members from this area, pointing out that blacks in the United States are not, traditionally, Roman Catholic.

The Catholic lay leaders also have an ongoing concern over the role of the Family Mass group in parish life. This group was formed seventeen years ago by people who wanted more democratic control, alternative liturgies, closer relationships, and more of a welcoming atmosphere for children in the service. The confusing status of this group was reflected when I asked members what I thought would be a straightforward question, "Is this group a part of the parish?" Some people denied that it was, while others said that it was integral to parish life. Most seemed aware that this group can potentially draw members away from the main services and are uneasy about its role in parish life. But no one talked of this group as causing conflict or being a source of conflict.

Something not talked about as "conflict" but as a "significant event" was forming the Parish Council. Begun two years ago, at the pastor's urging, to involve laity more in congregational decision-making, the group draws resources and control away from traditionally powerful groups like the women's organization. Moreover, there was a period of some confusion over the Council's role and functioning that caused some discomfort.

These issues or incidents are all recognized by many members as being at least a potential source of conflict, yet none report any actual conflict events arising around any of these sensitive issues. This seems to be because, when specific decisions have to be made, they are resolved by routines that utilize formal administrative and religious authority structures and they do not cause congregation-wide debate. Nor is there any sense that the outcome or the legitimacy of the leadership is in doubt. Members of this congregation are happy that they are not constantly torn apart by the kinds of turmoil that they see in other churches.

These two churches have this pattern of conflict because of the limited nature of the commitment implied by a house of worship model of congregational life. Members do not have the attachment to the congregation as an important, effective, face-to-face community that members of family and community congregations do, so there is no interpersonal conflict over who is "inside" or "outside." They are not engaged in social issues, nor do they tend to see the congregation as an arena in which to express their own social and political values, so they do not have issue-based conflict. Routine changes in the distribution of resources or power do arise, and disagreements about specific courses of action do, too, but these are contained by legitimate organizational routines and not perceived by members as conflict.

Maintaining a House of Worship

Each congregational model, once it is in place, seems to generate its own set of organizational contradictions. The chief and ongoing problem for the house of worship is "mission-creep," the push by leaders, both clergy and laity, to load on more and different priorities and core tasks. This is a kind of institutionally driven pressure. Clergy in most denominations are trained to fight against parochialism in local congregations and to try to move the congregation from thinking of itself as a sanctuary from the world to a more active and socially aware engagement with it. This is particularly true for liberal Protestant clergy or for rabbis of the Reform tradition, but it is becoming more true even for evangelical Protestant clergy and for Catholic priests in the post–Vatican II era.[5]

It may be that the house of worship model fits less well with the theology of some denominations than with others, adding even more pressure to take on other tasks in some congregations. While members of the Methodist church can cite the historical incident that pushed them toward a house of worship model, members of the Catholic church cannot. Rather, they seem to take it for granted that this is a natural thing that needs no specific historical reason. This means that the question of, "Is this the right model for us?" is something that people can ask in the UMC church but that is not even raised in the Catholic parish.

This is not to say that a house of worship model should be conflated with the model of the Catholic parish. Clearly some Catholic parishes do provide intimacy, some are forums for debate about controversial issues both inside and outside the Church, and some are leaders in their local community and beyond. This may be true even of parishes that maintain a more formal or distant ritual style in the Mass and that nevertheless provide locations for activism and intimacy in other parts of their program. But it may be fair to say that the house of worship model is compatible with one historically prevalent and institutionalized way of thinking about what a Catholic parish ought to be like,[6] while for a Methodist church a house of worship model has not, historically, been a legitimate model for the local congregation.

In addition to pressure from clergy, lay leaders whose experience with other congregations in the past leads them to want a more socially engaged or a more friendly congregation may try to move the house of worship to adopt functions that the bulk of current members see as marginal or irrelevant. The house of worship model, while definitely preferred by some congregational members, may be less stable than other models, and this may particularly be true in this kind of highly educated, professional, politically aware community. The best example of this was in the splitting off of the Family Mass group from the main Catholic parish about thirty years ago. This group was constituted entirely by laity who wanted a more intimate congregation and who, in effect, created one out of a subgroup of the larger parish. Their worship service, conducted in the large parish gymnasium, features not only informal seating (folded chairs) but also a moveable altar, a priest facing the congregation, and public prayers that mention private aspects of members' lives in detail, including instances of suffering, grief, and illness. It also features children, sitting on parents' laps or playing quietly together in the back, on the floor behind the folding seats, watched by several parents, mostly fathers, standing in a loose ring at the very back of the improvised worship space.

The Family Mass group attests not only to the desire of lay members for a different congregational model; it also illustrates how particular denominational forms can either foster or suppress certain models of congregational life. For the members of the Methodist church who want a more intimate worship experience, one is to be had in at least two of the small UMC churches in Oak Park and Forest Park. That is to say, finding an intimate worship experience would be as simple as leaving this congregation and looking for a Methodist church with a different congrega tional model, a fact of which the pastor is quite well aware. For the Catholic parishioners who wanted a more intimate worship experience, a much more radical break with standard parish life was necessary.

In both of these congregations, a certain ritual nod is made to other mission priorities, but they never touch the core of the common life (cf. Meyer and Rowan 1991). Compassionate outreach is achieved through donations to programs run by the denomination or organized with other congregations through the local ecumenical organization. Issue-based activism is left entirely to denominationally sponsored special-purpose groups that are active at other levels of the organization or carried out through other community organizations besides the church. Anyone at the Methodist church who is interested in them can find out about them at the information table at the coffee hour or through the pastor, just as the Catholic parishioners can be referred by the priest to other places where they can find an outlet for service, activism, or outreach. Programs like the "Sharing of Joys and Concerns," spread through the seminaries in which pastors are trained, can be instituted, but no one can force the members to share truly intimate things.

Another ongoing organizational problem for the house of worship may be a difficulty in adapting to changes in the environment or membership. It seems to be difficult to mobilize lay support and enthusiasm when change occurs or new programs need to be initiated. The only areas that receive sustained resources are worship and religious education; and for most of the congregation's business, members rely heavily either on the clergy and staff or on a central administrative committee. The pastor of the Methodist church noted that, after the big conflict in the late 1960s, the mentality of "We're a dying church" hung on a long time in this congregation. He thinks that this is partly due to the laity not quite knowing what to do to revitalize the congregation, not knowing how, as a group, to set new priorities, try new programs, or in general make collective decisions.

This makes it difficult to make certain kinds of changes. At the Catholic parish, the Parish Council has initiated a four-year capital improvement plan that has no hope of success without a high level of lay financial support but that also needs lay volunteer labor to work. This is not terribly easy to achieve. One Council member notes that, in this congregation, people need to be taught that, "Just showing up is not enough." But convincing people that more is required than their presence on Sunday morning and their weekly tithe is not so easy in a congregation where "showing up" has long been the only norm or imperative task that members agree on.

House of worship congregations foster the most individualistic style of religious commitment, seeing religion not as something that overlaps and reinforces ties of friendship, affection, and community, nor as a publicly oriented "player" in local affairs. Hammond (1988, 1992) has called this "individual-expressive" religion. The programming that is in place is minimal and focused on doing only what is necessary to foster individual spiritual growth and training individuals in the rituals and doctrines of their tradition. Decisions are made by the pastor, the staff, or the appropriate committee using the formal routines set out in the denominational guidelines.

This form of congregation may only be unusual in the American context. Most scholars of American religious history, like Martin Marty (1976, 1986), Nathan Hatch (1989), and E. Brooks Holifield (1994), emphasize that in this country religion has generally been an institution that is about community and friendship and has always played an important role in civic life. On the other hand, it has also always had a strong pietistic and devotional strand, as well. Whether the house of worship is a new form that is expressive of a new religious individualism is something that will be considered further in Chapter 9. In any case, it is a form that bears out Simmel's observation that conflict flows out of caring and commitment, and lack of conflict can signal a more limited form of communal engagement.

Notes

1. The historian Dorothy Bass (1994) develops this argument at length in an essay that considers the historic role in the United States of congregations in bearing, continuing, and changing religious traditions.
2. Of course, there are more activist Catholic philosophies, such as liberation theology. But for examples of works that document the strong emphasis on pietism and transcendance throughout American Catholic history since at least the nineteenth century, see Orsi (1985), Taves (1986), Gremillion and Castelli (1987), and McDannell (1995).
3. This quote was taken from a Web-page posting of the *Book of Discipline*, copyright 1992 by The United Methodist Publishing House, http://www.netins.net/showcase/umsource/umdoct.html#basic, visited 5 June 1996.

The quote is from Paragraph 65, Section 1, "Our Doctrinal Heritage," which goes on to say:

> In asserting the connection between doctrine and ethics, the General Rules provide an early signal of Methodist social consciousness. The Social Principles . . . provide our most recent official summary of stated convictions that seek to apply the Christian vision of righteousness to social, economic, and political issues. . . . Our struggles for human dignity and social response to God's demand for love, mercy, and justice in the light of the Kingdom. *We proclaim no personal gospel that fails to express itself in relevant social concerns*; we proclaim no social gospel that does not include the personal transformation of sinners (emphasis mine).

For a longer discussion of connectionalism, see Campbell et al. (1997).

4. See Roozen et al. (1984) and Carroll and Roof (1993).
5. For a discussion, see Blau (1976), Roozen et al. (1984), Wertheimer (1987), Carroll and Roof (1993), and Marty (1994).
6. For a good discussion, see Gremillion and Castelli (1987).

4

FAMILY CONGREGATIONS

From the time he came to the church in 1989 until the spring of 1992, Pastor West was the center of conflict at Community Church of Christ. Soon after he arrived, he was diagnosed with Alzheimer's disease. The disease itself made some people uncomfortable. Others were concerned that, being ill, he might not be able to give the congregation vigorous leadership. But from compassion as well as a sense of obligation, many of the lay leaders — particularly the older ones — rallied around the pastor. They let it be known that they would support his tenure as long as he was healthy enough to do the job. Early in 1992, he announced his intention to retire in June, and the church formed a committee to search for his replacement. Although people saw this as a difficult, painful, and frustrating time, the dispute did not concern how to deal with an ill pastor.

Members understood the conflict to be about the pastor as a person — his style, and particularly his inability to become close to people. A small group of vocal lay leaders made their dissatisfaction with him widely known. Two events in particular bothered this group. Soon after he arrived, Pastor West performed a joint service with the former (interim) pastor. The service included a christening, which the former pastor was supposed to perform. Instead, Pastor West "took over and ran the service and performed the christening." The parents, a very active couple, were offended and upset, and they eventually left to attend another church. Others were bothered when Pastor West was unwilling to give a children's sermon on Sunday morning. One or two left, but most were satisfied when the pastor arranged to have two lay members handle the children's sermon each week.

More generally, there was widespread dissatisfaction with the pastor's interpersonal style, which was described as "cold" and "formal." Some added "uncaring" to the list, while others were more apt to use phrases like "he's reserved" or "he's a very private person." One person, who supported the pastor throughout, nevertheless conceded that he

> makes people feel formal. He is not [pause] relaxed. I mean, I could never go to him for Christian advice and counseling.

Others reported that "it's hard to talk to him" or said that he is "aloof, not personable."

The pastor told a very different version of what was going on. He said that the congregation is inward-looking and complacent. Instead of worrying about children's sermons, he felt they should spend more time talking about issues of peace and justice, especially those close to home, like racial equality in the village or poverty on Chicago's West Side. He said that he had repeatedly tried to spark more interest in these kinds of issues, but it was frustrating, "like beating my head against a brick wall."

By March of 1992, reports varied on how many people had left the congregation – from four to twelve people, out of about sixty active members. Some members, who themselves were not pleased with Pastor West's personal style, nevertheless disagreed with the particular way in which the departing members had expressed their dissatisfaction. One council member noted that some people were openly rude to the pastor, which she termed "inexcusable." The members who left, and some who stayed, were called "troublemakers" and "complainers," in part because they met in small groups in one another's homes to discuss the pastor. Some people felt that they had "overreacted to silly things." Several council members were annoyed with the fact that, despite their dissatisfaction, people made no report to the Council or the Pastor–Parish Relations Committee, giving the church no formal means to address the disagreements and work things out.

At least part of the problem was an unfavorable comparison with two former pastors. The first was a long-term pastor who had left the congregation in 1981. Older members reported that this man, gone now for over ten years, had been "idolized." The congregational history gives a long and glowing account of his tenure. Since he left, they have had two full-time ministers and two interims, but to the older members no one else really seems to measure up. One woman described the dilemma this causes for Pastor West:

> [They'll say] he's not doing this, he's not doing that. And as I say, everyone is still being compared against a man who had been there for years, and everyone is coming up short.

She described Pastor West's problem when confronted with a decision on whether or not to begin leading the adult Bible study group or to allow the layman who was currently leading it to continue. This is a specific example, she feels, of a more general problem.

> We have a Bible Study group, and one complaint was he was not involved in it. But we do have a man that's led it for years, and he just felt that [that] man should be left alone to lead it. So, no matter what he did, he would have been criticized. If he'd gotten in actively, well he'd be [pause] some

would say, "Well, he's trying to take over." By leaving it alone, though, he "wasn't interested."

Younger members, meanwhile, had formed an attachment to the most recent interim pastor. He was quite popular. "We loved him," says one man. But they were not allowed to offer him a permanent job because of denominational guidelines against hiring interim pastors into full-time positions.

While some are critical of the way the more vocal members reacted to Pastor West, there are few people in this congregation who will be sorry to see him retire. He is showing early signs of his illness. He now writes out his sermons and reads them, because without a written text he sometimes wanders. Between this and the larger conflict, it has been a draining experience for the whole congregation. Although, as one man said, "no one wants to be mean," they are relieved at a chance to move on. And lay leaders anticipate the return of the members who left because of their disagreement with Pastor West. As one man, who is on the search committee for a new pastor, said:

> We're an extended family. It's more than a place to worship, and it's hard to find what we have elsewhere. So, they'll come back when they can.

Who We Are

Out of twenty-three congregations, six had what I call a family model. They spanned several Protestant denominations, including two Episcopalian parishes, and Nazarene, United Methodist, United Church of Christ, and Presbyterian Church, U.S.A. churches. Choosing the metaphor of family for this model is choosing to reproduce an element from the discourse and imagery of congregational life.

In these congregations, "family" is by far the most common metaphor used to describe what the congregation does well and what it means to members. Phrases like "we are a family church" or "come join our family" are highlighted in church bulletins, flyers, and newsletters. A typical promotional leaflet asserts that, "Worship has always been central to the spiritual life and nurture of the family" – referring to the congregation. Newsletters have a "family news" or "church family" section, telling of weddings, members who are ill or hospitalized, and summer vacation plans. When asked to tell me what brings the congregation together, the pastor of one Presbyterian church immediately said, "They see themselves as a family." The pastor of an Episcopalian church replied, "We are a pastoral family here." All of the pastors gave a similar answer.

In interviews and informal conversations, members also described their congregation as "a family," "my family," or "an extended family." When asked, "What role does the congregation play in your life?", members most often gave an answer similar to this woman's:

> It plays a very important role in my life [pause] an extended family.
> . . . It's just an extremely important part of my life.

Through the repetition of familial language and imagery, the understanding of the congregation as a family becomes institutionalized. Being a family, or family-like, has become a key element of the public identity of these congregations, a widespread and common understanding among members and clergy and a part of the congregation's reputation within the neighborhood. That is what the man at the Community Church of Christ meant when he said that "it's hard to find what we have elsewhere."

The Sunday morning service provides a ritual confirmation of the congregation-as-family. The prayer time is an especially important way of expressing the family metaphor. In all twenty-three congregations, public prayers sometimes include mention of individual members, especially of those who are ill or grieving. But family congregations are distinct in the degree to which this kind of prayer is elaborated, in how long it takes, and how big a percentage of the public prayer time is devoted to members' concerns. They are also distinct in that prayers that are common in other types of congregations – for political leaders, for peace and justice, for healing from racism, for an end to abortion – are either absent or given here in the most cursory terms. In family congregations it is common for a dozen to twenty individuals to be mentioned by name in each Sunday's prayer.

Sometimes, the count is much higher. At one Episcopalian congregation, on the Sunday before Ash Wednesday, the pastor began the litany of the Prayers of the People. After following the text in the prayer book and adding no specifics for most of the prayer, the pastor reached the part where he was to pray "for this congregation." First, "for those in our parish family," he recited fifty names in groups of five, in the same rhythmic singsong as the previous stanzas. Then, "for those away at college," he named two men and four women.

After the first few, I could not keep up with the names. On my bulletin I wrote, "For David, for Amy," but then I stopped and concentrated on counting. For those "serving in the armed services of our country," he prayed for seven people: one was "Brenda," a woman, and the rest were men. "For those in special need," he mentioned twelve or thirteen names;

and "for the children," he prayed fifteen names. There were prayers of celebration for six or seven birthdays and for two couples celebrating anniversaries.

By the end of the prayer the pastor had mentioned, by first name, over ninety individuals who were members of or associated with "our parish family," on a Sunday when about seventy members were present for worship. This was in keeping with the theme of the sermon, which focused on the renewal of the parish during Lent, in preparation for Holy Week and Easter. In the sermon, he spent most of the time talking about the power of prayer and the joint celebration of the Eucharist to achieve renewal and reconciliation of the parish family. He purposely mixed the "family" metaphors, linking the renewal of the parish family to the renewal of the parish's families, and he encouraged families to consider coming to the daily Eucharist as a way to celebrate birthdays or anniversaries. He also encouraged people to attend the Wednesday Bible study and the adult and children's confirmation classes.

This service took to an unusual length something that is a common practice in family congregations every Sunday: using prayers and announcements to incorporate the daily life events of the individual members into the worship life of the congregation. Family congregations do this at length and in detail, giving far more ritual space and time to individuals and their births, deaths, and daily lives than any other type of congregation. They achieve, regularly and seemingly without effort, the kind of intimacy and involvement with one another's lives that the Methodist pastor, profiled in the last chapter, found impossible to achieve in his church.

In addition to the prayers and announcements, the fellowship time after the formal service is an important enactment of the congregation-as-family. In these churches, people talk about the coffee hour as a part of Sunday morning worship. In every family congregation, the pastor, in our first interview, told me that if I really wanted to understand the congregation and know what the people were like, I should come to worship and stay for coffee afterward.

The coffee hour I attended at the Episcopalian church one cold January Sunday in 1993 was typical. The streets had been cleared, but there were about ten inches of snow on the ground. The sidewalks had been partly shoveled to about one-half their normal width. After the service, all but two or three of the people who had been at worship gathered in the basement. There were eight or nine small, round tables covered with white paper. The coffee cups were porcelain, heavy, and heavily used. The yellow cake with white frosting and the raisin cookies were on small, white paper plates. There were also paper cups of sweet red punch. Most people got something to eat and then sat in groups of six or eight at the round tables. There was a small group clustered right up by the coffee table, talking. They were in the way, right in front of the coffee urn, but they would move aside with a smile when anyone came up for a refill.

When I got my cake and made my way to an empty seat at a table, the older woman on my right took charge of me and introduced herself and her friends, who filled up the rest of the chairs. They asked me if I was married, where I grew up, and whether I had children. One woman told me that she had a daughter about my age, who used to go to another Episcopalian church in the area but then decided to come to this one. The woman explained that her daughter was not here this Sunday, but she would remember to introduce us the next time I came to church.

The rest of the time was spent talking about who in the congregation was away, who was sick, and upcoming events. It was icy out, despite the plowing and shoveling, and toward the end of the hour a younger woman, probably in her mid-thirties, came by to see if anyone at the table wanted a ride home, rather than walking on the slippery sidewalks. Two older women accepted, and, because things were breaking up, I left.

In family congregations, coffee "hour" lasts at least an hour, and often closer to two. Most of the membership stays; my fieldnotes from these visits show that only three or four people, out of an attendance ranging from forty to over seventy, would leave immediately after the service. More people stay for coffee hour, and it lasts longer, than in other congregations. And there is no feeling of hurry or rush, as people linger and talk companionably about private lives and personal interests.

The family metaphor crops up all the time in these six congregations, in sermons, prayers, and bulletins, and it was a dominant theme in my interviews with members. But the term "family" is a multivalent one. It can mean different things in different times and places; there are all different kinds of families. Of all the different meanings that can be associated with the metaphor of the family, what ones apply to the family congregations in and around Oak Park?

When clergy and members used the term "family" or "family-like" to describe their congregation, they seemed to mean a limited set of fairly specific things. The best summary is to say that their congregation fosters a general sense of well being, acceptance, and belonging. The phrases "a sense of belonging" and "I feel like I really belong there" recurred in many interviews. The most common adjectives people used to describe their congregation were "warm," "caring," and "friendly." These congregations form an ongoing set of connections that are primarily personal and social, not religious or ideological (cf. Coser 1956; Warner 1994). As one promotional leaflet assures prospective members,

> Our Congregation may be SMALL, but we are very warm and caring people in a BIG way.

This is a diffuse and functional way of thinking about what a family is. This definition does not imply a group of people performing well-defined and specific roles; rather, it is a family defined by the emotions that link members together, the feelings that are inspired in the members.

In family congregations, people know and care about each others' personal lives. It is hard to stay out on the edge and be uninvolved. They share together private joys, troubles, and major life events. When asked, "What brings this congregation together?", members virtually always give an answer similar to this woman's:

> the worship service . . . funerals, weddings, the birth of a child. The people here pull together. We celebrate the good things, and help in the bad times.

Ninety percent of the members I interviewed in these six congregations said that what their congregation does especially well is being close and supportive of one another. Nothing else comes close; about one-half said that they have a good worship service, one-half mentioned fellowship activities like annual dinners, less than one-half said good religious education. When asked what the congregation has meant in their lives, ninety-five percent said that it is a source of close and family-like connections with other people. The next most common answer (53%) uses religious language – the congregation provides them with a place to express their beliefs, learn about God or their faith, or find spiritual comfort.

This closeness seems to occur without a great deal of discussion or conscious effort. People refer to the congregation as a family, but there is no elaborated discourse on what it means to be a family. There are no sermons or pastor's columns in the newsletter devoted to the topic. People do not lead Sunday School classes on "community-building" or "what is our family like?" However, they do drop by on a snowy day to see if an elderly church member needs a ride or any errands run or if a new mother is feeling overwhelmed. They do this on an informal, ad hoc basis, without a formal committee structure and without relying on the pastor.

Being caring is especially important in times of illness or other crises. In one Presbyterian congregation, a member discovered that she was very ill. This older woman, who could not drive, would need to go to the hospital every day for two months for treatments and monitoring. Within two days, congregation members had been on the telephone and had put together a schedule of drivers to cover the two-month period. In family congregations, such things are not only more likely to happen than they are in other places, they are also more valued, more likely to be reported with pride and thought of as characteristic of the best part of what the congregation is like.

However, being caring and close-knit does not necessarily imply that members spend their social time together outside the congregation. Of course, some people do, particularly longer term members. But many members draw a distinction between the kind of family-like connections they have in their congregation and friendship.

The woman who is quoted above as saying that the congregation is her extended family and an extremely important part of her life also told me that very few of her friends are from the congregation. Without prompting, she elaborated for me the difference between friends and her congregational family:

> When you say friends, maybe I should go backtrack a little bit, too, because [pause] even though they're not like, I'm not sure what you meant by friends, going out with this group or something, they're not that way, but I would consider them more like family.

Another woman, from a different congregation, reported that none of her friends is from the congregation, but she likes the "sense of belonging" and feels like "they really want me there." A woman from a third family congregation reported that about ten percent of her friends are from the congregation and went on to say that the church is "intimate and friendly . . . very important to us now. It's like our extended family."

However, the emphasis on being close-knit and caring, and the fact that members keep track of each other's personal lives, does lead some newcomers to expect that they will automatically find friendships in the congregation and that it will become the center of their social lives. Some people told me that they had been disappointed to find that this was not

84

the case, or that they had to work hard to find such friendships in the congregation (cf. Olson 1989). Newcomers to one small Episcopalian congregation found it "cliquish," for example. But even these people affirmed that the congregation was a warm and caring place and an important source of support for them.

The kind of attachment that people find in family congregations, then, is not the same thing as having an active social life or a group of friends to engage in activities with, although many people find that in family congregations as well. But it seems more accurate to describe the common understanding of what it means to be a family congregation as a feeling of belonging, a knowledge of the important events in each others' lives, and a sense of caring and support in times of crisis.

How We Do Things Here

"Who we are" and "how we do things here" are interconnected ideas, at least in these congregations. The metaphor of the family implies certain things about the congregation's relation to its social and physical settings. It has implications for what activities the congregation engages in and which of those are positively valued. It makes some ways of doing things, some styles of decision making, more plausible than others, and it creates some typical organizational problems or contradictions.

Families have homes. Family life is home life, domestic life. In congregations where the chief metaphor of common life is "family," the church building is valued like a home is valued. People are proud of it, talk about it, and have an emotional attachment to it. When asked about the congregation's history, in four of the congregations over eighty percent of the people talked about the church building, and in two congregations thirty percent did. Older members are more likely to actually call the building "a home," but younger ones also talk about the building as an important part of the congregation's history.

This is in contrast to other types of congregations, where discussions of history generally center around when the congregation was founded, important leaders or outreach programs, and founding families. In other congregations, when the building is mentioned it is generally to point out some architecturally or artistically famous feature (stained glass windows by a famous artist, for example), to note that they have plenty of space for their activities, or to lament the size of the mortgage.

Members of family churches talk about when their building was built and are knowledgeable about the style of architecture. Some know the actual date that the mortgage was paid off and tell about how it was burned or torn up in the dedication ceremony. One woman, when talking about how their church building had been destroyed in a fire, broke down and cried, the only person in over 200 interviews to become so emotional about anything. My fieldnotes on this conversation make it clear that, for her, the burning of the church was similar to the loss of a home:

> I asked her what the hardest thing had been. She said, "It was *ours*." They had put in a lot of equipment – a movie screen and a huge kitchen. She said, "the nicest kitchen, it had been remodeled, it had two double sinks, it had everything to work with." They had just spent over $6000 to remodel the church. They had had people give things as memorial gifts – nice lighting in the sanctuary (cathedral lights). She says, "We ladies not only lost the whole kitchen, but the linens in the dining room, the cutlery, everything." They had an electronic bell tower with chimes and would always, her husband said, be careful not to disturb the neighbors with it on Sunday. They had a real brass, heavy, old-fashioned cross. She said, several times, "It was home" and "It was, quite simply, our home." When I asked her how they had gotten through the loss, she said, "We cried together and we worshipped together."

Of course, all congregations meet somewhere, and all of these congregations except for one had their own building at the time I was doing fieldwork. Sometimes, in one of the nonfamily congregations, a member would say that they have a nice building or a good worship space. And written histories always tell about the building. But family congregations are the only ones where the building itself is valued as an important part of the congregation's identity. They are the only ones where people are as proud of how well kept the building is as they are of the building per se, talking to me at length about things like landscaping and upkeep and decisions about lighting and decorating. They are the only ones where members regularly refer to the people who live near the church as the church's "neighbors."

If families have homes, families also avoid politics and other controversial issues, or at least middle-class families do (Baumgartner 1988). Coser (1956) suggests that, more generally, groups where members have a close and family-like attachment suppress disagreement and avoid debate on political or social issues. One of the consequences of the thinking of

86

the congregation as a family, at least in this predominantly middle-class community, is the avoidance of issues and persons who seem overtly controversial, political, or ideological.[1]

Pastor West, who was profiled at the beginning of this chapter, found out how difficult it is to spark a public discussion of social issues in his family congregation. Other pastors are more accepting of the inward orientation that such a metaphor implies. The pastor who described his congregation as "a pastoral family" went on to tell me, "We don't confront each other over issues. That's not what we're here for." And he went on to say that providing a space that fostered intimacy and caring, as well as religious seriousness, was its own important goal and should not be risked by the divisiveness that a focus on "issues" can bring.

When I asked people what their congregation's stand was on abortion or homosexuality, people would report that the congregation had no official stand. One woman explained, "We don't talk about that." Another said that what she likes about her church is that "No one will tell you what to believe" on any given issue. Although many people would identify their congregation as either liberal or conservative, no one went on to say that that was important to them or something for which the congregation was known in the community. Some refused such labels entirely — as one woman said, "We don't take sides, we're here to worship."

One Episcopalian pastor did say that his congregation supports the ordination of women and gays, although they have no official policy statement. After telling me this, the pastor quickly noted that the identity of the congregation revolves around liturgy and a warm, family-like feeling. He contrasted this specifically with other Episcopalian churches in the area — one in a neighboring community that is known as "the conservative congregation" and others where the identity revolves around social justice issues or being evangelical or charismatic.

Another pastor of a family congregation described how he deals with the issue of lesbians and gay men in the church:

> I have always ministered to gay and lesbian members of this church, on a one-on-one basis, on an individual basis. I've engaged in pastoral care and counseling, and I've been very successful in that.

This did not satisfy one gay male, who left this church to attend a different parish in a neighboring community. The pastor told me that the man had said to him, "You're not sympathetic to gay and lesbian rights." The pastor paused and said,

> We don't, for example, have an Integrity group. . . . We don't do
> that, we wouldn't do that here.

"Integrity" is the name of the denomination's gay/lesbian advocacy group, and advocacy was not welcome in this parish. To the pastor, this distinction between individual compassion and care-taking and politicization is characteristic of how his congregation deals with all potentially controversial issues.

People who want issue-based debate find this atmosphere frustrating. One man, a relative newcomer to his Episcopalian parish, told me that he resigned from the vestry[2] after realizing that he had an entirely different view of what the vestry was for than did everyone else. Based on his experience at the last church he had attended, he saw the vestry as a forum for debate and discussion, and disagreement if necessary, on issues ranging from the budget to homosexuality to whether to rent the building to non-Christian groups. He told me, with some visible upset, that after a while he came to the painful realization that the other members saw him as difficult and obstructionist. After about a year, he resigned, concluding that he was not going to change anyone's mind. Other vestry members reported to me that they were relieved, that he had been a "troublemaker." Two revealed that they had asked the pastor to ask the man to step down (the pastor had refused). Now, they reported, they could go back to having "productive meetings."

At first, the "troublemaker" said he tended to attribute this unwillingness to debate the issues to a lack of caring. But he told me, after his resignation, that he had changed his mind. He concluded that maybe it was better that "things run smoothly" than that decisions be debated and questioned.

When religion is discussed in family congregations, it is generally not talked about in doctrinal terms. People talk about spirituality and inner strength, and they say that their religion comforts them or gives them guidance in everyday life. In the Nazarene and Methodist churches, one or two members used typical evangelical Christian language of personal salvation – for example, "I love Jesus" or "Jesus is my Saviour." In fact, there is a great deal of religious seriousness in these congregations, with an emphasis on individual spirituality and renewal, but also on more old-fashioned ideas like repentance, reconciliation, and spiritual discipline. For example, the pastor at an Episcopalian church told the congregation that their Lenten observance would be successful if it resulted in more

88

character, stature, and perception . . . a quiet awareness of the growing influence of Jesus in our daily life.

But this religious seriousness is not expressed in doctrinal terms, and the members of these six churches do not say that they attend because their congregation embodies some specific doctrine or ideological stand – being fundamentalist or concerned with social justice. This is true even in the Nazarene congregation. People in this church would talk about being "a holiness church," particularly when they were talking about their history. But doctrine, or being part of the holiness tradition, was not central to their identity or to many individuals' reasons for belonging. As one woman said, "We agree with the doctrine. But the people are more important than the doctrine." Members of this church mentioned in other parts of the interviews that they do not believe in smoking or drinking and that members seem to uphold this life-style sincerely. But no one mentioned doctrine, or being a holiness church, when asked what the congregation means in their lives, what it does well, or what brings it together. The responses here echoed those in the other family congregations – there is "a real closeness," "they're my Christian family," or "it's our family."

Family congregations focus on three core tasks: worship, religious education, and providing a close and family-like place for members. These three things are the only ones mentioned consistently in bulletins, newsletters, and promotional materials. They also are the only three things that people identify as things the congregation does well.

Worshipping well in these congregations involves having an aesthetically pleasing service. People are particularly proud of their pastor's preaching and the music program. There is general agreement among members and clergy that these congregations worship well within their tradition. Aesthetics count, and a poorly run service or bad music would not be tolerated. Lay people are actively and enthusiastically involved in worship service guilds or planning committees, and many reported that the worship service gives them inner peace or makes them feel closer to God.

Worshipping well in these churches also implies a conservative stance toward the liturgical tradition of which they are a part. Worship services in family congregations are not usually subject to the kind of experimentation and eclecticism that some have associated with contemporary congregations (Carroll and Roof 1993). They usually use denominational hymnals, prayerbooks, and other materials. Religious education is often conducted using denominational materials as well. Religious education includes the adult and children's Sunday School, confirmation and membership classes, and one or two weekly Bible studies.

From the foregoing description it would be easy to conclude that family congregations have an exclusively inward focus, concentrating solely on their own members and not being concerned with or involved in the community. This is not exactly the case. As is true of the house of worship congregations discussed in the previous chapter, each of these six congregations engages in outreach to the community. Particularly well supported are the local food pantry, a tutoring program for children in a nearby and very poor urban neighborhood, and a rotating community homeless shelter. Members support these mostly with donations of money, but also, sometimes, with their own volunteered time. Also, these congregations give money and provide volunteers for denominational and ecumenical outreach programs.

However, it is fair to say that none of this makes much impact on the identity of these congregations, at least at the level of discourse – the identity they talk about and publicly symbolize. Members do not mention these activities when asked what the congregation does well or what it means to them, and they are not highlighted in promotional materials or Sunday bulletins. They are things that the congregation does, but they are not remarked as the important things about what it does, nor are they part of what members think of as distinguishing their particular congregation from any other. Rather, they take service and compassionate outreach for granted.

More generally, members and pastors of family congregations do not think that their congregations have much of a presence in the community at large. People identify their congregations as neighborhood churches, and a few members say that their presence in the neighborhood is as a witness. One pastor articulated this, saying that they feel that they meet together and worship together on behalf of the local neighborhood. But there is no sense of leadership or even a vital presence in the village as a whole.

Patterns of Conflict

Family congregations do not have very much overt conflict. In six congregations, only ten conflicts were reported as having occurred during the last five years, and four of these were in one congregation. There are only two kinds of conflicts reported: conflicts over the church building and property and conflicts among lay leaders or between lay leaders and the pastor that are understood as and spoken of as personal. These conflicts are listed in Table 5.

Four conflicts in three churches centered around the church building or property – one over whether to rent out the building to other groups, two over selling the parsonage/rectory, and one over what to do after a church fire. Proposals to sell the parsonage (or rectory), rent out the building, or merge with another congregation after a fire caused great distress. This makes sense, considering that in family congregations members take a great deal of pride in the building and have an emotional attachment to it.

These conflicts were framed as pitting the demands of efficiency ("watch the bottom line") against preserving the congregation's history, identity, or status in the community ("preserve our tradition"). In three churches, it was the pastor who took a strong bottom-line approach, and this was

Table 5. *Conflicts in the six family congregations*

There were 10 conflicts in 5 congregations. One congregation reported no conflict.

* 4 conflicts in 3 congregations over property

Factions:	in 3, pastor and lay leaders
	in 1, older and newer members
Understood as:	conflict between efficiency and preserving congregational tradition
Participation:	widespread
Resolved by:	congregational vote

* 3 conflicts in 2 congregations among lay leaders

Factions:	none
Understood as:	personal
Participation:	narrow, contained within a board or committee
Resolved by:	in 2 cases, when one person resigned,
	in 1 case, when new procedures were instituted

* 3 conflicts in 3 congregations over the pastor

Factions:	pastor and lay leaders
Understood as:	personal
Participation:	widespread, emotional
Resolved by:	pastor resigned

seen by members as yet another indication that the pastor was still an outsider. In the fourth conflict, it was a group of newer lay leaders who proposed renting out the building to other churches and groups. These conflicts occurred in both centralized (hierarchical polity) churches and in congregational polity churches.[3]

For example, the pastor of one small Episcopalian congregation told me that he had no idea of the trouble he would cause when he told the vestry that he did not want to live in the rectory but to buy his own home. When he further suggested that it might make better sense, financially, simply to sell the rectory and invest the money to provide a housing allowance, he told me that some of the older members were outraged. My fieldnotes on this conversation read as follows:

> He reported that people would come up to him after the service and explain that they had "had that rectory for years" and that it was "part of our presence in the community." They saw no need for change and said, "We've always done it this way." The pastor told me he saw this as "a simple business decision," but he found himself in the position of having to explain, repeatedly, that he had not meant to insult the rectory, it was very nice, it was just too small for his growing family.

While sensitive to the fact that he had hurt people's feelings, he did not really seem to understand why it had been such a problem.

After a long series of meetings, the vestry did decide to follow his advice, but only reluctantly. One of the wardens of the vestry told me that the older members had only agreed, finally, because they were reminded that the rectory issue had come up with the last pastor, too, and was likely to be a continuing source of strife. Few younger men with families would want to move into the smaller, older rectory, and the church would come out ahead, financially, to sell the building rather than rent it and pay for taxes and upkeep. I spoke with one of those older members, also on the vestry, who told me that he understood all of the good reasons they had to sell it, but that it still hurt to get rid of it. When I asked him why, he looked at me in surprise and said, "Why, because it was ours."

In addition to struggles over the building and property, there is a group of conflicts in these churches that were understood from the beginning to be interpersonal. One example occurred in the Presbyterian church. A conflict between the church treasurer and the rest of the board began when the pastor and some of the newer lay leaders asked the treasurer to adopt more formal accounting and reporting procedures. The treasurer told me that he felt that they were questioning his honesty, while the newer board members said that they could never plan anything because no one but the treasurer could figure out the accounts. The board voted to adopt more formal bookkeeping and reporting procedures, and the man complied. Apologies were offered and accepted, and the man remained treasurer, but there were many hurt feelings that took a long time to heal.

What is particularly relevant here is that this was understood as an interpersonal conflict between the treasurer, on the one hand, and the pastor and other lay leaders, on the other. It was seen as a matter of trust and caring, not of accounting practices. This is similar to the conflict on the vestry of the Episcopalian church discussed previously, in which one man wanted more debate and confrontation over issues. These differences in style were immediately labeled by other members as him "making trouble" or "being a troublemaker." He even came to see himself this way and to talk about the conflict as an interpersonal difference, rather than being about different styles of decision making or different ideas of church governance. The differences were only resolved when the man left the vestry.

The three conflicts centering around the pastor were also framed as personal; they involved questions of the pastor's competence or differences in style between the pastor and the lay leaders. These conflicts were resolved in each case by the pastor resigning.

The example of the conflict surrounding Pastor West, profiled at the beginning of the chapter, is typical along many dimensions. The conflict was understood as being about interpersonal style, that is, an inability to interact well with congregation members. The pastor's attempt to frame the conflict as being about a difference in mission orientation was completely unsuccessful. None of the lay members who spoke to me even mentioned the pastor's desire for a more outward mission focus. And the pastor himself, after a while, adopted a kind of personal language in describing the conflict. From talking about mission, he went on to report that the lay leaders were "lazy," "uncaring," and just "want things their own way."

Conflict and Culture

The conflict over Pastor West was typical of the overall style of conflict in family congregations. Most of the conflict revolves around control of things that have become valued in their own right by lay members who have great feelings of ownership of the congregation. Routine procedures, the church building, the rectory – all become valued for their own sake, because that's "how we do things here." Even when some conflicts arise around things that might inspire issue-based debate – differences in mission orientation, for example – they are immediately translated into personal terms. The problem is publicly identified as residing in persons, in personality and temperament, not in ideas or ideology. People are labeled as uncaring, as troublemakers, or as lazy.

This has several consequences. For one thing, it forecloses the possibility for issue-based debate. When Pastor West tried to get the congregation to take more of an outward focus, engage in the community, and tackle social issues, he was seen as devaluing exactly those things that lay members value most, namely, the inward focus on the church family. And he was unsuccessful in getting lay members to talk about these issues. Rather, members decided that the problem was with the pastor himself, as a person.

Of course, if the problem is rhetorically defined as residing within persons, a specific kind of solution is implied. In family congregations, conflicts do not lead to changes in decision routines, and mission orientation is not debated. Rather, people understand that the natural resolution to conflict is a personal one. The person in whom the problem resides needs to change or leave. The reasoning is this: If the person would just stop being so cold, such a troublemaker, or would just go away, then the problem would go away, too.

And conflict in these congregations can take on a kind of interpersonal intensity that I did not find in house of worship, community, or leader congregations. After proposing that the congregation sell the parsonage, the pastor at the United Methodist church received anonymous threatening phone calls and hateful letters. This was an extreme incident, but it can be seen as a logical extension of conflict that is understood as being "about" persons and not about ideas or procedures. In several congregations, anyone who wanted to change the way things were done was branded a "troublemaker," and the pastor especially was vulnerable to a label of being "uncaring" any time he or she wanted to put business considerations to the forefront of decisions about property, money, or administrative procedures.

The tendency to label those who disagree as troublemakers can lead to an atmosphere of mistrust and resentment that simmers under the surface of the family-like closeness of the congregation. The treasurer at the Presbyterian church was quick to suspect that a criticism of his account-ing and reporting practices must really be a personal criticism, indicating a mistrust of his honesty. This may seem to the outsider like an overreac-tion, but it makes sense given the context of the family congregation, where it becomes reasonable to assume that people who criticize what you do may soon begin to find fault with you as a person or with your per-sonality or character.

The pattern of conflict in family congregations is generated by the emphasis that members and the culture of the congregation place on being a close-knit community. There are few incidents that people themselves understand and interpret as conflict. Even the kinds of routine adminis-trative conflicts that are mentioned regularly in other congregations – disagreements over the budget or whether to start a new program – are not understood as "conflict" here.

As Coser (1956) notes, groups that value close, emotional ties tend to suppress conflict. Actual families, especially middle-class ones, often sup-press and avoid conflict, or ignore it when it does happen (Baumgartner 1988). In congregations where people think of themselves as a "family," people are very good at handling most things by vote and other routine procedures that resolve disagreements before people come to think of them as conflict. People may avoid or suppress conflict in family congregation because, when it does occur, it tends be understood as personal and to disrupt the relationship. In four cases, one party left the church; in two cases, one person either resigned from the board/vestry or did not seek another term.

Implications of the Family Model

There is a tendency to sentimentalize the family and to think of the family as a "traditional" institution. And in some ways, family congregations are traditional organizations; but in other ways, they are really quite modern. Families are about blood ties, but they are also about emotional ties, and these can be made by choice (cf. Stacey 1991). As Friedland and Alford (1991) argue, the "institutional logic" of the family can also be found in other groups besides biological families. They use this term to describe a kind of social logic in groups where members are valued for their own sake, where the attachment is personal, unique, emotional, and idiosyncratic (cf. Simmel 1955; Coser 1956; Warner 1994). In groups that are not based on biologically determined ties, this social logic is driven by and sustained by choice.

Many of the churchgoers in Oak Park, River Forest, and Forest Park have experienced in their own lives the effects of contemporary social arrangements that erode attachments to one's place of birth and to primary, blood connections. As professionals and businesspeople, most of them have experienced geographic mobility themselves or else have seen their children move all over the country pursuing college degrees, graduate degrees, spouses, or careers. One response to these conditions, as documented by Hammond (1992) and others, is to eschew local ties altogether, becoming a cosmopolitan who avoids local rootedness. Another is to become an "elective parochial" and to choose to re-create the connections of community and family life through other institutions (cf. Tipton 1982; Warner 1988). Members of these six family congregations are using the church as the institution through which they can create a set of connections that meet the needs that, in other contexts, are met by close neighbors and extended family. The way they talked about their churches reminded me most of my own experience of family growing up in rural Ohio, where my nuclear family was part of a tight-knit circle of aunts, uncles, and cousins.

By using the church in this way, the members create a social and religious space where certain kinds of religious values are privileged. These churches, like houses of worship, provide a place to express the individual's faith and to have experiences of renewal. But more than that, these churches carry on the tradition of pietism that has been such a strong strand in American religiosity.[4] In these churches, faith is not primarily about doctrine, but it is instead about rituals that interweave the symbols of God with the fabric of everyday life. Health, happiness, family, joy, illness, suffering, and grief – all are celebrated or mourned through and in these congregations. Through this, private experiences of joy and suffering are brought into the public space of the congregation and form part of the common life. And the congregation becomes a place where relationships of help and care are expanded beyond the confines of the nuclear family to encompass neighbors and friends, a form of social capital, in Putnam's (1996) terms.

Values are also carried in practices and ways of doing things. The ways in which family congregations conduct business, make decisions, worship, and foster members' interactions indicate a traditional approach to authority, where a history of doing things a certain way becomes a moral imperative to continue to do them in the same way. This leads to a traditioalism in worship as well as in other aspects of congregational life. Interpersonal authority and the authority to make decisions are not invested in formal qualifications or a specific role; the pastor, for example, is not really in charge by virtue of being the pastor. Long-term lay leaders make most of the decisions, and people who have been members for ten years can still be considered newcomers.

In family congregations, the emphasis on being a close-knit community generates two central and recurring organizational problems. The first is the incorporation of the pastor into the "family" on an interpersonal level. The pastor of the Presbyterian church told me that *"They* see *themselves* as a family." I noticed immediately the implication that he was not part of the family. Most of the pastors I spoke to were aware that they were coming into a preexisting and close-knit group, and that as the pastor they were, at least at first, outsiders.

This sense of the pastor being an outsider was compounded by the fact that all six family congregations were small. In such a church, the pastor often becomes the focal point for a more general distrust of or dissatisfaction with the denomination. Lay people often told me that the denomination as a body drains local resources while setting policies that are unresponsive to the needs of small local churches. Most denominations do assign better trained and more competent pastors to larger and more influential congregations, and most lay leaders are aware of this, leaving members of small congregations to feel that they may have been subjected to a series of pastors who are less well trained and therefore less willing or able to meet the congregation's needs than they ought to have been.

So making the transition from outsider to part of the family can pose serious problems for the pastor in a family church. And the failure to make this transition can, as in the case of Pastor West profiled at the beginning of this chapter, lead to a great deal of distress within the congregation. If the pastor continues to be perceived as an "outsider," he or she will struggle with the congregation over decisions about things that have great symbolic value to the congregation – their own building, their property – and less value to the pastor.

In such a situation questions of competence arise, and differences between the pastor and membership in education, age, or culture are highlighted. The older members of the Nazarene church were appalled when their former minister made references to television programs and popular music in his sermons. What the people at the Community Church of Christ thought of as Pastor West's coldness may have had something to do with differences in age and class, the pastor being older and coming from a higher socioeconomic background than many of his parishioners. These divisions, mentioned in the literature as generating clergy–lay conflict, do so only in the six family congregations in this study and not in any of the other seventeen congregations.

It is worth spending some time on the one family congregation that reported no conflict. In one Episcopalian parish, the much-loved pastor who has been there for over twenty years was able to introduce both a moveable altar and the idea of women priests to a congregation that is rather conservative in terms of ritual practice. Not only did the pastor report that this caused no conflict, but the lay members seemed to agree. Either they did not mention it, or they said that they like it when the pastor makes them think about things in new ways. This was the only family congregation that had a long-term pastor at the time of the study. It was also the only one in which the pastor spoke of himself as part of the family and in which members consistently mentioned that they have confidence, trust, and a liking for the pastor.

Far from cold or aloof, this pastor is involved in the lives of the members, particularly so in times of trouble. After church one Sunday, I asked a man I had previously interviewed what made this pastor so special. Jackson thought a while, and then he told me a story, recounted here in my fieldnotes:

> Jackson's father-in-law was ill with Lou Gehrig's disease. The rector visited him and saw that he needed a haircut. So he trimmed the man's hair, trimmed his toenails, and gave him a bath. Jackson had tears in his eyes as he looked at me and asked, "How many men – or women – of God do you know who would do that?"

Although at some of the other family congregations members liked their pastors and spoke of them fondly, there were no other congregations where the pastor was so accepted, so loved, and on such intimate terms with the members.

If family congregations have a particular problem incorporating new pastors into their close, family-like group, their second, more general, problem is one of organizational maintenance. All six of these congregations are small. When I asked members and clergy about their short-term goals, most people mentioned "growth." But when asked to elaborate, it was clear that in family congregations there is great ambivalence about growth. Many people want the resources that growth would bring, for example, more money and time donated to committee work and other activities. But they are also uneasy about newcomers, noting that with too many the church would change its character, perhaps becoming less warm and more indifferent. All agreed that they would rather grow "naturally," which seemed to mean slowly, welcoming new people one at a time. Certainly, when I attended, I was warmly greeted, encouraged to stay for coffee hour, and invited to come back. One on one, newcomers are welcomed.

However, too many newcomers might bring troublesome changes. One Presbyterian church had recently seen a small influx of new members after a Presbyterian congregation in a neighboring community shut its doors. As a result, about ten new people came and joined their congregation. Old-timers were pleased to report to me that they "fit right in" and did not want any changes in the worship service or Sunday School. But this influx of several new people did lead to the controversy over renting out the building. Resolved by vote, this conflict did not seem to have left lasting bad feelings, but it did cause in older members a kind of rueful acknowledgment that newcomers, with all their energy and enthusiasm, are a mixed blessing.

Notes

1. In a way, it is possible to think of Baumgartner's and Coser's interpretations as different alternatives. If Coser is right, any small, affective, face-to-face organization is likely to suppress conflict; Baumgartner suggests that this may only be true for middle-class ones. The question for this study then becomes, would a family congregation in a non–middle-class setting have a different orientation toward debate and conflict? Or is the congregational model itself based on a middle-class ideal that would be the same even if it were institutionalized in another setting? Without comparative analysis it is impossible to tell; I would suspect that in other settings congregations with a family model might operate in a different way.
2. The main administrative board in an Episcopalian parish.
3. And so it seems to me that it is not due to the specific property ownership characteristics of any given denomination or of hierarchical denominations more generally.
4. The discussions of pietism in American religion are far too numerous to recount here. A good historical overview is provided in the work of Nathan Hatch (1989) and Martin Marty (1976, 1986, 1994). See also Wuthnow's dis-

cussion (1988) and McDannell (1995). Caplow et al. (1983) provide a good empirical study of how pietism informs individual religious sentiments in both the early and the latter parts of the twentieth century in their continuation of the "Middletown" studies begun by the Lynds.

5

COMMUNITY CONGREGATIONS

At Bethlehem Congregational Church, "Congregational" means something very specific. When I asked one man, a highly involved lay leader in his forties who works as a midlevel manager at a downtown company, to describe what brings the church together, he emphasized themes that other members would talk about again and again:

> It's a good *congregational* church. We do a good job of being driven by the interests and needs of the members. We don't have many cliques . . . and we'll confront each other, it's very confrontational. We'll confront all kinds of issues that other churches avoid. But the guiding principle is always to be more open, to include *more* people and more points of view, not to exclude.

He went on to tell me about a debate over whether to use Styrofoam or paper cups at the coffee hour, brought about by some people who "felt strongly about the environmental issue." He said, ruefully, that a lot of energy was expended over what was in fact a small thing. Openness to all of the members' needs all the time can lead to exhaustive debate. He said that sometimes "We worry too much. We beat ourselves up over things." Still, he is glad that this is a place where one or two people can start a public conversation over an issue that they care about.

This is what happened when some women in a discussion group brought up the issue of inclusive language. Mostly well-educated professional women, they felt uncomfortable with gender-exclusive language in the Sunday services. After a discussion in a Sunday School class, they approached the deacons and asked, "What can we do about changing things?"

This began a process that lasted over a year and a half. The deacons ran a series of public meetings to try to find out what other members felt about this issue; the meetings were well attended and highly participatory. Many people were uncomfortable with changing traditional language and were made more so by the fact that some of the women proposing inclusive language were openly lesbian.

Unwilling to confront the issue of sexual orientation at the same time, the congregation dealt first with the issue of gendered language.

After the first few meetings, it became clear that, while many people favored adopting gender-inclusive language, some were opposed. The deacons decided that their first step was to map out the common ground. They came up with a statement on "Areas of Agreement" that recapped the points brought out in the congregational meetings. The first part of this statement acknowledges that this is a tense and difficult issue, because liturgy matters so deeply to people. The last part discusses the strategy to be pursued:

> The committee feels that we as Bethlehem members need to be made continually more aware of God's fullness and God's nature through some modification to our language of worship and other educational opportunities. However, any such modification needs to honor and respect the feelings and spiritual needs of all members. Bethlehem's growth in the area of inclusive language needs to be sensitive to the needs of the members. Any changes to our language, our liturgy, and our worship must be sensitive to the needs of all members. Accordingly, such changes must be gradual, with repeated opportunities for discussion and feedback. Our destination is still unknown; only our objective – to ensure an inclusive attitude in our worship and community life – is sure.

The pastor attended but did not run the congregational meetings, and he took no stand on the issue of inclusive language. He told me afterward that he had understood that his role was to ensure that the process of making the decision was itself caring and open – and therefore moral.

Eventually, the congregation adopted a new policy on inclusive language. Elements of the service that were highly meaningful to people because of their tradition and their beauty would not be changed. These included the Lord's Prayer, the Doxology, and the Gloria Patri. But the pastor "offered to use inclusive language in other prayers and in the sermons," and the congregation bought new hymnals with inclusive language.

People were very pleased with the decision. The lay leadership reported that they had been able to address everyone's needs in a genuinely caring atmosphere. In fact, the same process will be used now as the congregation tackles another issue – whether to adopt a policy statement that the congregation is officially inclusive of lesbians and gay men.

This issue had come up briefly in the previous discussion over inclusive language, but it was put on the agenda again later, and more forcefully, by one gay man who convinced the moderator of the congregation (the head of the lay administrative council) that it was right to assess the congregation's stand on this issue. The moderator explained to me why he had taken the urging of just one member so seriously, risking conflict over an issue that has torn apart more than one liberal Protestant congregation:

> I feel like, that it's the church's responsibility to somehow include its members. That doesn't mean it has to do everything everybody wants; it means it has to react to them as part of the community. And that its responsibility is not to declare an openness toward gays, but its responsibility is to go through a process that is directed to members' needs. If the outcome is "we're not gonna do anything," that's fine. I don't care. I understand, that's the nature of the church, but we can't just ignore it, because that's irresponsible.

He went on to explain why the process had to be a long one of exploration and why shorter, more cut-and-dried measures would not be legitimate:

> You see now, in a church, you can't vote. It's not a democracy, that's what's very interesting about a church, it's a community, and to me it's a very delicate balance between individual needs and the needs of the body. . . . So, we're going to make a decision. I don't know what it's gonna be, but we're going to make it.

Who We Are

Out of twenty-three congregations, six had what I call a "community" model. A term taken out of congregational discourse, it is an appropriate metaphor for these six congregations because it connotes the close interpersonal relationships, the widespread participation, and the inclusive and democratic decision processes that are important parts of each congregation's identity.

At the heart of the community model is the commitment to balance caring for each member's needs with exploring what stands to take on potentially divisive moral, social, and political issues. Accompanying this commitment is an emphasis on process – how do we make decisions, how do we conduct worship, how do we do things – that is absent in the other congregations.

These congregations have the largest number of core tasks of any of those that I studied. Members want the transcendent worship atmosphere of the house of worship, although they achieve it quite differently than houses of worship do. Instead of relying on the pastor or paid staff and denominational materials, they foster a creative, participatory, and eclectic style in which many lay people take on leadership roles on a revolving basis.[1] They want the interpersonal intimacy of the family congregation, and they have large numbers of small fellowship groups to help achieve that intimacy and friendship.

In addition, the members want to figure out, together, how their religious traditions are relevant for their contemporary lives. They see their congregations as the venue through which they can explore and express the social, political, and religious values that are important to them through public discussion and corporate action. They see having a group of people to care about and having a place where shared values are important and talked about openly as the two most important aspects of religious community, and they do not see these two imperatives as being contradictory.

When asked what the congregation means to them, eighty-five percent of the members of each congregation reported that they find close and supportive relationships in the congregation. Sometimes they said that the congregation is "my family" or "my extended family," but the most common terms they used invoked a metaphor of community. They did not tend to make the distinction between "church family" and "friendship" that some members of family congregations make, and they were much more likely to tell me that they have found their closest friendships in the congregation. They like how easy it is to get involved in the congregation, and they are proud that newcomers can also find close and supportive attachments there. One woman, who told me that "nearly all" of her friends are from the congregation, said that what the congregation does well is this:

> We do a good job of plugging people into the life of the church. That's how you get people to stay, if they're wanted and needed.

Forming close and loving connections between members is a core task in these congregations. About seventy-five percent in each congregation say that their congregation does a good job of being a caring and supportive community, and they were able to articulate in some detail what this means in their particular context. Usually they spoke of the congregation as either a "community of like-minded people" or "a caring community."

Community-building is an explicit focus here, a subject of conversation that is not left to chance but is carried out through organized programs. Beyond making some effort to care for those members who are experiencing a personal crisis, and beyond the informal groups of friends that are found in all congregations, these congregations engage in a conscious attempt to provide members with experiences of community and an opportunity to discuss what that means. There is an explicit language of community-building employed here, an elaborated discourse about what it means to be a community. This is in contrast to the family congregations, where "family" as a term is used frequently, but what it means to be a family is seldom explicitly articulated.

Part of this attention to community-building is a response to the life experiences of the highly mobile professionals and business people who make up the bulk of the membership in these congregations, particularly the bulk of the lay leadership. One woman, in her early forties, told me a typical story of moving four times in the last eight years as her husband's career kept advancing. They were finally going to be able to stay awhile in one place, but she did not think that meant it would be easy to meet people and make friends. She told me with some sadness, "As you get older, it gets harder to make friends and to meet people you really have something in common with." The Congregational church was the only place she had been able to find a group of people her own age, with similar interests and values, with whom it was easy to make friends.

Community congregations consciously foster the type of environment where that kind of thing happens. Large or small, all six of these congregations have age- and interest-based fellowship groups. Moreover, in all six the leadership points to these activities as an important part of the congregation's identity and something that it does well. In contrast to members of family congregations, members of community congregations generally find their close and family-like attachments in small groups, rather than spread throughout the congregation as a whole. This is true of both the large and the small community congregations.

Worship services are a place where what it means to be a community is publicly defined. Pastors and lay leaders who participate in the worship services are the major sources of this part of the public discourse of community in these congregations. The pastor of the Lutheran church gives sermons that challenge people to be more committed, authentic, and loving in their interpersonal relationships. In doing so, he is echoing a language that is a common theme for sermons, mission statements, small group discussions, and interviews throughout these six congregations. For example, my notes from one Sunday morning worship service at the Lutheran church in August of 1992 contain the following summary of one of the sermon's main points:

He doesn't have much patience with people who always smile – that's not real. To be real is to experience all of the pain, as well as the joy, of real emotions, and to find people to share those real emotions with is a real blessing. Our culture gives us stereotypes of real men and women, and they are often straightjackets, harmful. We need the courage to be who we really are and not to be caught up with these useless images from the culture.

Lutherans believe that the communion materials are really the body and blood of Christ, that there is a real presence here, not just a historical symbol. Having friends and being friends, sharing the real joys and pain, helping the poor, and reaching out to help the community, that is real.

He went on to draw a link between authenticity ("being real") and community:

God – his gift [pause] her gift – is to weave us together into the beautiful tapestry of life, of community.

At first, I attributed the use of this kind of language to the fact that this congregation is liberal and that the leadership is largely composed of Baby Boomers. Roof (1978, 1993) has shown that a language of authenticity and religious seeking are typical of Boomer spirituality, as a preoccupation with community is of liberal Protestants.

However, this kind of language was also found in the fundamentalist independent Baptist congregation, in the Assemblies of God congregation, in the Plymouth Brethren congregation, and in the Conservative Jewish synagogue. Each of these conservative congregations has a community model, and all but one of them has a lay leadership that is not dominated by Baby Boomers, but includes both younger and older cohorts in leadership. Like the Lutheran and the Congregational churches, these congregations use a language of authenticity to describe interpersonal relationships, and they focus heavily on community-building in sermons as well as in making the small fellowship group a major part of their programming.

Community congregations have a distinctive approach to worship and religious education. Over sixty percent of the members named worship as something they do well. But they are particularly pleased that their worship services are creative and innovative. They are more eclectic than any of the other congregations I studied, combining traditional and innovative elements in the service and using nondenominational materials. And they encourage lay participation, not only in performing traditional tasks like Bible readings or prayers, but also in coming up with innovative ways to structure the service itself. In these congregations, the most important thing is that the services and classes meet members' needs, not that they pass on a specific doctrine or ritual tradition. The emphasis is on lay involvement, self-expression, and creativity.

The Lutheran congregation has no official inclusive language policy. When one of the small discussion groups decided that some of the gender-exclusive language was offensive and getting in the way of the worship experience for some participants, they took matters into their own hands. They went through one of the two books of liturgy that the congregation regularly uses, and they changed all of the gender-exclusive terms to inclusive ones. Sometimes the congregation uses the gender-inclusive book and sometimes the more traditional book, and the pastor goes back and forth in the language he uses in sermons and prayers. This congregation has experimented with creative worship in other ways as well: A special outdoor service saw the pastor give the sermon in dialogue with songs that one member of the congregation had written about his experiences as a gay male in a straight society.

Not only is participation and creativity valued in these congregations, but there is a respect for the feelings of ownership that people have regarding the worship service. Innovation and tradition are balanced carefully; everyone's needs are addressed. This style of worship, sometimes thought to be associated with liberal Protestant denominations, is found in both liberal and conservative congregations in this community.

For example, the independent Baptist congregation includes in its Sunday worship both traditional Baptist hymns and contemporary praise choruses. They also include gospel and spiritual songs. They have a diverse congregation along the lines of age, race, and socioeconomic status. After much discussion, they have made a conscious decision that everyone can listen to everyone else's music, not only to educate people about other traditions and worship possibilities, but also so that everyone can have part of their own cherished traditions present in the worship ritual.

One member of the Plymouth Brethren congregation notes that she was looking for a place that welcomed an eclecticism and a participatory approach by members when she joined this congregation, in contrast to the church where she had been before:

I guess for me it's meant something more free . . . [we're] able to use our talents more. And the elders are very open to doing new things to enhance worship, and so that's allowed us to use our talents in different ways [pause] in drama and things like that. So it's been very freeing, in that sense.

I was able to see what she meant when I attended a worship service at her congregation. The call to worship was a poem composed by a woman in the church, read by her from the back of the sanctuary. The service featured a film clip from a movie about street gangs in Los Angeles that would be screened at the church later in the week, and the children's "sermon" was in the form of a skit performed by several of the younger adult members. The music ranged from nineteenth-century hymns to twentieth-century Christian folk to contemporary praise choruses. Several members did inspirational readings that included Bible passages as well as Christian poetry.

The recently retired rabbi of the Conservative synagogue attributes the emphasis on discovery, involvement, and self-expression in his congregation to the high number of professionals in the Oak Park–River Forest community. He says that his congregation became "more interesting" in the 1970s as businessmen were replaced by doctors, teachers, lawyers, and social workers. He talked about how members are now much more involved in governance and are more demanding about the quality of religious education and worship services. When I asked him why this was so, he answered,

The emphasis changed completely. The others wrote checks [pause]. And when I say [the congregation] became more interesting, it became more challenging to me. So [pause] the sermons had to be – there was an intellectual bent to the sermon. And I had to prepare, and that was a great joy, I had to prepare for lectures that I gave and the classes that I taught. And I enjoyed it much more.

They wanted more participation in the decision making. For example, they became much more interested in participating in the education of their children. Those were the beginnings. There was more of a sense of, well, "we're really a democratic institution," whereas before, you know, the guys who wrote the checks, they had much greater influence.

He attributes this to the presence of professionals. But while many of the congregations in this three-community area are dominated by professionals, they do not all have this emphasis on lay involvement. What makes community congregations different is that the members expect their congregation to be a place where they interpret what their religious traditions mean in their own lives. As one of the women on the board of the synagogue explained to me,

> I think [pause] I think to be Jewish these days is to be confused. You have to sit down and figure out what you're going to be and how you're going to do it. If I want to upset my husband I'll [ask] him, which kid do you think is gonna marry a non-Jew? [pause] But the probability is very high, intermarriage is very high, you can't take it for granted any more. These kids are gonna have to *decide* whether they want to be Jewish, and how.

Members of community congregations believe that one does not make these decisions alone. Prayer, and experiences of transcendence, are important, but they are not enough. To make this kind of decision, one needs to be an active part of a community of shared values. Members of these six congregations see themselves as engaged in the communal enterprise of interpreting a living faith.

Of course, the situation of the Jewish community is in some ways quite unique. But in none of these six congregations is the passing-on of religious tradition seen as a straightforward matter, nor is it taken for granted. Rather, it is seen as something that members must "figure out," grapple with, and struggle for. The pastor or the rabbi can be a guide, but he or she is not the ultimate authority. And while the religious tradition — doctrine, theology, ritual practices — is valued, it is not seen as straightforward or as the only source of religious authority.

At the Lutheran church, the classes for new members used to concentrate heavily on Lutheran history. But now, the pastor has one short session on that. He spends much more time talking about congregational history and programs. And he has open discussion sessions to try to discover where the new members are at in their own spiritual lives and what needs they are looking for the congregation to meet. He told me he made this change because what matters is how *this* Lutheran congregation, here and now, carries out its ministry and meets the needs of its members, not Lutheran history. The moderator of Bethlehem Congregational Church told me that it was both Christ-centered and congregational, religiously serious but not dogmatic, or even traditional.

Members of community congregations want both this sense of religious seriousness and the freedom to interpret the important religious truths for themselves. Even members of the independent Baptist church emphasize that doctrine does not give them a very specific guide to how they should conduct themselves as a twentieth-century church in an urban-density suburb on the edge of one of the poorest neighborhoods in the city, drawing on black and white, well-off and poor neighborhoods. The task of being "the New Testament church" here and now is something that they try to figure out together. The pastor is their leader, but much of their interpretive activity takes place in small discussion groups or among the lay leadership, especially the deacons and elders.

In addition to community-building and creative worship, members of these congregations care about values. Over seventy percent of the members I interviewed in these congregations said that the congregation is meaningful because it embodies some value that they hold dear. They would say that it is Biblical, or that they like the fact that it passes on the rituals of Conservative Judaism. Many used an expressive language. When I asked this woman what her congregation does well, she replied:

> I think we do a good job of [pause] of expressing the values of the members, the professional people who make up our membership.

She is not alone; in three congregations, over one-half of the members I spoke to said that what the congregation does well is express the values of the members.

How We Do Things Here

Although values are seen to be important in these congregations, the members shy away from dogmatism. Values are interpreted and applied at the local level, and there can be more than one truth. Values and community are linked in the discourse of these congregations; being a community that expresses members' values is the rationale behind most of the congregation's activities and policies.

In each congregation, over one-half of the people said that their congregation is "tolerant" or "very tolerant," which is held to be a good thing, in and of itself. In all six community congregations, members value tolerance highly, although it is interpreted in slightly different ways in different congregations. The head of the board of elders at the Brethren congregation expressed tolerance this way:

> We are committed to multiculturalism, to decentralized leadership, and to loving counsel rather than judgment.

This is not the same kind of tolerance as in the Lutheran or UCC congregations, with their commitments to inclusive language and openness to lesbians and gay men. But it is important to note that congregations from more theologically or doctrinally conservative traditions can still embrace tolerance and diversity and avoid dogmatism. As the pastor of the Baptist church is fond of saying, "It's alright to be different, as long as you're not different from the Lord." When I asked him what that meant, he explained that there were really only a very few core truths that everyone needed to agree on. The nature of Christ, and salvation through a personal relationship with Him, were essential truths. But most other things Christians could, in good conscience, debate.

Tolerance also meant a commitment to integration across traditional lines of social division. The Plymouth Brethren congregation, the Assemblies of God church, and the Baptist congregation had much higher percentages of nonwhite members than the other community congregations, which is one very important measure of tolerance in a community where residential integration has not always led to institutional integration. But the other community congregations were trying to include people from more diverse backgrounds as well. A lay leader at the Lutheran church emphasized tolerance of racial, economic, and age differences when he said,

> I like the racial diversity. And I like the fact that you can walk in in jeans or in a three-piece suit and be treated with equal respect.

In the Conservative temple, tolerance meant trying to attract mixed-marriage couples.

One of the values that receives attention is intimacy, and when intimacy or community become an explicit goal, this makes a difference in congregational life. One respondent was very articulate about this difference. I asked Janet, a vivacious woman in her forties who works as a researcher for a large organization, what kind of person would feel uncomfortable or unwelcome in her Lutheran congregation. I was trying, in that part of the interview, to get a sense of how open the congregation really was, for example, to persons of color, to lesbians and gay men, or to those with less money. Janet's answer surprised me, as did the frequency with which this type of answer came up in subsequent interviews. She began by talking about diversity, but ended up talking about intimacy. She said:

> I think out-of-bounds behavior would be [pause] blatantly discriminatory. I think that the congregation has a high tolerance for diversity. [pause] Interesting. There are just social norms that are in place. One social norm is intimacy. If people are not comfortable with it, they just won't come back.

One man in this congregation told me that, although he wishes that his wife would attend with him more often, he usually attends alone because his wife finds the atmosphere at his congregation too close for comfort. He said that people she barely knows will come up and hug her or ask her about their personal life, and she does not like this; she finds it, he reported, "cloying." Unlike the house of worship, where friendship is optional, here it is hard to avoid.

This intimacy, while genuine, is also highly planned. One Sunday morning coffee hour at this church was typical of all six community congregations. Initially, about one-half of the congregation stayed. For the first twenty minutes, people were chasing each other down, making connections for the coming week: "Did you know our meeting was moved to 7:30?" or "If you're interested in music, we should talk – can you have lunch this week?" After this whirl of activity, most of the people left. Many of the remaining were staying for a committee meeting. The pastor explained to me that the people were busy and hard to track down later in the week, so Sunday was a time to make connections. People were quick to greet me as a newcomer and to ask especially what kinds of activities I enjoyed so that they could put me in touch with the right contact person. "Plugging in" to one of the congregation's many organized activities was a key to making friendships and being part of the community.

Trying to balance the goals of maintaining community and being involved and aware on social issues is not always easy. The imperative to being a caring and tolerant community that expresses members' values leads community congregations to be engaged in social issues, but in a reactive and partial way. They are heavily guided by the passions and commitments of particular members, and they are likely to act only when broader social issues directly impact on their local community or constituency. This balancing act also leads them to value process over outcome. Only in a community congregation could the pastor say, as he did at Bethlehem Congregational Church, that it does not matter *what* decision the congregation makes, as long as the *process* is open and inclusive. And only in community congregations is the process itself viewed through this moral lens.

These six congregations are concerned with social issues, but they actively resist activity that might be deemed radical, and overtly political language or rhetoric is not well received. Compassionate outreach, about which there is no disagreement, is a favorite way to engage with social issues but not cause division. A growing awareness of homelessness in Oak Park and River Forest led many of these congregations to participate in a revolving shelter, usually at the urging of one or two committed members or ministers.

In this community, race is the most historically salient social issue, and in community congregations people will talk about race and racism. But when they do so, they do not use political or economic language; rather, race and racism are discussed in communal or personal terms. That is, racism is defined as a problem for the local congregation because it can get in the way of maintaining a genuinely close and loving community. The pamphlet introducing the Assemblies of God (AOG) church has, on the inside front cover, a statement of welcome and several sentences describing the congregation. The first describes Jericho AOG as a place "where there is a friendly spirit" and shows a black hand clasping a white hand. There is no mention anywhere of the words "race" or "racism," or even "tolerance." But there is an indication that community across racial lines is valued.

The Baptist church and the Assemblies of God congregation both have over forty-five percent black and Hispanic membership. They are both situated on the border of Oak Park and the city of Chicago, and they have the greatest socioeconomic diversity of any of the twenty-three congregations. Forced to confront race and racism as more than a symbolic issue, these two congregations still shy away from political or ideological interpretations. When I asked the pastor of the Baptist church why the congregation had moved toward a multiethnic ministry, he gave me a copy of a sermon he had preached in which he had consciously attempted to articulate their rationale for this ministry:

> The ministry here is not trying to be traditional in its values and it's not trying necessarily to be progressive in its values . . . we're trying to be honest exegetically to the Bible and relevant with the community. The lifting up of Jesus Christ is our goal. We are not show-

casing the fact that we're multiethnic. We just happen to be multi-ethnic. God has given us the privilege to be a multiethnic congregation. We are pleased of the Lord that He's done that. . . . I also realize that there are groups that center upon the reconciliation of groups. That's what's important to them. But really, is that what the church is for? No. The church is to lift up Jesus Christ.

Interestingly, he understands race as a problem that must be confronted to build religious community and points to interaction as the key to resolving the issue of race successfully. The "problem" of race becomes the problem of racism that interferes with the establishment of their congregation as "the New Testament Church." As this sermon says:

> I began to preach when I came here that it's alright to be different, as long as you're not different from the Lord. What I was saying is that the focal point of our experience, and our multiethnic ministry, *must be* Jesus Christ! *We're not carrying on some sort of social experiment here. We're just focusing on Jesus Christ.* . . . But how do you do this practically? . . . If I say that I indeed want to practice the word of God and submit to my brothers and sisters in Christ, what I'm going to do is do what *they* want to do, not what I want to do. If I prefer them, I'm going to want to sing what *they* want to sing, not what I want to sing. I'm going to be interested in what they do and how they live. And I will want *them* to do what interests *them*, not what I demand for myself because of my fear or comfort. (emphasis in original)

Racism is evil because it interferes with the Biblical mandate to "lift up Jesus Christ." To be racist in their particular setting would keep them from the task appointed to them, which is to draw the people in their immediate surroundings to the Lord. They feel that mere tolerance pales in comparison to the genuine community that they are trying to achieve.

Race is not the only issue that is understood in these personal and communal terms. The letterhead of the Lutheran church's stationery proclaims that they are "Embracing the diversity of God's creation and celebrating our oneness in Christ." Their mission statement begins by talking more explicitly about inclusiveness, saying that they

> welcome in the spirit of Christ all men, women, and children without regard to race, nationality, marital status, family composition, sexual orientation, or socioeconomic status, inviting all to par-

ticipate fully in the life and ministry of our parish. We encounter Christ in each person and therefore treat one another with trust, love, care, and respect.

Of course, mission statements can be symbolic gestures, nodding to all the right values, saying the correct things, and influencing very little in congregational life. But this congregation illustrates that taking a formal and official stand can have some utility. As one member of the church, a lesbian who searched a long time before she found a church she was comfortable attending, stated:

> See, I'm just so impressed with this congregation and the issues that they are addressing. Just by having our mission statement out there, and recognizing minority groups and welcoming them all, come one, come all – that's just not common. I think the fact that their social ministry is involved on the West Side,[2] is involved with the food pantry, they're tied in with the AIDS group Community Responds. ... They're addressing some needs there of people in the community.

Most of the activities she mentions are things that the congregation participates in because of personal ties or the strong commitment of a few members. For example, their major new "partner" in outreach to the city of Chicago is a church in a poor Hispanic neighborhood that is pastored by a man who is their former student intern.

But there are real limits to what can be done when social issues are understood in communal and personal terms, and this sometimes frustrates members. One man noted that the same church that allowed him to use his songs about his experiences as a gay male in the Sunday service was resistant to forming a small group for lesbian and gay members and even felt some resentment at passing an "open and affirming" resolution. When I asked him why, he said it was because they felt it inappropriate to treat this as a political issue within the bounds of the congregation. The pastor confirmed this, stating that, because gays and lesbians were already welcome and knew they were welcome, why did they need a formal policy? He said it was like being told, "You're not doing enough."

Where tolerance, diversity, and creativity in matters of symbolism and ritual are valued, many people reject "liberal/conservative" labeling. In their tendency to shy away from dogmatism and politicized rhetoric, the leaders of these six congregations are not comfortable choosing sides in the culture war. At the Plymouth Brethren congregation, the Bible teacher told me that most of the people in his church, including himself, do not like or identify with either the label "conservative" or the label "fundamentalist."

> More significant would be – the description would be "Biblical" rather than identifying with a – with a political or a religious label or tag.

One of the members of this congregation laughed when I asked her if she considered herself liberal or conservative and said,

> I always say to my liberal friends "I'm conservative" and to my conservative friends that I'm liberal.

This answer may seem flippant at first, but it does show a real unwillingness to be pinned down by categories that are highly charged in the larger society but not so relevant in this congregation.

The moderator of the Congregational church gave a good characterization of the larger motivation behind this rejection of liberal and conservative ideological categories. When I asked him what kind of church he had been looking for when he came to Bethlehem, he said he wanted a church that was

> socially minded, open, not overly dogmatic or fundamentalist, loving and Christ-centered. . . . I wanted to be free to look for my own truths.

The sense of inhabiting a middle ground, and that theological or doctrinal positions do not lead in any necessary or determined way to particular stands on social issues, is characteristic of members of community congregations. In addition, it is not particularly legitimate in these congregations to engage in political rhetoric or in social activism that tends to have a polarizing effect on the local congregation. This wars with the style of commitment, which leads members to want to institutionalize their own values, and drives much of the conflict in these congregations.

The style of commitment in these congregations is very reminiscent of the style found in the pilot study for this project, a study conducted in an urban Chicago neighborhood (Becker et al. 1993). People in these churches have made a serious commitment to their congregations, and they feel a great deal of loyalty. That loyalty, however, is due as much to the particularities of the local congregation as it is to tradition or ideology. Most of these members view the congregation as important for self-expressive reasons. They are willing to fight to institutionalize values, programs, or symbols that are important to them, but they try hard not to fight in a way that causes members pain or leaves hurt feelings. And they try to prevent the most serious conflict by negatively sanctioning overtly radical or politicized rhetoric.

Patterns of Conflict

In community congregations, members value the congregation as a place that institutionalizes their values, in everything from the ritual life to the social issues the congregation addresses. This leads to a great deal of conflict and widespread participation. Community congregations report twice the number of conflicts as family congregations, with twenty-one conflicts in six congregations over the last five years. These conflicts tend to be understood as moral conflicts rather than personal conflicts (see Table 6). The overall style is that of a participatory, expressive moral community, where religious authority is diffuse and rooted in members' experiences as much as in the pastor or the doctrine. The most salient division is not a liberal/conservative ideological split, but a struggle between older and newer members to institutionalize their own sets of values. Conflict is not feared but is viewed as positive and healthy, up to a point.

In nineteen out of twenty-one conflicts, participation was widespread. In fourteen conflicts, the factions were groups of older and newer members. At least two conflicts between older and newer members occurred in each of the six community congregations. Members themselves put issues on the agenda in community congregations. Fifteen of the twenty-one conflicts were begun by the proposal of a member. Community congregations fight about anything from renovating the building to what kinds of songs to sing, from inclusive language to whether to hire a new Bible teacher. Thirteen conflicts were framed entirely in moral terms, and all six community congregations had conflicts that were understood entirely in moral terms.

The conflict over inclusive language at Bethlehem Congregational highlighted in the opening vignette illustrates some typical features of conflict in community congregations. First, it featured moral arguments about how to balance doing "what is right" with doing "what is caring." Conflicts over premarital sex, inclusive language, and being inclusive toward

Table 6. *Conflicts in the six community congregations*

There were 21 conflicts in 6 congregations.

* 4 conflicts in 4 congregations over budget and staff

Factions:	in 1, older and newer members
	in 3, none
Understood as:	administrative
Participation:	2 narrow, confined to board or committee
	2 widespread, at congregational meeting
Resolved by:	vote

* 13 conflicts in 6 congregations, including conflicts over music, inclusive language, inclusive policies towards homosexuals, hiring a new rabbi or Bible teacher, sexual morality, renovating the church, changing the congregation's name

Factions:	in 10 conflicts, factions of older and newer members
Understood as:	moral, mostly with religious arguments
Participation:	widespread
Resolved by:	usually a long process of consensus-seeking, congregational vote

* 4 conflicts in 3 congregations over delegating resources

Factions:	in 3, older and newer members
Understood as:	conflict between efficiency and some religious principle
Participation:	widespread
Resolved by:	unresolved, or board vote

---

homosexuals were argued in these terms. In these conflicts, clergy and lay leaders affirm the taking of a moral stand, but only if it is done in a way that does not hurt people needlessly. Both "what is right" and "what is caring" were understood and spoken of by many in religious terms (see Becker 1997a).

Some moral conflict features other kinds of arguments. The decision to renovate the Lutheran church was argued in terms of mission orientation. Ought we to spend money on our own worship and educational needs, or ought we to give the money to outreach activities? Aesthetic and symbolic concerns were also voiced. Those in favor of remodeling wanted a free-standing altar, so that the pastor could face the congregation during prayers and communion, which is more in line with their egalitarian preferences. They also wanted more space up front for the children's sermons and special music that take place almost every Sunday.

Still other moral conflict is argued in expressive terms (Tipton 1982). In the synagogue, hiring a rabbi was talked about as an expressive struggle between older members who wanted a good speaker and fund-raiser, an urbane and well-spoken man, and newer members who wanted someone informal and comfortable with children. Members reported this as a struggle to symbolize the whole congregation. In two other congregations, two conflicts over the style of music used in the worship service and one over renaming the congregation were also argued in expressive terms. Whose identity was to be expressed in the music? The Baptist church decided to express the identity of blacks and whites and young and old members by having an eclectic mix of music, including traditional Baptist hymns, songs by the Gospel choir, visiting jazz musicians, and praise choruses.

The conflict over inclusive language at Bethlehem Congregational was typical in another sense. In community congregations, it is usually a lay person or a group of members who puts issues on the agenda, not the pastor. And these issues are likely to be ones that are important because of the personal experiences of members – being gay in a straight world or a professional woman who has experienced sexism but also understands how to bring about change. Aesthetic interests, for beautiful music or a sanctuary that is a better symbolic worship space, for example, are also legitimate bases on which to begin a public discussion.

At Bethlehem, the pastor and several lay people told me that the outcome itself was less important than the process. In general, community congregations tend to be process-oriented. The three liberal ones featured an "exhaustive process," which seeks through a series of meetings and drawing up of draft resolutions to include a majority of the laity and which takes from one to two years. The conservative congregations have shorter decision periods, but they are also highly participatory, with congregation-wide meetings and votes being the most popular ways of resolving conflicts.

The process of decision making is itself valued and talked about in moral terms. In five of the community congregations, the pastor[3] told me that he did not care what the outcome of a specific conflict was, as long as the process itself was caring and honest and therefore moral. This was true for a range of conflict issues. Pastors in community congregations were the *only* pastors in the twenty-three congregations to speak of their role this way or to view the process itself as moral.

The reason that the process is viewed as moral, and important, is that members believe that it is possible to achieve some form of genuine consensus if the process itself is open. At the Lutheran congregation, many people told me that the older people, who had opposed the renovation, all "came around" during the course of the congregational meetings to discuss the issue. I spoke to one older member who said that this was not true. She said that she never agreed that the renovation was a good idea; she simply realized, at some point, that it was going to happen anyway. At Bethlehem, the moderator of the congregation, when I asked him directly, told me that there were "probably one or two people" who left over the inclusive language issue. And at the Baptist church, the pastor conceded that they lost a few people to Main Street Baptist, the church in the center of town, when they decided to engage in a consciously multiethnic ministry focus.

It is not necessary to conclude, however, that the leadership in community congregations are insincere when they talk about consensus. They genuinely attempt to create a process that is open enough for everyone to express their views. And the fact that one-half of the conflicts end in compromise indicates that there is some sincere attempt to meet everyone's needs when possible and to incorporate views that are not in line with the majority. It is also the case, however, that even after a long and open process, at some point a decision is made, and there are sometimes people who disagree. In community congregations, the remaining disagreement finds no legitimate or public form of expression, and people either learn to live with that or they go on, usually quietly, to another congregation.

It is tempting to see the process-oriented, inclusive, tolerant nature of Bethlehem stemming from their liberal heritage. But, in fact, it is a mistake to think that all liberal churches have such little emphasis on doctrine or theological content. Also, not all liberal congregations locate religious authority so diffusely in the lay members; some have strong pastors. At the other Congregational church just down the road, the same issue of inclusive language came up and was resolved through a process of open meetings. But in contrast to Bethlehem, the pastor took a vocal role, telling the congregation that he felt that they should adopt an inclusive language policy because he felt that their theology told them they must take a stand against sexism or any other institutionalized form of discrimination. The congregation followed his advice and adopted inclusive language to apply to all parts of the service. This other Congregational church is discussed in Chapter 6, which profiles the leader congregations.

The conservative congregations that have a community model look a lot like the liberal ones in the way they make decisions and resolve conflicts. Just like Bethlehem, they emphasize tolerance, inclusiveness, and meeting the needs of members over doctrine or theology. For conservative congregations, this works better with some issues than with others. It works well with race, as is illustrated in the sermon excerpts from the Baptist church previously quoted.

It is a little more difficult to manage with a topic that hits closer to the core of fundamentalist social morality, like homosexuality or abortion. When asked about homosexuality, members and clergy from this Baptist church said that they would welcome and accept homosexual persons. They said that they would never make a homosexual person who came to the church feel unwelcome and that they would be accepting, even loving. But when I pressed the assistant pastor on this issue, he did say, finally, that continuing in the life-style would be antithetical to their beliefs. Still, they would hope, he said, to build strong relationships with that person, to lead him or her, in love, to a point of new understanding. Again, their approach is pragmatic and partial, not ideological and totalizing. In our conversation, the Baptist pastor said that homosexuals are sinners, but so is everyone else; abortion may be wrong, but probably there are some women in the congregation who have had them; it was very painful, and why talk about it, really? If you want to protest abortion, do so, but the job of the local church is not to man the barricades. The head pastor explains it this way:

> We're conservative theologically, but we're tolerant. More than tolerant. I don't like the word tolerant. . . . There are people here for instance who [pause] are a little different in their social values, like on abortion and so forth. Now, the general stance of the church is that it's pro-life. But the people who are not, I don't think they feel rejected at all. I think they would feel like they fit in. Now I think that if homosexuals came here, which [pause] that does not happen openly, but I think they would be accepted, and that would be demonstrated. I think people would say, "We accept you." And it wouldn't just be a toleration thing.

And by concentrating on racial tolerance, an issue on which there is consensus in the congregation, and avoiding taking official stands on more controversial issues, the Baptist community congregation can maintain both its emphasis on being loving and supportive and its commitment to engaging with relevant social issues and institutionalizing members' values. The Plymouth Brethren congregation has adopted the same strat-

121

egy; they concentrate mostly on racial tolerance and have successfully built a mixed-race congregation, something that more liberal churches have not, for the most part, been able to achieve.

The Community Congregation

It is common for religious leaders to rail against local churches for being parochial and internally focused. The kind of engagement with social issues that community congregations achieve would strike some theologians and denominational officials as inadequate (see Gilkey 1994), although it would perhaps find a more sympathetic reception in some quarters. They seem to be living out, regardless of their denominational affiliation, something similar to the Methodist doctrine of connectionalism discussed in Chapter 3, in which the personal life of piety is linked to a concern with social issues and social justice. Private faith and private life are not seen as being in a realm apart from public life and social issues. The two are seen as informing one another, and the role of the congregation is, in part, to serve as a venue for thinking through how it is that they inform one another and what are the requirements of moral action that flow from this interconnection between private lives and public issues.

It is important to note that this connection between private faith and social awareness is made not only in the congregation's symbolic forums, like the sermons and the music, the mission statements, and the letterhead slogans. It is also made in some very practical ways that should not go unremarked. A focus on community and interaction has led the Baptist, the Assemblies of God, and the Plymouth Brethren congregations to stable racial integration; it has led the Baptist church and the Assemblies of God congregation to the integration of members from vastly different socioeconomic backgrounds, something that is quite uncommon in local congregations. It has led the Lutheran and the Congregational churches to their reputations in the tri-village area as welcoming places for lesbians and gay men, and it has led the Conservative temple to develop programs for mixed-religion couples that are not featured in most Conservative synagogues.

The religious values that these congregations express are very modern and in many ways very American. They are the values of a pluralistic democracy, emphasizing tolerance, diversity, and widespread participation in decision making. These congregations take seriously the doctrines and the history of their religious traditions, but liberal and conservative congregations alike take a progressive, not an orthodox, view of the tradition (see Hunter 1991). The task of the believing community is to reason together to interpret the relevance of historic faiths to contemporary life. This task is seen as thoroughly moral in and of itself. In this process, both caring and compromise are important to the ongoing life of the community and are moral imperatives in their own right.

The role of the pastor in a community congregation is largely that of a professional hired to perform ritual and administrative tasks and to facilitate the process of congregational consensus-seeking. Pastors exert a formal and process-oriented leadership, but they tend not to put issues on the agenda or take substantive stands during conflict. The pastor's formal authority translates into very little religious or moral authority in actual congregational decision making. That authority springs from the membership and is conceived of as residing in the community as a whole. The expressive style of community congregations and the fact that members themselves put issues on the agenda is why they are prone to conflict between persistent groups of older and newer members (cf. Becker et al. 1993). These conflicts over generational transitions in leadership can be made worse if the newer and older cohorts also exhibit differences in age, socioeconomic status, or ethnicity.

In two congregations, Jericho Assemblies of God and the independent Baptist church, the division between older and newer members is overlaid by differences in race and socioeconomic status. The older members tend to be mostly white and middle to upper middle class, although there are some African American middle-class older members as well. The newer members are young white professionals who value a multiethnic environment, along with African Americans and some Hispanics and Asians, who tend to be poorer, younger, and to live in Chicago and not Oak Park proper. These differences have resulted in conflicts over the liturgy, particularly over the style of song used in worship, in both congregations. In addition, at Jericho, it led to a conflict over renaming the congregation.

In the case of the Lutheran congregation and the Conservative temple, the older/newer member division led to conflict over how to spend resources such as time and money, driven in part by generational differences in needs for specific services, as well as by different attitudes toward worship and liturgy. In the Lutheran church, this resulted in a conflict over the renovation of the church building, begun when some younger members suggested renovating the sanctuary space. In the Conservative temple it drives ongoing conflicts over the scheduling of the religious school and the use of temple space for it and the role of the Sisterhood, a traditional organization for the temple women.

The older/newer transition is made more difficult at four of these six congregations – Jericho, the Lutheran church, the independent Baptist church, and the Congregational church – by the fact that each congregation had undergone a period of severe decline and had some concerns about surviving at all. All have stories of remarkable turnarounds during the 1980s, and all are now thriving. In all four, that core group of people who would not give up, who steered the church through its darkest time in recent history, are still around. And their presence makes the transition to new leadership especially difficult.

It is of course normal for congregations to experience changes in leadership. But for community congregations, this type of transition is particularly difficult to accomplish, and it generates more conflict than it does in other types of congregations. In these congregations, the tendency for people to feel ownership of the congregation is enhanced by the individual-expressive nature of the congregational commitment. So is the tendency for new members to attempt, fairly quickly, to institutionalize their own values and preferences. Issues on which there are likely to be generational differences – the role of women in the church, worship style, attitudes toward lesbians and gay men, how to spend money – are particularly likely to trigger conflict.

In community congregations, there is a sense of members discovering and implementing together a local and negotiated application of the core values of their religious heritage. They figure out, together, in an ongoing way, what it means to be a Conservative Jew or a Biblical Christian or a Lutheran. Members can spark congregation-wide debate on things that matter deeply to them. Disagreements arise and must be addressed in a way that is compatible with their emphasis on being a loving and affirming community, where everyone's needs are met. Members find this exciting, frustrating, and challenging, and to them that is what authentic religious community means.

Notes

1. See Carroll and Roof (1993) for a discussion of the trend toward eclectic worship services in liberal Protestant churches.

2. Of Chicago.
3. In the Plymouth Brethren congregation, it was the head of the elder board; they do not have a pastor. They hired a Bible teacher to give the Sunday sermon, but he has no administrative power and is a full-time student who is relatively uninvolved in the life of the congregation.

6

LEADER CONGREGATIONS

Main Street Baptist Church traces its roots back to the Protestant fundamentalist movement of the early twentieth century. The congregational history says that
the fundamentalist/modernist controversy "was a primary force in making Main
Street Baptist Church what it is today." The church was formed by members from
five local churches of different denominations who left their original churches
because of doctrinal differences. The history says that

> The framers of the church constitution and statement of faith worked to
> create a church that would be independent of any denominational ties and
> faithful to the cardinal doctrines of Scripture, particularly those currently
> under attack in liberal churches and seminaries.

In interviews, members echo this understanding of their congregation's history.
For example, one of the elders told me that

> The church was [pause] formed as a reaction, seventy-five years ago, to its,
> what it perceived as a drift from the fundamental evangelical position of
> the other churches in the area.

Until 1977, the congregation had a different name and was housed in a small
building on a side street in Oak Park. When a fire destroyed that building, the
congregation eventually arranged to buy from a struggling Presbyterian congregation the impressive Romanesque building on Main Street where they are housed
today. They changed their name and, in 1979, Rev. Billy Graham conducted their
dedication service.

Just as everyone I spoke to was aware of the congregation's fundamentalist heritage, so too did they agree that the move to this building at this location changed
the congregation's identity. Before, they were a smaller, older, less affluent congregation on a side street, marginal to the community's life. The assistant pastor
told me that before their move it was easy for people in the community to disregard them or to write them off as "weird or shabby."

But by 1991 they were drawing over 700 people to their two Sunday morning services. They have all age groups, but by far the largest group is younger professional families with children. People from the community's Episcopalian, Congregational, and other main-line churches send their teenagers to the youth group here, which is one of the few in the area that is thriving. The congregation is now perceived as a leader in local and regional evangelical Protestant circles. It is active in outreach in the community, and its pastor and lay leaders speak out publicly on community affairs. Main Street Baptist is neither weird nor shabby; it is an impressive presence in the community. As the head pastor says, they are now "on the map, in the big leagues."

The move to Main Street brought a new constituency into the church. When I first walked into this congregation on a Sunday morning, I was struck by what I perceived as their homogeneity. The vast majority of the over 350 people were white. They were well and conservatively dressed: the men and some older women in suits, the younger women in cotton print summer dresses. The parking lot and several tiers of the municipal parking garage across the street were filled with expensive, newer cars. But congregation members perceive things differently; they see great diversity. Lay leaders and the pastoral staff were especially prone to point out just how different the new constituency is from the older, pre–Main-Street membership. As one of the board members told me:

> We don't have a homogeneous congregation. We have a very diverse congregation. We have a lot of people like Jane and I who come from a strong evangelical background, and who tend to be more traditional. We have a lot of younger people . . . in their twenties and thirties, who come from a nonreligious background, who may have been converted through a college ministry . . . who do not have any traditional church background. How do we integrate these people? Or, how do we integrate as a congregation without ending up in two separate camps?

The newer members are younger and more cosmopolitan. They have more money and less time. They come from widely divergent church backgrounds or have been unchurched, unlike the older members, who mostly had traditional Baptist upbringings. This has led to tension over a variety of issues, including the style of music, the timing of services, preferred programs, and whether it is okay to borrow money to renovate the church.

The only serious conflict has been over women's roles in the congregation. The conflict began when a woman was elected to the church board. At the time, the board was a joint board, functioning as both an administrative body and as a body of elders, who gave spiritual guidance and direction to the congregation. No women had been elected to this board for several years, and then two were elected in a row. Most fundamentalist Protestant churches reject the idea of women pastors and elders, although there are some exceptions to this general rule.

The pastor reacted to this election by leading several adult Sunday School classes on the issue and wrote a position paper on women in the church. This position paper is eleven single-spaced pages. It includes a brief history of the rise of evangelical feminism and has a short bibliography, in which the pastor included both works that support his traditional stance and just as many by evangelical feminists who hold an opposing view. However, in the text of the paper, the pastor makes clear that his interpretation is that women should not teach or hold authority over men in the church, specifically that they should not be elders or pastors.

The board, already in the process of revising the church constitution, decided to move to a two-board system, at the urging of the pastor. The new arrangement would include a board of deacons, which is an administrative board, on which women and men would both serve. And there would be a board of elders providing spiritual guidance, and on that only men would serve. The congregation ratified the new constitution by a large majority vote.

Estimates vary on how many people disagreed with the policy, ranging from ten to thirty people. Certainly, the core was a group of professional women, and some men, who thought that if women could "do the job," then they should be allowed to do so. Drawing on their experience in the working world, they did not "want discrimination in any form."

The pastor was quick to point out that the standards of the world and the standards of the church are different. The head of the new elder board, a businessman in his forties, agreed. He told me:

> Well, of course, our society is changing dramatically. There are women in other denominations, there are women ministers, there are women elders. . . . When it comes to excluding women from *anything*, we have to understand that we're swimming against the stream of our society. The decision we have to make is, are we gonna follow what we perceive are Biblical principles, or are we gonna try to mirror what we find in society? I think this is the main issue.

He, and others, trace the controversy over women's roles directly to a group of younger professional women who have joined since the move to Main Street:

> There are some women in our church who feel strongly, and maybe men, too, who feel strongly that women should be, perhaps, should be elders. And, see, that's the thing that we have, because we have people coming through of diverse backgrounds. We have a lot of people from liberal denominations, denominations where there was no distinction made.

Another lay leader agreed, saying that it is the "doctors, lawyers, women who have positions of authority and leadership in the outside world" who want the changes. This description fits the profile of a good portion of the newer female members.

At least one of these professional women rejects the idea that the traditional stance is the Biblical one. Her support for women elders is not based entirely on worldly or work experience. Referring specifically to evangelical feminists who make Biblical arguments for including women in leadership, she noted that the board

> needs to study more, because they can't refute some of the very good arguments that women have.

Some of the newer professional women think that women in leadership has a Biblical, and not just a worldly, basis.

None of those who disagreed with the policy have left, and none are likely to go, according to my interviews. While some disagree with the pastor's position, none question his authority to make the decision. This distinction – disagreeing, but accepting the pastor's authority to make the final decision – was a distinction that members themselves made, unprompted, during our interviews. It helped that the pastor was quick to make other changes to incorporate women into positions of administrative and ritual leadership where possible, including hiring a female director of Christian Education and having more women give prayers and read Scriptures in the Sunday services.

Also, the general tone that the pastor maintained throughout the public discussion helped to ease any tension. One woman who disagreed with the new restrictions on women's service told me that there was broad discussion and respect for opposing views. This quote from his position paper is typical of all of the pastor's public pronouncements on this issue:

> While I make no apology for having strong convictions, I wish to say that I have deep respect for those who may disagree with me. Believers often disagree on sensitive issues.

This convinced many people that the pastor supported the congregation's mandate to work things out peacefully and fostered "an honest desire not to hurt each other." As one older woman, a Sunday School teacher who believes that women should not serve as elders or pastors, told me, "We don't always agree . . . but let's find something we can live with." The pastor made a point of saying that this matter was not a fundamental point of doctrine, but rather "something about which Christians, in good conscience, can disagree."

It is tempting to see all conflicts over women's roles in local congregations as a struggle between liberals and conservatives, but that is difficult to do in this case. People on both sides embrace fundamentalist doctrine. The woman who supported expanding women's roles to include serving on the elder board nevertheless told me that she shares the broad congregational consensus around the issues of the verbal inspiration of the Scriptures, inerrancy, the virgin birth, salvation through the acceptance of Christ and his substitutionary death.

The desire to see women's roles expanded, for this woman and others in the congregation, is not rooted in a broadly liberal approach to theology or a liberal political discourse, it does not coincide with liberal stands on abortion or homosexuality, and it generally cannot be adequately understood as "liberal" as that term is conventionally used. It is also not rooted in a democratic or expressive understanding of religious authority in the local church. No one has challenged the basic governmental structure: The pastor decides about doctrine, the boards formulate policy, and major nondoctrinal issues are voted on by the entire congregation.

One older laywoman who was against expanding women's roles told me, referring to the women who had initiated the public discussion, "if they're really unhappy, I suppose they might leave and go somewhere else." She was glad that doctrine would not be compromised to keep just a few people. But, in fact, faced with a pastor and a board with whom they disagree, but who also managed to disagree respectfully, those who wanted to see the congregation consider women for the role of elder, or even that of pastor, have been content to stay at Main Street.

Who We Are

In these five congregations, members and clergy told me repeatedly that their congregations are leaders. To say that immediately raises some questions. Leaders among whom? In what area? To what purpose? As the term "leader" is used by the members of these congregations, it implies a typical set of answers to these questions. To be a leader congregation means having visibility and status within the local community and having a public voice in community affairs. It means having a reputation for leadership within the denomination or among similar congregations, being a church or a synagogue to which others look in formulating policy or developing programs. It means having a rabbi or pastor who is well known and well respected in the local community and beyond. And it means not compromising on important issues of doctrine and religious tradition.

One important sense in which the term "leader" is used has to do with the congregation's reputation in the local community. Members know that their congregation is considered to be *influential* by residents, community leaders, and other churches. Part of this is simply a sense of visibility and status. Main Street Baptist and the United (UCC/Presbyterian) congregations across from one another on Main Street are visible because of their impressive buildings on a major thoroughfare. The Presbyterian congregation in River Forest makes itself visible to community leaders by buying its pastor a membership in the country club and by its substantial stone buildings that dominate a large corner lot. The synagogue is more visible because it is the only Reform temple in the immediate area and because of its large physical plant on a major cross-street.

The four large leader congregations have something of an advantage in this aspect of visibility. However, not every large or affluent congregation in this community thinks of itself as a leader. Rather, size and resources are better understood as plausibility structures for thinking of the congregation as a leader.

One of the most important means of visibility is having a pastor who is a known and respected "player" in community affairs. The pastors of all five of these congregations are public spokespersons on a variety of issues. They attend and speak out at public meetings on issues ranging from the appropriateness of Christmas carols in school pageants to the village's policy of granting benefits to same-sex partners of village employees. When African American community leaders spoke out about what they perceived as institutionalized racism in the local high school, the rabbi of the Reform temple wrote an editorial in the local paper supporting their position. Main Street Baptist formed an AIDS policy task force and organized an all-day conference on AIDS outreach in the village that was open to the community. They invited health-care professionals to attend and told people how to get involved in AIDS outreach. They also spoke out at school board meetings against the decision by the village board to add sexual orientation to their antidiscrimination policy.

Leader congregations do not shy away from local politics, especially on sensitive or conflictual issues. The head pastor at Main Street Baptist gave a sermon that was designed to mobilize people to go to the school board meetings, including the following passage:

> Isn't this sermon an attempt to mix politics and religion? Answer: Absolutely. All political decisions are ultimately based on ethical considerations. . . . Occasionally there arises an issue which touches the moral foundations of our society. At that point the church of Jesus Christ has a solemn responsibility before God to speak His Word clearly. In the day of controversy God's church must not be silent.

The visibility of the pastor is a resource that is available to small and large congregations alike. The members of the small Disciples of Christ congregation still talk with pride about how one of their former pastors was involved in the Civil Rights movement and worked tirelessly to pass the integrated housing ordinance in Oak Park. They were proud when the local paper ran a profile of their new pastor, which named him as a leading local activist in peace-and-justice issues. The paper profiled the new pastor's own work in the Civil Rights movement and, more recently, in promoting better race relations in Oak Park. For example, in 1988 it came to light that the village board had tried to block the sale of a local Christian Science Church building to a black congregation from Chicago. In response, this pastor organized a series of town meetings to discuss race relations and persuaded several congregations to engage in pulpit exchanges across traditional denominational and liberal/conservative lines, to create a dialogue about race.

Sometimes, it is not only the pastors in these congregations who are involved in community affairs, but also lay leaders. When asked what her congregation does well, a lay leader of the Disciples congregation said that they

> reach out to the community. And the leadership provides leadership for the community.

A man from the United (UCC/Presbyterian) congregation said that he thinks that the church should be about justice and dignity. He likes his church not only because he thinks it embodies those values better than the other congregations in the community, but also because

> it embodies part of the power structure of the community. So our commitment to justice and peace can actually have some practical consequences in the community.

Being politically involved is a form of witness, not only for the pastor, but for many of the members as well.

But even members who are not themselves involved in community affairs take pride in their pastor's visibility. The woman who said that the congregation provides leadership for the community went on to say,

> And while not a lot of members are active in doing that, they support [the pastor] and are proud of him.

For those who are politically involved in village life and for those who are not, being a member of a leader congregation is a way to feel part of the local community power structure and involved in important civic affairs.

Speaking out on community affairs and wielding power in the village is one aspect of what these congregations consider to be their outreach. Another is compassionate ministry, like supporting the local food pantry and rotating homeless shelter. As has been noted, all of the twenty-three congregations engage in outreach in some form, and compassionate outreach is by far the most common form. But leader congregations are the only ones where members consistently name outreach as an important goal, as something that the congregation does well, and as something it is known for in the community at large. Outreach is valued more in, and is more central to the identity of, leader congregations than it is in any other type of congregation.

The chairwoman of the worship committee at the United congregation gave a typical response to the question, "What does your congregation do well?" when she said

> It has a very strong social conscience and a very strong mission. And those things certainly help people to feel that they are less of a single voice.

When I asked her specifically what the congregation was doing, she said that they had just voted to become a "church of light," welcoming lesbians and gay men, that they are trying to attract more people of color, and that they have been active in working with the Community of Congregations, an ecumenical organization, to organize the homeless shelter.

Also, there is a difference in how the outreach is carried out in these congregations. Leader congregations do not just give money to ecumenical or denominational organizations. They tend to organize and fund outreach activities, and more of their lay members are involved in such activities than is the case in other kinds of congregations. These congregations give their members a sense of being connected and involved personally in their communities and, more broadly, a sense of

> being aware of issues, what needs to be done, whether it's letter-writing to your congressman or, you know, seeing a need in our own village or other places.

Being a leader is a relational idea. To say "We're a leader" implies that these congregations are distinguishable from other congregations in their

133

community that are not leaders. Sometimes members and clergy are very explicit about this. A deacon at the Presbyterian church says that her congregation does not define and measure itself against the other Presbyterian congregations in the area, but rather against two other leader congregations, Main Street Baptist and the United church. Another member acknowledges that they now feel some competition from the Baptist church for the position of foremost evangelical congregation in the area.

People in other congregations are also aware of this distinction. I asked the pastor of a nonleader church, also a fundamentalist Baptist congregation, whether they were going to send representatives to the community meeting to discuss offering health benefits to same-sex partners of village employees. He said that some of their members would probably go, but that the church would have no organized presence there, noting that, "We tend to leave things like that to Main Street Baptist."

When members of these congregations say that they are leaders, then, this relates to a distinctive visibility and influence in the local community and an active outreach into that community that is highly valued by congregation members. All five leader congregations have this sense of leadership at the local level springing from status and visibility, from outreach activities, and from having lay leaders and particularly pastors who are "players" in community politics and affairs. This is strongest in the United church, the Disciples church, and the fundamentalist Baptist church, although members of the Presbyterian church and the Reform synagogue also report this.

But in each of these congregations there is also an awareness of being a leader in ways that go beyond the boundaries of the tri-village area and engaging in nonlocal outreach. For example, the rabbi and members of the Reform synagogue talked about being a leader within the Jewish community. Sometimes, "the Jewish community" referred to the larger metropolitan area, as when several members told me that they were proud to be members of "*the* Reform synagogue in the western suburbs."

But they also referred to exhibiting national leadership among Reform congregations in working out a policy on the participation of intermarried couples, particularly the non-Jewish spouse, in temple life. The president of the congregation reported that they had shared their policy on intermarried couples at a recent regional conference. Her column in the temple newsletter the following month includes this passage:

We were surprised that there were but a handful of congregations that have tried to address this issue at all. Some, who tried to deal with the issue in their constitutions, gave up, leaving their membership in confusion. . . . At this Biennial we were able to share our process and our conclusions. We were proud to have tackled this difficult issue early.

The rabbi routinely shares with other synagogues his insights into the problem of intermarriage through lectures, extending the congregation's leadership outside of the tri-village area to include the whole region. The fundamentalist church and the conservative Presbyterian congregation are considered regional leaders in evangelical/fundamentalist circles. The United congregation is known as a regional leader among liberal churches, and the Disciples of Christ congregation is a leader among congregations in the larger metropolitan area that are concerned with issues of racism and peace and justice.

And although local outreach is important in each congregation, they also have a global orientation to mission, being concerned with outreach across national borders. At the Presbyterian and fundamentalist congregations, this is accomplished largely through the support of global missions. At the liberal Protestant churches it takes the form of supporting peace-and-justice organizations and initiatives in Africa and Latin America. And at the Reform temple, it has to do with outreach to persecuted Jews in other countries and support of the State of Israel.

Leader congregations tend to see themselves as stewards of larger traditions or values that do not spring from common congregational life or individual experience, but that have their origin outside of the preferences and needs of congregation members. It may seem obvious that religious congregations are, by definition, about the business of preserving and transmitting religious traditions, moral guidelines, and ways of life (Bass 1994). But while house of worship and family congregations place value on preserving a ritual and liturgical tradition, leaders place more emphasis on preserving doctrine.

In each leader congregation, there is a specific set of values from their religious tradition that is highly articulated and that shapes much of the rationale for how and why the congregation thinks of itself as a leader. These traditional values also provide a rationale for outreach. And while each of these congregations has widespread member participation in decision making, there is not the sense that one finds in community congregations of interpreting the tradition in light of members' own needs and experiences. Their approach to tradition is more orthodox; they see religious values as having a validity apart from historical context or personal experience (cf. Hunter 1991).

At the synagogue, it is the Reform tradition that provides this set of values. The rabbi spends a great deal of time in sermons and informal communication stressing that part of what the congregation is about is applying the values of the Reform tradition to their current setting in Oak Park. The policy on intermarried couples must be in line with the Reform tradition. The renewed emphasis on religious education and ritual practice must be true to Reform, not Conservative, principles. This includes a principle of strong lay control and democratic decision making, but also the principle that the rabbi is the sole religious leader. For the Disciples congregation, maintaining tradition means advocating a "peace and justice" ministry in this community, specifically, being true to their denomination's leadership in advocating racial and economic justice.

The United congregation passes on the denominational heritages of both the United Church of Christ and the Presbyterian denominations, with which they are affiliated. The pastor says that they face

> a continuing challenge to remain rooted in our denominations. The people who come in now come in from other denominations or come in from no denominations at all, and are coming back to the church again.

Just like Main Street Baptist, they want to maintain a sense of doctrinal and ritual heritage in the face of a diversity of members' religious backgrounds, including members who have been previously "unchurched." The United pastor uses the broader idea of the Reformed Protestant tradition to articulate a message that is relevant to both their UCC and their Presbyterian affiliations. The pastor keeps a continual emphasis on "that sense of being rooted in the Reformed tradition, which has always been very strong here."

For the Presbyterian and fundamentalist Baptist congregations, the challenge is how to make their conservative, evangelical Protestant message relevant to contemporary concerns without compromising the central tenets of their faith. Main Street Baptist is happy to draw a younger professional crowd, but it draws the line at letting women's religious authority be influenced by ideas about gender equality that spring from the feminist movement. They welcome working women, but they reject the ideology of merit that says that positions of authority should be assigned by universal criteria, according to merit, instead of using ascriptive characteristics like sex. The Presbyterian congregation was undergoing a pastor search at the time of this fieldwork, and the very first sentence in the church profile given out to prospective pastors emphasizes the need to put doctrine first:

> Our congregation has a strong desire to see the foundational doctrines of our faith become real in our lives and, through us, to our communities.

How We Do Things Here

These congregations embrace a "public religion" model of religion. Their clergy and members reject the strict division of religion from other spheres of life associated with modernism. They believe that, at the local level and beyond, religious organizations have something important and public to say about social and political issues. They actively maintain their public voice, their "seat at the table," in community affairs. And they engage in outreach out of a sense of connectedness to the public realm and other institutions.

Unlike the community congregations, they do not consciously interweave the public and the private aspects of religion. On the contrary, these congregations display some ambivalence toward the more "private" aspects of religion. Members of leader congregations rely on them less for feelings of intimacy and community, for fellowship and friendship, than do the members of family or community congregations. Only about one-third (35%) of the members of leader congregations reported that they have close and supportive interpersonal relationships with other congregation members, and just under one-third (about 30%) say that they like to be with like-minded people on a Sunday morning. Older, long-term members are the most likely to report that they find good friendships in the congregation.

Lay leaders and clergy are especially distrustful of the emphasis on meeting individual needs for emotional and spiritual support that they find to be very common in this community. Clergy are aware that there is an imperative, or at least a widespread expectation, for congregations to take on the responsibility of providing these relationships and a sense of family or community for members, and they are uneasy about this expectation. The rabbi of the Reform synagogue told me that more of the newer members

> are looking for an extended family. Many have been grafted from other locations and are looking for support systems in a congregation that at least *promises*, at some level, to be that.

But he went on to say that his congregation is unable fully to meet those needs and that he rejects the view of the congregation as "merely a social service agency." He feels that trying to meet too many individual needs takes scarce money and staff time away from traditionally important tasks like religious education or outreach.

The pastors and lay leaders of the United, Presbyterian, and fundamentalist Baptist congregations also felt torn. Confronted for a demand among some part of their members for ministries to meet individual needs, they feared being swamped by "needy people" who look to the church for social and emotional, as well as religious, needs. The two evangelical congregations were more likely to report some success in this area, particularly in the form of having small groups targeted to specific kinds of needs, like singles' groups and parents' groups. However, even in these two congregations lay leaders expressed concern about being overwhelmed by increasing numbers of people who look to the church not just for Biblical preaching and leadership in the community, but also for intimacy and friendship, for help in crisis, and for social and emotional connections.

I initially assumed that the Disciples of Christ congregation would have an easier time of meeting these demands for support, friendship, and caring, because they are a small congregation. Unlike the other leaders, who draw hundreds of people to a typical Sunday or Saturday service and have many more on the mailing list, the Disciples church runs an average Sunday attendance of between sixty-five and eighty, depending on the time of the year. How could that not be intimate and friendly? But lay leaders told me consistently that they are not very good at providing for people's needs and that people often "fall through the cracks" at their church.

For example, members who attend regularly can suddenly miss church for several weeks and not have anyone from the congregation follow up. This had happened to one long-term member just before I began fieldwork, and it was clear when I interviewed her that this had caused hurt feelings. The woman had "dropped out" for a time because of a combination of work stresses, small family crises, and illness, and no one from the church tried to find out why. Gloria, an African American woman in her forties, had grown up in a close-knit black church where such an absence would have generated, she told me, numerous calls and visits until she had gotten herself on her feet again. This incident prompted some discussion of forming a visitation committee, but during my fieldwork this did not happen, nor had it happened six months later when I made a follow-up visit to this church. And Gloria's experience was a fairly common one. No one in this congregation referred to it as "family-like" or "my extended family," and the family rhetoric is not a prominent theme in newsletters or Sunday bulletins. Members told me that, when they were newcomers, they had a hard time getting to know people in the congregation.

The clergy and lay leaders of these five congregations are aware that there is an expectation that the congregation will provide both support in crisis and a sense of community for members. Some of them have tried to make a symbolic gesture toward community by putting a "family news" section in the monthly newsletter or trying out different new fellowship activities. In interviews, when I asked about short-term congregational goals, lay leaders and most of the clergy in these congregations said that they would like to be better at "community-building" than they are now. But to my follow-up questions, they replied that they really had no plans for any specific actions to implement this goal.

For leader congregations, community-building is the same kind of goal that growth is for family congregations. Aware that some people want it and that newcomers, especially, expect the congregation to care about it, they are willing to talk about it or to make small deployments of resources toward it. But the clergy and lay leadership explicitly reject an inward congregational focus that would make forming a family-like community the main goal.

The pastors play a different role in the life of these five congregations than they do in congregations with other models in place. The emphasis in these congregations on transmitting specific doctrines, religious practices, and other parts of their religious tradition bolsters the authority of the pastor on ritual and doctrinal matters. At Main Street Baptist, church members told me repeatedly that "the pastor sets doctrine." The Presbyterian church was engaged in a pastor search at the time of my fieldwork. According to their congregational profile, one of their top priorities was to find a pastor to

provide spiritual direction, teaching, admonition and encouragement to the congregation.

In fact, of course, decision making tends to be a fairly open process,
with lots of congregational input, as the example of the conflict over
women's roles at Main Street illustrates. The Reform temple saw the rabbi
play a similar role in formulating their new policy on the participation of
non-Jewish spouses in the life of the synagogue. The rabbi told me that,

> It was a long process, characterized by a lot of discussion. . . . Even
> the people who are unhappy with the end result know that they were,
> and in fact were, involved in the discussion. It's not as if they had
> been cut out.

However, there was consensus among the congregation members that "the
rabbi, in fact, has a lot of influence" and that he is in charge of the ritual
life of the congregation. The policy on intermarried couples is talked about
by members as "the rabbi's policy."

All of the pastors in these congregations were called to be stewards of
the denominational, ritual, and doctrinal traditions of the congregation.
And all of them conduct their role as public spokesperson for the congregation with great consciousness of their responsibility, not only to provide
spiritual direction within the congregation, but also to use the congregation's tradition and heritage to provide a rationale for outreach and leadership within the local context.

Patterns of Conflict

Members and clergy report eighteen conflicts in these five congregations
over the past five years. At a very general level, these can be divided into
two kinds. There were six small-scale conflicts, mostly confined to the
board or a committee, that were resolved by vote. These were understood
by all to be administrative conflicts over procedure or allocation of scarce
resources. A typical example occurred at the Presbyterian congregation,
over whether and how to let a Boy Scout troop use church space. But two-
thirds of the conflicts, or twelve out of eighteen, were framed and argued
in moral terms and concerned, for the most part, either the allocation of
resources or the ritual life of the congregation (see Table 7).

Three of the twelve moral conflicts were about questions of worship
style. In the United congregation there was a conflict over which hymnal

Table 7. *Conflicts in the five leader congregations*

There were 18 conflicts in 5 congregations; 6 were small-scale administrative conflicts, and 12 were more widespread and understood as moral conflicts.

* 6 conflicts in 4 congregations over budget and staff, including whether to sponsor a Boy Scout Troop or participate in a homeless shelter, not renew contracts of assistant pastor and choir director, fund-raising for repairs, budget and space for religious school

Factions:	in 1, older and newer members
	in other 5, no factions
Understood as:	administrative
Participation:	5 narrow, confined to board or committee
	1 widespread, at congregational meeting
Resolved by:	vote

* 3 conflicts in 3 congregations over worship style

Factions:	in 1, factions of older and newer members
	in other 2, no factions
Understood as:	moral, preserve our tradition vs. meet contemporary needs
Participation:	widespread
Resolved by:	pastor made decision, or decision put off

* 9 conflicts in 5 congregations over inclusive language, inclusive policy for homosexuals, pastor's outreach, women's roles, role of intermarried couples, missions, install elevator

Factions:	in 4, older and newer members
	in 5, none
Understood as:	moral, at least one side making religious argument
Participation:	widespread
Resolved by:	5 by vote, 4 by pastor

to choose; in the fundamentalist Baptist church it was over whether to use traditional Baptist hymns or change to more contemporary music. In the Presbyterian congregation there was also a conflict over whether to incorporate more contemporary, informal music into the worship service. This was potentially quite divisive, because those in favor of the contemporary music are a small group of charismatics in the congregation, and the charismatic movement has caused many conflicts in evangelical Protestant churches over the last twenty or so years. However, in this case, it was not understood as a conflict over theology or doctrine but simply over worship style.

In each of these conflicts, one side was making a set of arguments about the value of preserving the tradition for its own sake, while another side was arguing for changing the traditional way of doing things so that the worship service would be more meaningful. Because the leadership affirmed both arguments as valid, these conflicts were solved by incorporating elements of both preferred styles into the worship, by using more formal and traditional hymns alongside more informal, contemporary music. These conflicts were similar to those in community congregations.

The rest of the moral conflicts, nine out of twelve, were different. In these conflicts, at least one side was making a religious argument that rejected other alternatives as immoral or wrong. These conflicts played out differently than those in community congregations. Two of these conflicts were over resources, in particular, how to raise or spend money. At the Presbyterian congregation it was over the percentage of the budget that should go to missions. Those in favor of raising the percentage argued that the church's primary obligation is to support outreach, while those who wanted to limit the percentage and spend more money on upkeep argued that it was poor stewardship to let the building deteriorate. The conflict was resolved when the pastor decided that those who wanted to could designate all or part of their own tithe (financial contribution) to go directly to missions.

At the Disciples congregation, there was an argument over whether to spend money for an elevator, to make the church handicap-accessible. Those in favor said that they needed to live up to their peace-and-justice convictions and not discriminate against the handicapped, while those against said it was a poor time to spend more money. The elevator was put in place after a vote by the board.

These two conflicts were resolved by some well-established organizational routine. There were real disagreements, but the debate could be aired at a board meeting or within a committee. Although many people knew about these issues, few understood them to be dangerous for the life of the congregation. Rather, people were pleased to report that these were problems that had arisen and had been handled well and that had not disrupted the normal flow of congregational life or decision making. These were the kind of small-scale conflicts over money, space, and programming that would occur in any organization.

The other seven moral conflicts were more serious, in that they had more of an effect on the four congregations in which they occurred. They escaped normal decision-making routines, and special meetings had to be called to deal with them. They had a more widespread effect on the congregation; these were all conflicts that everyone knew about. And they were all conflicts that had the pastor and lay leadership concerned about people actually leaving the congregation.

The conflict over women's roles at Main Street Baptist is typical of these conflicts in several ways. First, the pastor himself placed this issue on the agenda for public discussion. After women were elected to the church board, he advised the board of the doctrinal consequences and urged them to move to a two-board system, and he wrote the position paper and led the Sunday School classes that began the wider process of congregational discussion. Not only did he begin the public discussion, but throughout it he sought to lead the congregation to accept his interpretation of the correct doctrine on this issue. He engaged in active leadership in an area that was legitimately his domain according to a broad congregational consensus – setting doctrine and providing Biblical leadership. It should be noted that he did this in a way that was relatively open and inclusive. He did not simply implement a policy, but instead he sought out an open forum for discussion. He acknowledged the legitimacy of the opponents' point of view, and he at no time attempted to make this decision a test of loyalty or of purity or to drive away those who disagreed with him.

However, the relative openness of this process is different than the open process in community congregations. In community congregations, the process itself is viewed as moral, and the objective is to come up with either consensus or compromise that incorporates everyone's valued objectives. And the outcome is in doubt until that process plays out. The pastor in community congregations is likely to see himself as the facilitator of that moral process. In leader congregations, the pastor and lay leaders never talked about the pastor's role in this way. While input is sought, it is in the process of educating the congregation about the pastor's point of view. And while compromise is sought where possible, compromise is not possible on the very basic points of doctrine or ritual practice that are at the heart of the conflict. In leader congregations, the process is not the point, and it is not viewed as moral in and of itself. The outcome is what matters, and the pastor or rabbi tries hard to lead the congregation to accept the outcome that he thinks is religiously correct.

The pastor at Main Street Baptist did not act like an autocrat or a zealot. He did not try to drive people away; instead, he tried to make sure that even those who disagreed with him might be able to stay. He acknowledged that sexism is wrong and incorporated women into more visible roles where it was consistent with his interpretation of doctrine. However, he was not willing to compromise on the part of the decision that was within his legitimate domain, the doctrine and ritual practice of the church. And people who did not agree were left with the alternative of staying even though they had lost this fight or moving on to some place that was more compatible with their own views.

One might think that this pastoral authority springs from the fundamentalist heritage at Main Street, but in the liberal congregations there is the same style of pastoral leadership in conflicts over issues that are understood by all as religious issues. For example, at the Disciples of Christ congregation, a religious conflict began when the pastor decided to begin baptizing infants. This had never been done in this congregation before. Several people told me that their tradition endorses believers' baptism by immersion, which requires that the person be old enough to make an affirmation of faith. The pastor's decision led not only to a discussion of baptism but also to a broader discussion of the role of children in the ritual life of the congregation and, in particular, whether children should participate in communion.

The pastor decided to begin offering infant (and child) baptisms because the congregation has many people from diverse religious backgrounds, including several ex-Catholics, who are used to the ritual of infant baptism. The pastor also felt that this was in line with the Disciples heritage, which is, he explained, extremely congregational and localized, allowing for a variety of ritual practices from congregation to congregation. At the same time, he decided that baptized children could take part in the communion rite.

His decision to do this caused a real uproar in this congregation, where communion occurs every week. Older members in particular were upset, and a few refused to serve communion to children when they were communion stewards. After several people complained to him, the pastor led some roundtable discussions and some adult Sunday School classes, explaining why he had done this and how he felt that it was a meaningful ritual in line with their denominational heritage. In addition, the elders, with the pastor's help, wrote a short, two-and-a-half-page paper on ritual practices.

As of now, the pastor decides whom to baptize, and parents decide if their children will participate in communion. There are still one or two members who raise this issue at deacons' and elders' meetings. They do not like the fact that the pastor did the first baptism without any warning, and they do not like it that children, who may or may not understand communion, are participating in it. One woman summed up her concern when she asked, "Do they know the *meaning* of it?"

Reports vary on how many members have left over this incident. One person told me that two or three have gone, while another said that, "The people who didn't like it said so, but no one was angry enough to leave." At least a dozen who were upset have nonetheless stayed in the church. When I talked to four of those who had stayed despite their disagreement, I asked them why they had not simply left, and they gave several reasons for their decision to stay. The foremost was that the pastor has the right to decide about baptism and communion because they are religious practices and rituals. They said that they felt that they had had a chance to speak their minds, and they liked this congregation too much to leave.

Members of leader congregations report that they find the congregation meaningful in their lives in part because it expresses specific social, political, and religious values. In this they are like the members of community congregations. They like being in congregations where values are important, talked about, and central to the life of the congregation. And in some ways, their pattern of conflict is similar. They are willing to engage in issue-based conflict over a wide variety of issues that are viewed as moral, not personal. People express their views, are articulate and involved, and value an open process.

However, there are also some important differences between community and leader congregations. In community congregations, members want to institutionalize their own values, which are interpreted at the congregational level and are based in large part on life experience. In leader congregations, the values that are institutionalized are doctrines, ritual practices, and beliefs that are seen as originating outside the congregation in some larger tradition or heritage. And the pastor is the steward of that heritage, having more control over the interpretation and application of those values to congregational life. In leader congregations, the pastor is also the representative of the congregation to the outside world, further bolstering his position as leader within the congregation (Zald and Ash 1966).

Implications of the Leader Model

Of the congregations in and around Oak Park, those with community and leader models both preserve what Martin Marty (1986) has called "public religion." Leader congregations do this by maintaining a traditional understanding of the private and the public as being realms that are relatively separate and even, perhaps, at odds. Clergy and lay leaders are uncomfortable with the idea of the congregation as being *primarily* about meeting members' emotional needs, providing intimate ties of caring, friendship, and support, because they see that as being contradictory to or undermining their public outreach, which is their primary mission focus.

Of course, it is not that these congregations are unfriendly or cold. When I attended worship services I was greeted warmly by those sitting around me, even at the temple, where it was clear that I was unfamiliar with the order of service and the prayers. When I attended coffee hour I found it easy to strike up conversations with people. But in leader congregations, coffee hour was not just about being sociable; sometimes it was a kind of informal continuation of the worship service. For example, at the Disciples of Christ church, one coffee hour included a prayer by the pastor, the singing of a hymn, and a short, ten-minute presentation by a visiting denominational official who was talking about the denomination's efforts to "plant" new churches in the western Chicago suburbs. In all five of these congregations, it was common for committees to have short meetings during coffee hour, saving the need to return to the church or synagogue later in the week.

These congregations do not reject friendliness and fellowship, compassionate outreach to the unfortunate, nor ministry to those in their own congregation who are ill or grieving. They have well-planned and well-executed worship services, paying a great deal of attention to having good liturgy and music. They use denominational materials for their Sunday School or other religious education. All of these tasks receive some attention and resources, and the strengthening of individuals in their own faith is valued.

What these congregations, and especially their leaders, reject is what Tipton (1982) has called a "therapeutic understanding of spirituality." He feels that this discourse has had a strong influence on American religiosity since the 1960s and has changed the way in which many people think about the nature of faith and the purpose of religious community. These congregations reject this new discourse and the accompanying idea that the congregation is primarily about meeting individual emotional and psychological needs. Concomitantly, these churches embrace a discourse and an ethic of service, which is expressed in their emphasis on outreach within their own community and beyond.

These congregations also place a value on religiously based political activism that is not found in the other congregations in the tri-community area. Together, these five churches have taken a strong, public stand urging ongoing racial integration of the community's institutions and on fighting homelessness. They have also spoken out about whether the village should offer health benefits to same-sex partners of village employees, albeit on different sides of the issue. They send members as an organized, vocal group to community meetings, and their pastors speak out, write letters to the local paper, and are known as moral advocates on social and political issues throughout the tri-village area. If community congregations live their religious values, leader congregations act on their religious values to try to change the political and social structures in the larger society.

These congregations emphasize community service, compassionate out-reach to the poor, civic involvement, and political activism in the service of religious values. They also preserve a more traditional concept of religious authority than other congregations. Authority in congregational life does not stem from tenure, as it does in family congregations, or from the life experiences of deeply committed lay leaders, as it does in community congregations. Rather, in leaders, authority is found in doctrine and in religious texts, in the historic tradition. The pastor or rabbi has authority not because of some formal administrative rule but because he or she is the steward of a historic tradition of faith.

Leader congregations have fewer organizational problems than the other congregations I studied. Because the pastor's authority is not based on being accepted by the inner circle of long-time lay leaders and because the pastor's sphere of decision making is clearly demarcated, there are fewer struggles between the pastor and lay leaders than in family congregations. Because there is no emphasis on creating a close-knit and personalistic community, growth is not a problem. Because member commitment is high, mobilizing people to perform needed tasks is not a problem.

Leader congregations also have less of a problem with the transition in lay leadership than do community congregations. While three of the leader congregations do have some tension between older and newer members, nobody reports that there are well-defined or self-conscious factions. Older and newer members tend not engage in ongoing conflict to define or control the life of the congregation. The pastor is more likely to put issues on the agenda and to lead the congregation toward his desired outcome. This, in combination with the pastor's position as representative of the congregation to the outside community, means that he is less likely to compromise. This is especially the case on matters that are understood by all participants to be "religious." Stewards of a tradition that is not just local, led by a pastor who has more authority than pastors in congregations with other models, leaders can ride out normal organizational transitions with some calm.

7

MIXED CONGREGATIONS

First Unitarian Church

The first thing I noticed about First Unitarian was the building, and the first thing I noticed about the building was that it does not look like a church. It could be a village hall, a cultural center, or a library. It is a low, square building made of concrete and framed by tall, old trees, across the street from the public library. It looks substantial, but understated, with no steeple or huge stained glass windows. The sign that identifies it as First Unitarian Universalist Church is small and set back from the street in a separate glass and metal case.

The sanctuary is in the center of the building. The entryway does not lead directly into it, but instead routes people to entrances on either side. Because other rooms open off of these passageways, a newcomer can wander a bit before finding the way to the sanctuary. When I first visited on a Sunday morning, I was a bit confused by the layout, even though I had been in the building before.

It was easy to wander about without drawing any attention. No one spoke to me as I entered the church, although after the worship service several people sitting next to me welcomed me and invited me to come back again. During the service visitors were urged to stand up and introduce themselves, which I chose not to do, although two people who were in town visiting family did so. We were informed that there would be someone in the entryway at the visitor's table after the service to answer any questions.

The sanctuary is not only at the physical but also at the spiritual and philosophical center of this congregation. Several people told me, before I had been in the church, that I would love the sanctuary, and that it would help me understand their congregation to see it. My fieldnotes from that first visit, describing the sanctuary, read as follows:

> People have told me that it is expressive of their governance and philosophy. The minister is no more than forty feet away from the farthest parishioner, and the people face each other, not just forward. It's like a town meeting, a discussion. There is a main floor, with two balconies above it. Facing the main floor, the podium is on a level with the first balcony. . . .

The seats form three sides of a square, and you can see most of the other people from any seat. Democracy, equality, discussion – all are evoked by the structure of the sanctuary. In this service, the introduction was made from the pulpit, but the rest of the service was conducted from the main floor in front of the pulpit, without any podium.

When I had interviewed the president of the congregation, he told me that the average Sunday attendance, based on hand counts conducted at each service, was about 175 adults in normal times. When I attended, I counted 130 adults. At that time, the congregation was between regular pastors, which is something that often causes a temporary drop in church attendance. But by the reports of the members I spoke to, attendance had dropped here before the interim pastor came, as a result of the previous conflicts.

The members have a strong sense of the congregation's heritage, both in terms of the architecture and in terms of religious tradition. This is not contained in any doctrine; quite the opposite. The tradition that is valued here is a tradition of doctrinal openness and spiritual seeking and discovery. These traits have received a lot of attention, both scholarly and popular, and are said to be broadly characteristic of the religiosity of Baby Boomers (Roof 1993). But they have always been part of the Unitarian and Universalist traditions and have been valued aspects of this congregation's history.

Members are aware of the jokes about Unitarian openness and will repeat them good-naturedly. The first person I interviewed here told me that "Unitarians believe in, at most, one god." It was clear from her intonation that "god" was the correct spelling, not "God." And although she laughed at her own joke, she also went on to explain that not everyone in the congregation is Christian, so one has to be careful of terminology.

Nevertheless, the members I spoke to had a strong sense of commitment to engaging in their spiritual search as part of a worshipping community. They had a religious seriousness that should not be underestimated because it does not lead to the kind of doctrinal certainty that one would find in a fundamentalist church. They were particularly concerned about communicating this commitment and sincerity to newcomers as a requirement for membership.

When asked what brings their congregation together, one woman said, "We are united in our quest for our own spiritual truths." Every person I spoke to echoed this reply. Some seemed aware that it is something of an oxymoron, a phrase that would provoke thought and shake up preconceptions. Some, particularly those in lay leadership, articulated the explicitly communal aspect of this, as did this board member:

> We're a strong community of people seeking their own spiritual path, unique to them. [pause] And as long as they want to join the seekers and don't harm anyone, they're welcome.

At least two strands of the local culture that are strong, stable, and agreed on are a valuing of the worship space and a discourse about and belief in spiritual seekership. This is true across the several segments of the membership identified by the lay leadership. Like those at Main Street Baptist, the members of this almost entirely white, middle-class, and professional congregation perceive a great deal of internal diversity.

The president of the congregation reported that the congregation is "different things to different people" and identified at least six different subgroups. These include parents who primarily want religious education for their children; couples with different religious backgrounds, for example, one Catholic and one Jewish, who want a church that is "neutral territory"; enthusiasts for the architecture; hard-core old-timers, the fifty-plus people who have been members for twenty years or more; single parents, mostly mothers, who find social and other support in the church; and a group of people who are primarily interested in social action. Another lay leader identified small groups of pagans and atheists, although she thinks that most members are theists and/or humanists.

Mostly, the things the president listed are motivations for attending that may or may not correspond to actual subgroups. That is to say, a person can be a single mother, an architectural enthusiast, and a long-term member all at the same time. And most of the people I interviewed combined several of these traits or motivations for attending. However, the group of people who are interested in social action and the group of long-term members are another story. These people not only belong to two groups that are mutually exclusive, but they are also aware of themselves as groups with opposing interests. And at the time of my fieldwork, they had engaged in a long and painful struggle with one another over the congregation's identity.

The older, longer term members have a family model of the congregation, and that is the model that was dominant here for many years. Susan, who has been a member since 1968, is an articulate member of this group and told a story about her own involvement in the congregation that is typical of this group.

She is married and says that seventy-five percent of their friends are from the congregation. When asked what the congregation has meant in her life, the first thing she mentioned was the friendships she has there. When she first joined, there were a group of other young couples. She said, "Then, we were the newcomers." Many have stayed, and they have since become the core group of church leaders. She also said that, "through all the adult education programs it's helped me get a handle on who I am." It has also meant "lots of opportunities for leadership." She and the other long-term members have led the church in developing a ministry that centers around fellowship and education.

Those who prefer a family model are aware that there is a strong tradition in their denomination of being more rooted in outreach, social activism, and community leadership on a variety of liberal social and political issues. They define themselves in part against other Unitarian Universalist churches in the area that embody this aspect of the tradition. In particular, members said over and over that they are different than the other nearby Unitarian congregation, which they described repeatedly with words like "activist" and "radical." This woman, referring to that other church, said:

> We just attract a different crowd of people. So I would say that we are more centered in spiritual things than [the other church], which is centered in social action.

Another woman, comparing First Unitarian to this nearby congregation, noted that,

> We, as a group, as a body, are less militant; we don't go marching for things. The church itself rarely takes a stand on a lot of things.

Susan ties these preferences for different models to historic differences between Unitarians and Universalists. She described for me what she thought it meant to be a Universalist and how that is different than the Unitarian heritage:

> Our church is Universalist. And it's not the Unitarian tradition. We were Universalist up until the early 1960s. Therefore, when we think of ourselves as a church we think of the Universalist tradition, rather than the Unitarian tradition. . . . Unitarians were more in big cities, in the early 1800s when they were first established here, and Universalists were more out in the country. So the Universalists were very concerned with their own, getting to their own salvation, and not waiting for anybody else to do it. I – I hate to use the word, because it sounds so seventyish, but "touchy-feely." Universalists have a lot more heart. And I've been members of both churches, and I joined as a Unitarian.

It is from the Unitarian tradition, she believes, that some Unitarian Universalist congregations get their strong concern with social activism.

Susan is a member of a potluck group made up of five couples that has been meeting once a month for twenty-three years and still meets as a group (two of the women have died, but their surviving widowers still come). Susan knows that there are other friendship circles that are equally active in her church, and she assumes that most members are a part of at least one of them. More generally, people who are part of this group of longer term members told me that the congregation is a social center for most members, that people find one-half to three-quarters of their friends there. They believe that their experience of close and intimate connections is typical of the church as a whole. Longer term members are more likely to talk about meals and social activities as important things that bring the whole congregation together. As one woman said, "We couldn't live without our coffee," referring to the Sunday coffee hour after church.

They also exhibit the same mistrust of the pastor as a newcomer and outsider that members of family congregations tend to display. They talk about the pastor as peripheral to the ongoing congregational community. Susan says, regarding the interim pastor:

> I don't agree with the minister who's there right now, so I'm not going. . . . I don't go on Sunday morning, I just won't put up with that. I am still loyal to the church, the minister I'll outlive. I have done it in the past and I will do it again.

In fact, she reported, she felt the same way about the last pastor, as did this woman, who noted,

> In a period of twenty-eight years of time, you're not always in sync with who the minister is.

This is related to the nondoctrinal heritage of the congregation. The president of the congregation, himself a newer member who is interested in social activism, reports that having no doctrine means that "there's no real religious authority, in the pastor or anywhere else." But while the newer members are more willing to endorse the pastor as a real leader, particularly in outreach, the longer term members are not. Some are even hostile to any manifestation of pastoral authority, like this man, a long-time member who told me that:

> Unitarian ministers are a very unusual group of people. They tend to have extraordinary egos. They tend to be extremely well educated, and they tend to have an exaggerated view of their own importance.

For those who think of the congregation as a family, the building itself is very important. Older members do not display the same ambivalence about it that younger members do, and they are not always aware that others have anything but positive feelings for the building. When asked what brings the congregation as a whole together, they are much more likely to mention the building and the fact that it is a "masterpiece." One woman said, "Everyone is madly in love with that building."

The group that prefers social activism is different on a number of dimensions. They are more likely to say that only ten to twenty percent of their friends are in the congregation and to say that this is true for everyone else. Most are not members of something like the potluck group or other friendship circles. One man did note that small groups and friendships are important in the congregation. But this man, who is forty-three years old, married, and has two children, said that he and his wife's "core group of lifelong friends" are not from the congregation, although they often go out and "do things" with congregation members. For him, there is nothing in the church that is equivalent to Susan's potluck group, nor is there anything similar for most of these newer members.

This group has more ambivalence about the building. Because it is a national landmark, the congregation has formed a restoration board, made up of both congregation members and outsiders, to oversee fund-raising and upkeep. The newer members have less confidence in this restoration board. While they are positive about the worship space, the newer members are much more ambivalent about the architecture as a whole and about the congregation's status as a landmark. As the president said about the building, "It's priceless. It's worthless." Someone else labeled it "an asset and an albatross," and another said that the building is "something between a source of pride and a burden that drowns us." This ambivalence pervades this group's talk about the building, along with concern about the amount of money and effort that must go into building upkeep that might instead go to outreach or social action.

Susan may have tapped into an important difference in speaking of this as a difference between Unitarians and Universalists. When I spoke to newer members, and particularly those who wanted the church to engage in more social activism and outreach, they did identify themselves as Unitarians, and they identified social activism as the important part of the Unitarian heritage. They related their Unitarian heritage specifically to their desire that this church develop a public voice in the community on issues like gay rights, AIDS awareness, and racial justice.

They also tell a different story about why they became members, what is important to the congregation now, and the future trajectory. When I talked to the man who is the board liaison to the social responsibilities committee, he said that there had been a lot of conflict, and he had found it very painful. When I asked him why he stayed, he reported that, despite the conflict, he and his wife have been happy there, because

> Our values are congruent with the congregation's. And they're becoming more so as the orientation of the congregation shifts more towards social responsibility.

When I asked different people I got several different versions of the conflict that had rocked their congregation over the last three years, but it was possible to reconstruct a series of events that began when the pastor announced that he did not want to live in the parsonage. A group of long-term members proposed tearing down the parsonage and building a new religious education center. Others wanted to tear it down and put in a paved parking lot, and still others wanted simply to remodel the existing structure as a multi-use center that would include classrooms and other meeting space. The last of these proposals was adopted by a congregational vote.

As one woman said, the outcome itself was legitimate. "We're a democratic body." And others seem to agree with this. What rankled, what is still remembered and talked about, was that the pastor had taken a vocal, public position against building a new religious education center, in opposition to the longer term members who wanted this. As a result, as one person reported, the pastor became a "lightning rod for criticism." For the first time, there was "an anti-pastor group."

This group grew a year or so later when there was a conflict over the congregation's relationship with the restoration board. The restoration board was developed so that donations for upkeep to the building could be accepted and have tax-deductible status. It manages relations with a local group that conducts tours, part of the money from which comes to the church for upkeep.

Managing this type of relationship is always difficult, and there had been tension for some time over who exactly was responsible for what. The congregation tried to renegotiate the agreement with the restoration board, and this process broke down over income from the tours. In August, at a church retreat, at the pastor's urging, the board voted to sever ties with the restoration board entirely.

This caused a huge and emotional conflict. In fact, many of the same people who had been upset with the pastor over the last conflict were also involved in this one, and to that group was added a large number of new people who thought that the board had not only been unwise but had violated the basic democratic tenets of the congregation by taking this action without a congregational vote. Some of them were themselves the congregational members who had been serving on the restoration board, and they felt that the church board's vote was a slap in the face to that service.

A group of members circulated petitions, got enough signatures, and called for a congregational meeting, at which it was voted to reinstate the relationship with the restoration board and continue negotiations. Eventually these negotiations were successful, and the congregation's relationship with the restoration board has improved steadily.

The congregational meeting and much of the public and private discourse surrounding this meeting was rancorous and personal. As one woman put it,

It was like a family squabble when things get out of hand. People say cutting, hurting things. The things said in the heat of the argument are not forgotten.

The pastor was not above the fray. For example, he called the group of people who circulated the petitions "dissidents" from the pulpit on a Sunday morning.

The relationship between the congregation and the restoration board could be mended, but the anti-pastor faction was now much larger, up to perhaps forty people. There was also an emerging consciousness of a pro-pastor faction, a group of roughly thirty people. One person in this group says, "We just loved him; we thought he was being railroaded." Or, as someone from the opposing camp put it, "They just thought he was God."

For the most part, the pro-pastor faction was composed of newcomers who favored a social action agenda and the anti-pastor faction of long-time members who opposed it. The pastor himself was a charismatic and powerful speaker, pro–social activism and pro-growth, and he had tried to use the pulpit as a means to promote both of these goals.

All of the people I talked to said that the pastor could be somewhat stiff or cold in interpersonal interactions. One of the newer members said that they thought that he was shy and that he could overcome it to speak from the pulpit but felt awkward interpersonally. But the long-term members did not put so generous an interpretation on his manner, calling him cold, controlling, or manipulative. One man told me that the pastor "was egomaniacal and paranoid." This man took the pastor's belief that people were plotting against him as a sign of paranoia, but in fact several people reported to me that it was true; people were meeting together and working actively to find a way to get him out.

The pastor himself provided that opportunity. He requested that the board find the money to hire a part-time business manager. The board was in the process of doing this when the pastor announced an ultimatum from the pulpit. Either the congregation would come up with the money for the business manager or he would quit. The congregation was at the beginning of a pledge drive. The pastor's supporters increased their pledges, but they tended to be not only newer members but slightly younger people, many with dual incomes but also with young children and mortgage payments. The pastor's opponents tended to be slightly older and had somewhat more resources. These opponents, and some people who had previously been neutral but who did not like the ultimatum, reduced their pledges. The money for the business manager did not materialize, and the pastor resigned.

Clearly, the conflicts in this congregation were about many issues. They were fed by personal dislikes and by different ideas about governance. Decisions like the one about how to dispose of the parsonage might happen in any congregation. And, of course, the tension between the congregation and the restoration board predated the arrival of newcomers with new congregational goals. Not everything about these conflicts is explained by reference to congregational models.

However, the specific conflicts – over the parsonage and over the restoration board and how it managed money – became, in this congregation, something more. They became opportunities for two different groups with two different visions of congregational identity to vie for control. This conflict centered around the pastor, who symbolized which direction the congregation should take. As the president of the congregation put it, it was between a group of people who wanted the congregation to stay more intimate, more "face-to-face," and those who wanted the congregation both to grow and to become centered around outreach.

People were aware of the stakes. When I asked the leader of the pro-pastor faction about the conflict, he told me that it was primarily about the older people, older members, not liking the last pastor. In general, I think they were becoming disaffected and had been for some time. This place has changed. Gradually, it's becoming more liberal. There's a consensus developing that social outreach ought to be the main responsibility of the congregation. That wasn't the case, say, even four years ago.

At another point he said that the older members "feel disproportionate ownership" of the congregation. One of the things he liked about the former pastor was that he drew in newer members, most of whom were more sympathetic with his social action goals. These people were also beginning to bring in more money and other resources, which would eventually tip the balance of control away from the older, smaller group of more affluent members.

On the other hand, the older members talked about the pastor and newcomers trying to "take over" and turn the congregation into something that it was not. Several people mentioned that those who preferred outreach and social action should go to the other Unitarian Church nearby, the one that is more "militant," and stop stirring up trouble in this one.

In fact, many people on both sides left the congregation, some for good. There was a great consciousness of winners and losers, but even the winners were exhausted and weary, and some of them left, too. When I ended my fieldwork in this congregation in 1993, there was hope that, with the congregation searching for a new pastor, there could be a time of healing and a sense of moving on. Those who preferred a family model had, at that time, won at least part of the larger battle. Most of the people remaining in leadership were emphasizing that spirituality, outreach, and providing a close and supportive experience for members are equally important. The new president of the congregation took pains to tell me that he would never emphasize social activism over either spirituality or the fellowship that most people find so important in the church.

However, when I checked back with the congregation in 1996, it had moved decisively toward a leader model and a more outwardly oriented and activist ministry. From being a small subgroup, those who were interested in social action and peace-and-justice issues have, in the end, changed the congregation's identity. It is now known throughout the Chicago metropolitan area for its leadership, particularly in gay and lesbian ministry and in AIDS and poverty outreach. I was unable to contact Susan for her reaction to this change, and I was told that she was no longer attending, so I do not know how she reacted to her congregation becoming, essentially, a different kind of church.

Congregations in Transition

The previous four chapters describe the nineteen congregations in which it was possible to identify a dominant congregational model in place. To say that a model is dominant is not to imply that there is complete uniformity or consensus at the level of individual belief. To illustrate with an example, the Eucharist has a set of shared, public meanings that the analyst can identify. Some of those are official meanings, which are spelled out in Catholic theology, explained by priests in homilies, and covered in catechism materials. Some of them may be local, communal meanings: The Eucharist may symbolize the parish's history of renewal and change. To use Griswold's (1987) phrase, the Eucharist is a "shared significance embodied in form." This is true even if, while some of the individuals at the altar rail are meditating on Christ's substitutionary death, some are reminded of private religious meanings that the Eucharist has for them, while still others are making up their grocery lists or worrying about a sick child.[1]

Likewise, it is possible to identify a certain set of core goals, valued tasks, and other shared understandings of identity in the public discourse and ritual life of the congregation that comprise important parts of the public culture of shared meanings and ways of doing things. This is possible in part because the center of production of official discourse and ritual activity is fairly small in congregations, comprising in most cases only the pastor and a relatively small number of lay leaders.[2] Information about this public culture is available through the observation of rituals, interviews with clergy, and review of "official" documents like promotional brochures, sermons, and mission statements.

Supplementing this by interviewing members both inside and outside of the current lay leadership and observing their interactions in a variety of settings provides a good way to assess whether these public understandings are reiterated in private discourse and member behavior. It does not provide a clear window into subjectivity, nor is it intended to do so. But it does indicate the degree of consensus about the public culture and whether it influences members' behavior and ways of talking about the congregation's identity.

Studying public culture is important because this is what shapes much of congregational decision making – which programs will be offered and which ones will be highly valued and garner resources. This is one of the faces of power – the ability to set and achieve goals and distribute resources to meet them, to set the agenda of corporate action (cf. Demerath and Williams 1992). Another face of power is more diffuse, but it has to do with the structuring of what can legitimately be said in the different contexts of public life. Conflict is a particularly useful lens into this aspect of public culture because it lets one analyze which issues arise, what rhetorics are used, and how public discussions of difference are conducted. Eliasoph's (1996) study of civic organizations notes the importance of both aspects of power for structuring public spaces and the capacity for different groups to use them as vehicles for effective participation in public life.

Congregational models are the basis of the congregation's public culture, a window into both faces of power – how resources are distributed and what can be legitimately said. While studying congregational models is not a good way to map the range and variation in individual experiences of and attitudes toward the congregation, it is a good way to identify the important features of the congregation as a particular kind of public space and to analyze how the congregation becomes a certain kind of moral community. The previous chapters analyze the congregational models that inform the public culture and structure the decision making in the nineteen congregations that have a dominant model in place.

But in four churches there was no dominant model. In these four congregations the public culture was fractured by ongoing conflict between two different groups of lay leaders who understood themselves to be engaged in a struggle with implications for the congregation's future and for its very identity. I call these four "mixed" congregations, and they are all congregations that have undergone some gradual transition in membership and have experienced some crystalizing or triggering incident that led to the current protracted conflict.

The vignette at the opening of Chapter 1 is taken from a mixed congregation, Hope Episcopal Church. It illustrates the central importance of these four cases for understanding all of the congregations in this study. When Martha reported that she "wasn't going to the same church" as the other people who had gone to the rector's evaluation meeting, she made me realize that people in local congregations both assume that there is a public identity and assume that their own perception of it is matched by others. It is in the context of conflicts within mixed congregations that individual members begin to discover that their own sense of the congregation's identity, and their own expectations for moral action within it, are not shared by all of their fellow members.

As a result, members begin to articulate and elaborate their own underlying assumptions about mission and identity that are at the core of the different congregational models. In the conflict at First Unitarian, members began to talk explicitly about what makes the congregation unique in different sets of terms, one group articulating the importance of a close-knit atmosphere of support, fellowship, and spirituality and the other the importance of an activist outreach into the community and a philosophical commitment to peace-and-justice issues.

It is here that one can see that congregational models can be understood as more than descriptive or heuristic devices for categorizing local congregations. In mixed congregations it is possible to see the link between culture and agency at the local level, as members orient their public and private behaviors toward defending the current model of congregational life or struggling to institutionalize a different one. Conflicts over identity are by definition conflicts over power in both of its faces – the ability to distribute resources and the ability to shape the rules for the public arena of discourse.

In these four cases, conflict between different groups of lay leaders provided occasions during which differences in members' understandings of mission and identity were first triggered, then discovered and talked about, and then sharpened in contrast to one another. Conflict was the process for articulating a challenge to the older model. In three cases, this challenge was successful, and new congregational models came into being. In the Missouri Synod Lutheran church, the challenge was unsuccessful, and the church retained a leader model.

The term "mixed" is not meant to imply that everything about the congregational identity is continually up for grabs in these four churches. Martin (1992) has noted that, in any organization, there are some elements of culture that are in flux while others are more fixed or stable. For example, even in the mixed congregations, denominational affiliation and heritage were valued and stable. In no case was anyone suggesting that the congregation leave the denomination and become independent or join another denomination. And some specific elements of belief or ritual practice were widely and publicly valued. For example, every person I interviewed in the Unitarian congregation used a language of religious journey or being a community of seekers, and they identified this as something that united the whole congregation.

So even in these four congregations there were some elements of the local culture that were relatively stable and agreed upon. But there were also two well-defined and self-conscious groups of people who had different ideas about what the congregation was like at present and what path it ought to take in the future. Specifically, they had different sets of assumptions about priorities, about what is important and valued in local congregational life, and about what are the core tasks and what are more peripheral concerns. And they disagreed about the specific implications for their own congregation of their more generally held common heritage, including denominational culture and governance.

The Episcopalian congregation featured in the opening vignette in Chapter 1 had a situation similar to the Unitarian Universalist church described above. The congregation had traditionally had a family model, and a newer group of lay leaders and a new pastor sought to move the congregation toward a leader model. This conflict was perhaps the most emotional and the one most damaging to the congregation of any of the conflicts that I learned about, and it became complicated when, after more than a year, the pastor was accused of fiscal malfeasance and abusive behavior toward some parishioners. It is difficult to remove an Episcopalian pastor against his or her will, and this pastor refused to leave for a long time. By the time it was over, between one-half and two-thirds of the membership was not attending, and some of them who had gone to other congregations in the area told me that they were not planning to return.

In the Catholic parish, the conflict was over liturgy, authority, and women's roles in the church. A woman religious, or Sister, had been accustomed to speaking from the pulpit. The current pastor retired, and the new one quickly put a stop to the noncanonical practice of allowing the Sister to preach. This resulted in a series of very painful events, including, at one point, a group of members picketing in protest on the doorstep of the congregation, to the great delight of the local news media.

Some members quickly framed the conflict as "about" the new pastor himself; others had no argument with him and directed their protest to the Archdiocese. Some, but not all, of the African American members of this racially mixed parish framed it as a racial matter, because the new pastor is African American and the former one is white. The Sister is also African American, though, and some black parishioners rejected any straightforward racial interpretation of the conflict. The pastor did not back down, and the Sister left the parish, as did a large group of members. Reports vary on just how many left; most people say 50 or more, but over 200 people had signed a letter in support of the Sister, and many who have not formally switched their affiliation are not attending. As of 1992, the parish priest reported 600 active parishioners, but I observed just over 300 people at the main Sunday Mass on the last Sunday in January 1993, after the conflict.

The group that challenged the new priest did so based on the congregational model that had been institutionalized up to that time. This was a leader model. This group was proud of having a woman speak from their pulpit. The leader identity had been institutionalized in the Sister's practices, in the approval that her activities received from the pastor and church council, and in the congregation's reputation both locally and in Catholic circles more broadly as a progressive and innovative parish. The congregation also had a history of community activism on racial issues.

The congregation had been led to adopt a leader model by the former priest, who disagreed with the Church's stand on ordaining women. The former priest created opportunities for the Sister to speak and lead services, encouraged her to do so, and encouraged the congregation to accept the practice. He created a climate of strong de facto congregationalism, despite the denomination's emphasis on standard practices and central control.

The new pastor favored not only a different stand on one issue – women priests – but in general favored a different set of goals and a different identity for local congregations. With his arrival, the congregation became a house of worship, rejecting a leader stance both in the community and beyond. At least a few members preferred the new state of affairs and had wanted a less activist congregation all along. Others did not agree with the new model at all, but they stayed because they had a history and friends there. Still others left when their parish became, for them, an entirely different place.

The Missouri Synod Lutheran Church in Forest Park had been for years a leader in the local community, active in outreach, and one of the first churches in the area to racially integrate both the congregation and the school. Most of the older members were proud of this identity as a leader and wanted it to continue. A few were not, thinking that the emphasis on outreach and racial integration had taken them away from the congregation's primary obligations of teaching Christian doctrine and providing a supportive community for believers – a sanctuary from the world.

These people for a long time had no recourse, but then a newer group of families started to attend, a group that did not live in the immediate neighborhood but commuted from farther away and that did not care so much about local outreach or the congregation's status in the community. They provided support for some longtime church leaders who had been upset about the congregation's direction, and a series of conflicts ensued. These included a conflict over whether to have a Lutheran pastor from a different, and more liberal, denomination speak at the anniversary celebration and a series of struggles over the school budget and the governance structure of the congregation.

Eventually, the group of challengers, who wanted to move the congregation toward a family model, conceded defeat. Some left, and some stayed. The ones who remain still vote their discontent at congregational meetings, especially over finances, but they are in the minority, and for the most part they are content to spend most of their time in fellowship activities in small groups of the like-minded.

Identity Conflict in Mixed Congregations

In these four congregations, there were some low-level administrative conflicts, but most were moral conflicts (see Table 8). At least some of these conflicts were caused by tensions or divisions within the larger denominational culture and history. The conflict at the Unitarian Universalist congregation and at the Catholic church are the best examples. It is also possible to interpret the conflict at the Missouri Synod Lutheran congregation as motivated by differences between conservatives and moderates, a distinction that may be as valid for that denomination at the moment as it was for the Southern Baptists at the time of Ammerman's (1990) study. Larger differences in theology or ecclesiology at the denominational level may become the basis for conflicts over ecclesiologies – congregational models – in local churches and synagogues.

But this kind of local identity conflict is not triggered in any straightforward way by larger divisions. Rather, it is triggered by the presence of two groups of local leaders who become engaged in a power struggle over the implications of their larger denominational culture and heritage for the life of the local congregation. In the Unitarian and Episcopalian congregations, these factions were composed of older and newer members, although in the case of the Missouri Synod congregation and the Catholic parish there were some older and newer members on both sides.

The groups of people and their interests predated the specific events that triggered the conflict, but it was through the conflict that they began to articulate and elaborate their ideas about the congregation's mission and core tasks, about how time and resources ought to be spent, and about the congregation's presence in the community (cf. Victor Turner 1974; Joyce Olson 1981). At the Unitarian congregation, one person reported that the congregation's identity centers around fellowship and spirituality, while

Table 8. *Conflicts in the four mixed congregations*

There were 13 conflicts in 4 congregations.

* In each congregation, one or a group of conflicts between groups with different understandings of congregational identity, difficult to resolve, resulting in the exit of a group of lay members and in two cases the exit of the pastor. This totals 10 conflicts.

    At the *Catholic* church, 1 conflict over women's roles

    At the *Unitarian Universalist* church, 3 conflicts, over the religious education center, over the restoration board, and over the pastor's ultimatum on hiring a business manager

    At the *Episcopalian* church, 2 conflicts, over how to minister to two men with AIDS and over the pastor

    At the *Missouri Synod Lutheran* church, 4 conflicts, over the school budget, over a guest speaker, over revising the structure of the boards and committees, and over hiring a business manager

* There were 3 conflicts that seem unrelated to the struggle over congregational models.

    At the *Episcopalian* church, 2 conflicts over having a woman priest as a guest speaker, and over how to deal with the former pastor's illness

    At the *Missouri Synod Lutheran* church, 1 over a family who wanted their son to be married in the church even though he and his fiancee were currently living together

---

another said that there is a new consensus that social activism is the central task. When I pushed them a little, asking if everyone would agree with how central these things are, they acknowledged that there were groups who disagreed, but they felt sure that their side – and their version of what is really important in congregational life – would win out in the end.

Whether defending the consensus or challenging it, lay leaders drew heavily on their interpretations of their denominational culture and heritage. However, denominational culture was not the only source that they drew upon. For example, in both the Catholic parish and the Missouri Synod church, people who favored a leader model drew on a language of fairness, tolerance, and justice that is rooted in a more generally liberal social discourse. A peace-and-justice mission orientation is articulated within many religious traditions,[3] but it also draws heavily on a humanistic discourse about dignity and a liberal political discourse about rights and citizenship.

Coser argues that "conflicts within the same consensual framework are likely to have a very different impact . . . than those which put the basic consensus in question" (1956:73). In these four congregations, conflicts that began over money, doctrine, or symbolism became conflicts where the basic consensus about congregational goals and identity was called publicly into question. When that happened, conflict processes changed in these congregations. Discrete events might be resolved by vote or some other procedure, but factions grew from event to event, as the buildup to the final conflict over the pastor at the Unitarian congregation illustrates. These were the only congregations in which conflict escalated like this, raging through a series of events, becoming more and more emotional, and finally involving a majority of the active laity. For 200 people to sign a petition at the Catholic church, or for several hundred people to turn up at congregational meetings at the Lutheran church over how much money to put into the school budget, indicates the widespread nature of the participation in the latter stages of these conflicts.

These were the only congregations where different people told me entirely different versions of the conflict. In the Episcopalian congregation, the first eight lay people I interviewed gave me eight different conflict narratives, and the pastor's was different still. In each of these congregations, people pointed to a multitude of issues and events and had different interpretations of what the real underlying issues were. What they were sure of was that there was another group in the congregation that was trying to "take over."

Powell (1991) notes that institutional change is usually quite costly. When the conflict is between two groups who cannot reach a common basis for resolution, it is likely to result in the exit of one group (Coser 1956; cf. Simmel 1971:70). Eventually, in these congregations, routine decision-making procedures were no longer able to contain or resolve the conflict, and the congregation only moved on after the leader and a large group of laity had simply left.

Members seemed aware that the conflict had somehow escaped their best efforts to manage it, and they were frustrated by this. Martha said of her Episcopalian church, "We don't have the tools, we don't have the skills, to deal with conflict constructively." Her congregation is comprised mainly of highly educated, professional people, some with extensive management experience – people who are likely to have some formal training in conflict resolution or the knowledge of where and how to seek out professional mediation if necessary. But normal conflict management techniques do not work in between-frame conflicts. Competing claims and arguments cannot be resolved by an organizational routine or by religious authority – which have both been called into question along with the rest of the bundle. They also cannot be subsumed by a larger set of under-standings, because participants are operating with two such large sets.

The conflicts in three of these four churches came to center around the pastor, and the role of the pastor was different here than in other congre-gations. When the pastor became associated with one of the two factions of lay leaders, his legitimacy was destroyed with the other group. The pastor often symbolizes the congregation as a whole; this is fine under con-ditions of consensus, but it can place the pastor in an untenable position when the basic consensus has been called into question. In the Catholic church, the arrival of the new pastor, with views in sympathy with those wanting more of a traditional, house of worship model, provided this group a chance to articulate views they had suppressed before to keep the peace. In the Episcopalian congregation, when the pastor used his sermons to articulate the view that the congregation ought to be more centered around outreach and social activism, he became a focus for conflict that had been brewing for a long time between groups of lay leaders.

The combination of a transition in membership and a triggering inci-dent that is articulated with the differences in the underlying congrega-tional models seems to have been that which pushed these congregations into a more destructive and escalatory cycle of conflict (cf. Victor Turner 1974). It seems logical to hypothesize that it is more likely for this to happen in larger congregations. In smaller ones, it would be more diffi-cult for a new group of lay leaders who were so clearly in conflict with longer term lay leaders to build up unnoticed.

Public or Private Religion?

In each of these four churches, the struggle was between a group preferring a family or house of worship model and a group preferring a leader model. Each of these congregations became an arena for conflict between priva-tized and public models of religious life among people who seemed to understand "private" and "public" to be mutually exclusive orientations. The four mixed churches saw conflict between groups operating with the assumption that the private and the public cannot coexist in a congrega-tion's mission orientation, that is, the church has to make a final choice about which one to emphasize. In this, they echo a common understanding in Western liberal discourse. In Oak Park, only the community congregations rejected this either/or, private/public dichotomy.

In one way, it is somewhat surprising that this kind of either/or orientation would be found in large congregations with large budgets and no crushing debt, which is an accurate description of all four of these churches. Surely, there would in fact be resources, in money and in member time, to do both. However, those who desired a more public model felt that the particular resources of larger congregations carry with them a moral obligation to do more than serve their own members. These resources include their high visibility and status, their large physical plant, their large membership and donation base, and even their clout in the denomination, which is likely to garner a well-qualified, up-and-coming pastor.

The severe conflict in these four congregations suggests that at the local level of religious life a public/private cultural cleavage may be more important than a liberal/conservative one, perhaps because of the specific way in which local congregations compete for members. Most lay leaders and clergy in this community talked about the need to define the congregation's identity vis-à-vis other local competitors who share the same denominational identity and the same basic ideology as one's own congregation. This is best illustrated by the conflict at First Unitarian. There were no conservatives here, whether that is defined politically, socially, or religiously. The longtime members did not think that social activism was bad and that churches in general ought not to do it. They just thought that some *other* local congregation ought to do it, the one "down the street." That church was already doing it and was known for it. They had specialized. This congregation had specialized in being warm, friendly, and caring – family-like. To engage in activism in *this* church would be in violation of their own history and identity, of what made this particular congregation special and valuable to them. It made them less distinct from the other Unitarian Universalist church in town.

Congregational Transition over Time

In explaining why these four congregations experienced this kind of severe conflict, several factors should be considered. They are all relatively large congregations. And while none of them was growing, they had been experiencing a gradual turnover in membership. At the Unitarian congregation, the membership committee had figured out that they had had an average of ten percent turnover in members per year for the last five years, some years as high as eleven or twelve percent. This resulted in a congregation with a stable core of long-term members and a group of more mobile newcomers. The other congregations were in a somewhat similar position, although at the Catholic church the "newcomers" had themselves been members for a relatively long time, most over five years.

In a large congregation, it is possible for newcomers to arrive who in fact have quite different ideas about congregational mission and identity and for longtime members not to notice this for quite a while. No one minded at the Unitarian congregation when the new members who were interested in social activism were content to work in the context of the social responsibilities committee. When they began defending the pastor and using public congregational meetings and votes over the budget to articulate a different vision for the congregation as a whole, things became more heated. At the Missouri Synod congregation, the proposal to have a non–Missouri Synod guest speaker provided a forum for members who were more internally focused and concerned with doctrine to criticize the congregation's priorities more generally. Then, when the congregation began considering a new governance structure and budget for the school, it provided an opportunity to continue the debate about congregational priorities.

The presence of mixed congregations in this small sample of only twenty-three suggests that congregational models, while relatively stable, are subject to a somewhat routine process of revision and change over the course of an organizational life cycle. Some theories of cyclical organizational development might suggest that the internalized models (family and house of worship) might be more associated with periods of founding or decline, while more externalized models (community and leader) might be associated with "middle" or thriving years of the organizational cycle. There is evidence that this is true for some congregations in this sample, but it is also clear that this general pattern does not hold in some cases. For example, the Catholic parish with the house of worship model is in a period of slight growth both financially and in terms of membership, and the Episcopalian church with the family model has been at a stable size and has kept a family model in place for almost twenty years without either significant growth or decline.

An adequate explanation for the relationship between congregational models and stages of the organization's life cycle is beyond the scope of the data gathered in this project, but this study can suggest some of the elements that such an explanation would have to include. First, at least two processes of cultural change would need to be explained: a normal or evolutionary process of change and a more rapid, crisis process of change associated with the kind of severe, between-frame conflict that is discussed in this chapter. Second, diverse measures of organizational success would need to be developed that are appropriate to the congregation as a form of organization and that would therefore allow for designations of the life cycle that are meaningful in this specific institutional context. For example, financial health would seem to be an undisputed measure of "success" for any organization, but the growth that increases the "bottom line" is problematic in this context because it is not recognized as a legitimate goal by many members. What are alternate measures of success? A long and stable pastorate? Membership stability (the ability to attract replacement members for those who leave) combined with financial health?

In addition, one would have to develop a way to take into account the differences in timing of the various processes of change that are more than merely descriptive or tautological. For example, why do some congregations seem to change with every new cohort of lay leadership, while others do not? Why do some congregations change in response to environmental factors like changes in community demographics, while others do not? Which model is in place might be determined by previous conditions, but it also might be determinative of how a congregation faces and responds to particular social and organizational changes at any given time, and this duality would need to be accounted for in any theory of organizational and cultural change.

One can see in the discourse surrounding the conflict in these four congregations that congregational models do in fact provide cultural frames or lenses through which members interpret the importance of specific events and issues in local congregational life. This is true for larger "denominational" issues like women's roles in the Catholic church or the strength of doctrinal and ideological boundaries in the Missouri Synod Lutheran church. It is also true for internal conflicts over money, resources, and governance.

Once conflict has been triggered by some salient event, the normally taken for granted is brought to the fore and articulated. For example, power is talked about openly in these congregations, in a way that it is not in any of the other nineteen. People discuss who is in charge and what is at stake in each conflict, topics that are generally avoided or that never arise in other kinds of conflicts in other kinds of congregations. Of course, the sociologist is not surprised to find politics – struggles over power – at the heart of conflict even in religious organizations, even if, in normal circumstances, members themselves do not frame conflict events in political terms.

What is surprising is that the political stakes in these conflicts do not vary along the lines of division that one might expect; racial differences do play into the conflict at the Catholic parish, as the black parishioners question whether a white priest would have gotten more respect. But for the most part the differences here are cultural and religious, not demographic. And these do not line up according to a neat left–right political division that the culture wars thesis would lead us to expect. Rather, the stakes here, or that which power is deployed in service of, are more publicly engaged ideas of local religious life versus more privatized, inwardly focused models. What is at stake is the construction of the congregation as a certain kind of public arena, privileging some kinds of discourse over others, and a certain kind of moral community, privileging some moral imperatives over others. What is at stake is the role of the local church in civic life and different visions of religiously informed civic involvement.

In Chapter 9, I will suggest that, while these divisions are religious, they also pervade white middle-class civic culture more generally in the United States. In local communities and in local congregations, this conflict over privatized versus public religion may be the real "culture war." I will also argue that, because there are more publicly oriented than privately oriented congregations in this community, and because even the privately oriented ones are engaged in compassionate outreach, we may need to rethink our assumptions that increasing privatization is the uncontested trend in American congregations.

Notes

1. This discussion draws heavily on Wuthnow's *Meaning and Moral Order* (1987:60–65, 97ff), on Martin's (1992) discussion of what organizational culture is and how to study it, and on Fine's (1984) description of organizational culture as a negotiated public order. In fact, congregational models can be thought of as a way to analyze the patterns or variations of negotiated public orders in a given institutional setting.

2. This too varies from congregation to congregation and depends in part on polity and denominational heritage. The "center of production" of official discourse and ritual life is both smaller and more uniformly articulated in, say,

a Catholic parish than it is in a Congregational church. At the other extreme in this sample of congregations was an independent church of Plymouth Brethren origins. They had recently hired a full-time Bible teacher, but until then Sunday sermons were delivered by congregational members. Even with the Bible teacher, the laity were more active than in any other church in providing music, devotional readings both original and from published sources, and extensive witnessing within the service, all of which contribute to a widening of the circle of people who participate in the creation of public understandings of what the congregation is all about. One might hypothesize that such congregations are more prone to transition from one model to the other, or even to schism, applying the insights from denominational studies to the congregational level (Liebman et al. 1988). But the Brethren congregation studied here illustrates that it is possible for even a congregation such as this to have a dominant public culture around which there is a high degree of consensus.

3. See the October 1994 and the April 1995 issues of *The Ecumenical Review* for examples of a peace-and-justice orientation that is articulated from more than one traditional perspective.

8

AN INSTITUTIONAL APPROACH TO
LOCAL CULTURE

I began this study seeking a better way of understanding conflict by seeing it as an entire pattern of interactions by people who are committed to an ongoing relationship with each other in a specific face-to-face context (cf. Becker et al. 1993). Cultural factors were built in from the start as both outcomes (what issues are fought over) and predictors (liberal versus conservative cultural orientation). But an explicit, comparative approach to understanding the relationship between local culture and conflict came out of changes that were made during the course of fieldwork. I progressed from thinking about discrete conflict outcomes being determined by a uniform set of underlying variables to understanding the variation in basic types of congregation that shape, and are shaped by, conflict and other aspects of group process. As was discussed in Chapters 1 and 2, this change was prompted by an interaction between the fieldwork and an evolving consideration of methods;[1] of the relationship between conflict and other features of group life, including moral expectations for action;[2] and of the structure of authority and commitment.[3]

Often the process of reassessment is kept "backstage" and receives little attention in the final published account of the research, which is generally written as though the analysis proceeded in a straightforward and uninterrupted way from the initial formation of the research problem and research design. But I believe that it can be valuable to give some attention to the process of developing an explanation, particularly when the result suggests a new approach. This study illustrates that an understanding of different institutional models of congregational life can be a useful supplement to approaches that use case studies, survey data on individual attitudes and beliefs, and studies of religious elites and religious discourses to analyze group processes like decision making and conflict, as well as such questions as the relationship between social change and forms of religious community and commitment (cf. Jehn 1997).

This builds on the work of others who adopt a comparative approach that takes the congregation or small group as a distinct level of analysis and incorporates both structural and cultural factors, especially the work of Ammerman (1997a) and Wuthnow (1994a, 1994b). Other scholars are beginning to make similar arguments about the necessity for comparative organizational studies to understand the dynamics of commitment, the civic habits of tolerance and caring, the styles of moral debate, and the structure of participation in a variety of social movements and voluntary organizations, as opposed to studies that privilege individual attitudes and beliefs or social movement frames.[4] Chapter 9 elaborates on why such research might prompt us to reconsider some of the basic frameworks that we use in interpreting the effects of recent social changes on American religion.

In effect, Chapter 9 uses the American religious field to explore how institutional forms, including things like the congregational models that I discovered in these congregations, mediate the effect of social change on individual organizations within a field. Similarly, this chapter develops the argument that these institutional forms have a mediating effect on social action and group processes within organizations. They mediate between larger cultural formations – like religious ideologies or religious traditions – and social action within a given religious organization. They also mediate the effect of structural factors, like the organization's size or its formal polity, on group processes like decision making. If the previous chapter concentrated on how the conflicts in the four transitional congregations shaped the congregational model that emerged as dominant, this chapter considers how dominant models, once in place, shape conflict.

Because an attention to congregational models does provide that better explanation of conflict that I had been seeking, I conclude that an attention to mapping the different empirical types of groups and organizations that occur in different institutional fields is a useful direction for further research on the relationship between institutions and social action within organizations. It can supplement our research on the forces that push toward isomorphism by helping us to specify the limits of isomorphism in various fields. It also can help us to further understand the institutional forms that mediate the relationship between larger cultural formations and structural factors, and individual preferences, beliefs, and decision making in organizations and groups.

As Nee and Ingram (1998) argue, this is the next analytical step in linking the study of institutions, local culture, and agency, and a growing number of scholars agree.[5] But some of the features of institutionalist approaches to organizational analysis, as well as emerging emphases in cultural sociology, have prevented many scholars from following this course. Institutionalists either emphasize the ways in which organizational culture is decoupled from core processes like decision making or they tend to focus on the forces that lead to isomorphism, not stable variation. In the sociology of culture, a new emphasis on systematic methodology has led some to favor methods such as survey research that aggregate individual responses to questions about attitudes, beliefs, and behaviors rather than methods that allow for the emergence of empirical typologies of cultural differentiation. Of course, as Abbott (1992, 1997) argues, it is not necessary to equate "systematic methods" with quantitative analysis; conversely, there is no reason to think that the mapping of empirical types – of careers, of organizational histories, of organizational forms – needs to be done with qualitative analysis.[6]

In short, there is no conceptual or methodological basis for thinking that we are not ready to begin answering the kinds of questions posed by Friedland and Alford (1991) and Nee (1998). How do organizations within a given field choose from, combine, or contest the various strategies that are available to them within their larger institutional environment? How do local practices – ways of doing things, cultural norms, and the conceptions of identity to which they are linked – constrain individual action in groups and organizations? How are these local forms related to larger institutional patterns in a given field? This specific study of how congregational models shape conflict in one set of organizations indicates how we might begin to go about answering these kinds of questions more generally.

Conflict

I began this study by asking, "What do congregations fight about? And why do some have more conflict than others?" The main strength of this study is that it allows me to develop and explore an entire pattern of conflict within each congregation. House of worship congregations have a few low-level administrative conflicts; family congregations have conflicts that are framed as personal and center around the building, the pastor's interpersonal style, or a struggle for control over decision making between the pastor and long-time lay leaders. Community congregations have many conflicts over a wide range of issues that are seldom understood as personal and generally are resolved by long and inclusive processes that seek consensus or impose compromise. Leader congregations also have many issue-based conflicts, but they have less compromise and a pastor who is willing and able to forgo consensus on important religious issues. Mixed congregations have conflicts that escalate through a series of events and are resolved only when some of the most involved parties leave the congregation (see Table 9).

The role of the pastor and lay leadership, the scope and the basis of participation in decision making, and the legitimate styles of decision making and forms of resolution differ in congregations with different models. People's willingness to engage in conflict at all, and the point at which they will exit, also differ not according to size and polity, but according to the institutionalized ideas about the nature and purpose of the congregation or the congregational model in place. This includes, of course, the set of ideas about the nature and purpose of conflict that are inherent within each model, like the preference for "exhaustive process" in community congregations or conflict avoidance in family congregations. Taken together, this suggests that differences in authority and commitment need not be examined by proxy but can be examined directly, because they are institutionalized within local congregational culture. It also suggests that the level of cultural analysis should not be that of the idioculture, but instead an analysis of the institutional structures that shape the formation of local idiocultures.

One feature of congregational life that directly affects conflict is the role of the pastor and the religious authority that inheres in the pastorate. The pastor in the family congregation is either an outsider or a beloved "member of the family." The former is more common, and this limits the scope of the pastor's ability to promote change in many aspects of congregational life, despite the fact that most of these congregations have a formal polity that is hierarchical and should reinforce pastoral authority. The pastor in a community congregation is primarily a facilitator whose job it is to promote inclusive processes and the seeking of a moral and practical consensus. The pastor in leader congregations is not only the religious authority and in charge of ritual matters, but can also exercise a great deal of direct control in other decision areas. In the house of worship congregation, the pastor's role is more determined by the formal polity structure of the denomination. In the Catholic parish, this means that the pastor

Table 9. *Comparing conflict in congregations with different models (including mixed)*

	House of Worship	Family	Community	Leader	Mixed
Fight over	money, staff	pastor, building	money, staff, worship, outreach, gender, sexual orientation	money, staff, worship, outreach, gender, sexual orientation	pastor, money, staff, worship, outreach, gender, sexual orientation, governance
Members make	administrative arguments	personal arguments	moral arguments	moral arguments	multiple kinds of arguments
Participation is	confined to board or committee	widespread, emotional	widespread	widespread	widespread, emotional
Process is	viewed positively	unremarked	viewed as moral	viewed positively	viewed with suspicion
Typical factions	none	pastor vs. lay leaders	older vs. newer members	none	groups preferring different models/mission
Conflicts are triggered	no pattern	often by pastor proposing change in administration or finances	by members proposing new policies/programs	by pastor or members proposing new policies/programs	by new pastor, by pastor proposing new policies/programs
Conflicts are resolved	by vote	by vote or exit of one or two people	1/2 by compromise, by vote	1/4 by compromise, by vote/by pastor	go unresolved or large groups exit

is heavily involved in administrative decisions, while in the United Methodist church this means that the lay Administrative Council is the most powerful decision-making body in all nonreligious matters.

An analysis of congregational models enables us to predict in which congregations latent divisions are likely to generate actual conflict events.[7] Latent divisions between clergy and laity, or between groups of older and newer members, may be common in all congregations. But a congregation with a family model is more likely to experience manifest conflict between the pastor and lay leaders than are other types of congregations. And the transition from older to newer members causes more overt conflict in community congregations than in other types, particularly as cohorts of newcomers take over formal positions of lay leadership. I argue that this is because of the feelings of ownership and the distribution of religious and other authority that go along with different congregational models. The community model fosters the most lay control over policy and the interpretation of official doctrines and symbols, so it is not surprising that more things become contested or that new lay leaders see the congregation as an appropriate context in which to institutionalize their own beliefs and preferences.

Likewise, a liberal–conservative "divide" has received much attention in recent years, largely as a result of declines in liberal and mainline denominations coupled with rising memberships in conservative religious organizations and an increasing left–right polarization of rhetoric in our national political discourse. However, there was little conflict in these twenty-three congregations between factions of liberals and conservatives. At a Catholic church there was one conflict over women's roles that could be characterized in this way. But at least some of the participants in that conflict did not participate because of a commitment to a liberal or a conservative ideological position per se. Rather, they joined in because of ideas about the proper location and basis of authority within the church, which they understood in different terms.

While conflict between liberals and conservatives is real, this study supports a growing contention that such conflict is more likely to be between religious elites or special-purpose organizations than within local congregations.[8] My interviews suggest that most members either think that a left/right dichotomy is unimportant or, if they find it to be so, that they self-select into a congregation in part on the basis of its liberal or conservative nature.[9] In any case, these twenty-three congregations did not tend to become locations for ongoing liberal/conservative conflict.

This study suggests a different approach in analyzing how religious ideology affects internal processes in local religious groups and organizations. Some scholars have assumed that liberal and conservative congregations operate differently, with conservative congregations fostering closer commitment, maintaining more religious authority, and suppressing internal conflict.[10] In Oak Park and its neighboring communities, I found that whether the congregation is liberal or conservative has some effect on the kinds of issues that arise and trigger conflict. Other than that, a liberal or conservative orientation has little effect on congregational conflict or on the dynamics of commitment and authority. This is because being liberal or conservative is not strongly related to the congregational model.

In fact, the only serious way that ideology seems to impact on conflict in these congregations is in the "yes or no" sense. Congregations that are more strongly ideological, be they liberal or conservative, have a different pattern of conflict than do others.[11] Community and leader congregations, being issue-oriented, have more conflict than other congregations. And leader congregations, which are the most ideological, are more likely to see the pastor as the steward of that tradition and their chief spokesperson. This informs the expectation that the pastor will be active in community affairs and also grants the pastor legitimacy within the congregation in conflict over the broad range of issues that are seen as directly related to the interpretation and application of the religious tradition.

This suggests that ideas about the nature and purpose of the congregation are determined, at the local level, less by a left/right dichotomy and more by broader institutional concerns that cut across this specific ideological divide. At the very least, the congregation's liberal or conservative cultural orientation needs to be thought of as only one of a set of schema that overlap and intersect within the culture of any given congregation, rather than as the fundamental divide that structures all of congregational life (cf. Sewell 1992). Other schema include the congregational model, and, for some congregations, another might be the pragmatic service orientation that Ammerman (1997b) has called "golden rule" Christianity.

A division between members caused by one group having a nascent religious experience has also been cited as a cause for particularly severe conflict over identity in local churches. This study shows that nascent religious experiences are not the only things that can trigger this kind of identity conflict. Events that give a self-conscious group in the congregation an opportunity to articulate an alternative vision of congregational life can trigger severe, between-frame conflict, even if it is rooted not in a nascent religious experience but in something more diffuse, like different mission priorities.

This study also allows me to differentiate between congregations that report "no conflict" because there are no underlying divisions or contentious issues and congregations that have these things but do not call them conflict. For example, one of the congregations in this study to report no conflict was a small Episcopalian parish with a family model. This congregation has a pastor who has been there for over twenty years and is well loved. Members report no conflict events, and they also report no underlying divisions, factions, or contentious decisions in recent memory. This is different than the large Catholic church with a house of worship model that reports no conflict even though one particular decision – to put in place a Parish Council – threatened those who had previously held other administrative positions of power and caused much private turmoil that was never spoken of publicly. And that is different still than the United Methodist church with a house of worship model, where at least some members feel that they have no conflict because they avoid any controversial issues, like race and homosexuality, to which their denominational heritage ought to speak. In short, a lack of conflict can indicate consensus or it can signal that there is no legitimate opportunity to voice dissent; some models foster the voicing of conflicting views, and others do not.

Congregational models give us a lens that explains more about conflict because it sees conflict as constituting and constituted by the moral order of local religious life, reflecting shared and divergent moral expectations for action, shaping legitimate discourses and forms of dissent, and expressing different modes of authority and commitment. But there are some limits to what can be understood by focusing on congregational models. First, not every single conflict can be explained completely by reference to the congregational model in place. All congregations, for example, have some amount of low level administrative conflict. And no doubt all have some amount of interpersonal conflict, as well, only differing in how legitimate it is to make interpersonal conflict a public issue. It is easy to imagine that some things, like fiscal malfeasance or abusive behavior on the part of leaders, would cause conflict in any congregation.

Because I did not go into the field expecting that these congregational models existed, let alone that they affected conflict, I was not able to sample on them as an independent variable. This makes it harder for me to argue that congregational models have an independent effect on conflict, because I cannot control how other factors vary across my congregational models, although, as Table 4 makes clear, there is no straightforward relationship between size, polity, and ideology and the four models. Instead of statistical generalization I can propose what Snow and Anderson (1991) call theoretical generalization, arguing essentially what I would have been able to argue for a case study. In this case – among these congregations – there is good reason to use congregational models as an explanatory framework because they leave no parts of the case – no congregations – unexplained, whereas other approaches do, and they provide an explanation that identifies specific mechanisms linking congregational culture to conflict in a theoretically satisfying way and in a way that can account for how members orient their own behavior and so produce conflict.

The comparative, qualitative design of the study allowed me to reject one explanation of conflict and to begin to develop another. But the question remains, what *kind* of explanation is this? At the most basic level I am suggesting that the same process is constitutive both of conflict and of the patterns of local culture that I call congregational models. That process is the negotiation of a local identity in relation to a range of institutionally structured alternatives (cf. White 1981). The rest of the chapter will explore the implications of this insight.

Understanding Congregational Models

Congregational models are a specific example in one field of a more general phenomenon, the institutional model of the group or organization (see also Becker 1998a). At the societal level, institutions provide cultural frames that define bundles of legitimate goals and appropriate means of achieving them. DiMaggio and Powell talk about the different kinds of goals in different institutional fields:

> Cultural frames establish approved means and define desired outcomes, leading business people to pursue profits, bureaucrats to seek budgetary growth, and scholars to strive for publication (1991:28).

The field of American congregational religion is characterized by cultural frames that privilege a set of core religious-institutional tasks that lead religious organizations to engage in worship, religious education, witness, and the fostering of local believing communities.

In congregations, the members and clergy negotiate a set of local understandings of the congregation's mission and identity in reference to these larger institutional imperatives. As they do so, they institutionalize a limited range of local cultures that provide the same kind of framing at the organizational level that DiMaggio and Powell (1991) talk about institutions providing at the societal level. As Friedland and Alford (1991) note, each organization in a field is in a position of choosing between the multiple or even competing logics that are available in that field to guide action. Congregational models are routinized solutions to this problem, bundles of things – programs, beliefs, ways of doing things – that go together. Members do not continually reconsider the nature of their congregation's mission, except at key turning points like the hiring of a new pastor. Usually, local members operate from one "bundle" of ways of doing things.

These bundles of understandings about what it means to be "us" and not some other congregation emerged from this analysis as empirical types. However, analytically it is possible to understand the models as bundles of core tasks and ways of carrying out those tasks. Worship and religious education are the most central, the ones without which the congregation would not be a congregation. For example, a prayer group or support group might involve providing members with religious community, and a special-interest political action group might see itself as providing religious leadership. These might both be small, face-to-face gatherings of religious people, but they would still not be congregations. More generally, a small religious group is not a congregation if it is not worshipping together to the end of perpetuating some tradition of faith.[12]

But while the models can be understood analytically as bundles of core tasks, in fact they are more than that. They are bundles of ideas about "who we are" and "how we do things here," informal understandings of mission and identity that permeate the local culture. The core tasks that congregations draw from their environment are not rules that they follow to avoid sanctions or routines that are in place to please powerful outsiders, which are two common ways of understanding institutional culture. Rather, these tasks provide the framework that defines the congregation's identity. In other words, mission, in these organizations, is constitutive of identity and moral order.

In local congregations and, I would argue, in other kinds of groups and organizations, core tasks are not separable from identity but are constitutive of it (cf. Giddens 1984; Douglas 1986). "Who we are" is defined by "what we do" and "how we do things here." This is exemplified in the interview with Martha, the lay leader at Hope Episcopal church, which was profiled at the beginning of Chapter 1. When I asked her why people were so opposed to the pastor's initiatives to speak out on social issues, she paused and then said that the opposition could be summed up in "two sentences of seven words each: 'We have always done it this way.' And 'We have *never* done it that way.'" Local culture and core tasks may be analytically separable, but in fact they are mutually defining for members' understanding of their congregation's identity.

This is an insight that institutional analysts have drawn upon in thinking about organizational identity since Selznick's *TVA and the Grassroots* (1949). More recently, Fligstein (1990) provides a compelling argument that "local" identity within subparts of large, complex organizations is tightly linked to the core tasks that the subparts perform and to the routines of accomplishing those tasks that become institutionalized and valued for their own sake.

Congregational models are embedded within and constitutive of local culture. They are institutionalized broadly in many aspects of congregational life, including norms of member commitment and formal and informal authority structures. They are found in rituals and repertoires of action. They are found in metaphors and official discourse of all kinds, from sermons to brochures to planning documents to letterhead slogans, and in the preferences for some types of programs over others.

However, while they are institutionalized broadly, they do not completely encompass or determine the whole of congregational culture (cf. Martin 1992). Rather, they determine the dominant features of the public culture, including the public discourse and ritual life. In conflict, they provide the rules for public discourse and interaction, shaping what kinds of issues congregations fight about and the forms of legitimate public argumentation. As Eliasoph (1996) argues, it is important to understand these rules of public discourse if we want to understand the institutional capacity of our civic organizations to sustain a robust and inclusive public discourse, and if we want to understand the dynamics of power that shape access to all kinds of public spaces. The models structure what issues – and whose issues – make it onto the table, as well as different repertoires of participation and contention. Power, which is often conceived of as a property of interpersonal interaction or control of material resources, also has an institutional face in who has access to participation in public arenas of discourse.

Thinking of congregational models as the constitutive rules for the formation of local religious cultures helps to elucidate the contrast between institutional culture and idioculture, as proposed in Chapter 1. Understanding congregational models would not allow one to predict which congregation would have a "donut program."

But understanding them would allow one to predict reasonably well which congregations are likely to have a social action committee or an official "greeter" program for Sunday morning, which ones might send representatives to the public meeting on whether to sing Christmas carols in the grade school recital, and which ones might send a Sunday School class to picket at the local Planned Parenthood clinic. It would allow one to predict whose issues can make it onto the public agenda of the congregation's discourse and be implemented in policies and programs. It could even help to predict the congregation's orientation to the state and to participation in public welfare initiatives, something that may become highly relevant if the federal government continues moving toward the use of private, voluntary groups to channel various forms of aid and charity.

Of course, there are some programs that virtually all congregations have. These include compassionate outreach, Bible study or adult education, women's or other fellowship groups, and annual "special" events like rummage sales or concerts. As Ammerman (1997b) notes, it is possible to understand a congregation as a bundle of practices; she argues that the bundle that makes up a dominant element in many congregations is a pragmatic approach to service and an understanding of the congregation as a place for fellowship. This explains why service activities and fellowship activities occur in all congregations, just as in every congregation there are some people who find fellowship and even friendship.

But in some congregations these and other activities are highly valued or are part of what the congregation becomes known for – they are part of the public identity and community reputation – while in others they are not. In some, they are a large part of what makes members loyal to this particular congregation, while in others they are budget items that go unnoticed and unremarked. It is the mix of programs that is associated with the congregation's identity – what people feel they are good at, which ones are valued, which ones figure in talk of goals or overall mission – that are included in Table 10, because they comprise what is distinct about the public culture of each type of congregation.

The presence of a dominant model does not imply complete consensus or a functional, unitary culture. The pattern of conflict in the "mixed" congregations indicates that it is possible for subgroups to develop,

Table 10. *"Bundles" associated with each model*

	House of Worship	Family	Community	Leader
Programs*	Worship	Worship	Worship	Worship
	Children's education (denominational materials)	Children's education (denominational materials)	Adult and children's education (eclectic materials)	Adult and children's education (denominational materials)
	Greeters	Coffee hour (long, informal)	Coffee hour (short, informal)	Coffee hour (short, organized)
	Committees for visitation, help in crisis	Committees for worship, special events	Interest-based committees	Interest-based committees
		Fellowship/fund-raising events (banquets, bazaars, bake sales)	Elaborate set of interest- or age/gender-based fellowship groups	Some small fellowship groups
Processes	Formal, short, follow official guidelines	Informal, long	Inclusive, long, but formal	Inclusive, short, many committees
		Lay leaders make decisions outside of formal structure or via main administrative body	Many committees, some issues discussed in congregation-wide meetings	

Pastor	Worship leader Other roles constrained by formal polity	Worship leader Outsider or "one of the family" Involvement in congregational decision making varies with acceptance	Worship leader Facilitator of consensus, debate on important issues	Worship leader Interpreter of the religious tradition, important leader in setting goals and developing policies
Lay leaders	Leadership based on tenure and expertise	Leadership based on tenure	Leadership based on expertise and interest	Leadership based on expertise and interest
Interaction – style	Friendly; members can be more or less involved with each other outside of the main worship service	Intimate; members tend to spend social time together and/or provide informal support in times of crisis; "extended family"	Intimate; members "plug in" to small groups that form friendship and support networks	Friendly; members can be more or less involved with each other outside of Sunday or Saturday service
Ritual – style	Traditional, formal	Traditional, informal, personal	Eclectic, informal, personal	Traditional, formal

* Refers to programs that are *highly valued within* or *typical of* a given congregational model.

particularly within larger congregations, who prefer different models. In the absence of a triggering incident like a change in official leadership or a major policy decision, it is conceivable that a "mixed" congregation could persist with some stability and not lead to a transition from one model to the next.

Also, the models may be more strongly or weakly institutionalized. For example, the models no doubt capture the commitment and decision-making style of the core group of active members and leaders more closely than that of occasional attendees and marginal members, which indicates that, in larger congregations, there may be quite a number of people "in the pews" whose own individual assumptions about the nature, purpose, and value of congregational priorities may be different than the dominant model. Also, it is clear that there are parts of every congregation's idioculture that are less task-centered and may therefore have little to do with the congregational model. One example is narratives of founding families and important early leaders, which almost every congregation has.

The United Methodist church profiled in Chapter 3 illustrates the possible ways of having a more weakly institutionalized model. It had many members who preferred a more activist or engaged mission style and who simply channeled this activity through other denominational or ecumenical organizations, not the local congregation. The Assemblies of God congregation (community model) had some people in leadership who would have preferred a family model that concentrates on worship, religious education, and fellowship. They channeled their activities in this direction and largely ignored the aspects of the congregation's life that were less important for them. But their presence almost made me, in my initial coding, place them in the "mixed" camp until a rereading of each previous interview, more observation, and a second interview with the pastor led me to realize that what I was finding was more of a residual model. They had been a family congregation until fairly recently, having made the transition to a community model with the calling of their current pastor a few years before and an influx of new, mostly younger, members. That is, they were no longer "mixed" or transitional but had come to the point where the congregation's leadership, its public rhetoric, and its programming and decision-making processes fit with a community model.

Why a particular church or synagogue has a particular congregational model is a complicated question about historical process that is not easy to answer with this kind of cross-sectional data. On the one hand, members of local congregations negotiate their identity in reference to some very specific carriers of institutional culture. Denominational policies, theology, and larger religious traditions are perhaps the most important tools in their tool kit, particularly for the clergy (cf. Swidler 1986). The pastor of the United congregation, for example, articulates the implications of the Reformed Christian tradition for his congregation's role as a leader. The pastor of a Lutheran congregation ties his congregation's community model to what he calls a Lutheran theology of community-in-Christ. Fifteen blocks away, a Baptist pastor uses the metaphor of "the New Testament Church" to articulate how his congregation is to be a community together and, specifically, to articulate a rationale for a multicultural community spanning traditional boundaries of race and class (see Becker 1997a, 1998c).

Some traditions, as Bass (1994) points out, privilege some religious imperatives over others, and denominations in their administrative structure leave more or less scope for local congregational innovation. It seems reasonable to think that Catholic churches would be more likely to have a house of worship model than United Methodist churches, because one has always fostered the centrality of worship as a transformative rite for the individual, while the other has a long history of emphasizing the link between personal piety and social activism.

On the other hand, it seems correct to view larger traditions and denominational culture as resources for the construction of local congregational models, rather than as determining of these models. This is more in tune with general ideas about how individuals and groups make use of larger traditions and ideologies in a pragmatic, partial, problem-solving way (Swidler 1986). And it is also more true to what I found in this community. In this small sample, one independent Baptist church has a community model while another is a leader. The four congregations in transition illustrate this point best; people at the local level can come up with more than one interpretation of which parts of their larger tradition or denominational ethos should be valued most in their particular congregation.

The mixed congregations illustrate that clergy are not the only ones actively involved in negotiating congregational identity and mission; lay members also play an important role. And in a context of high member mobility, with members switching even across denominational and traditional lines, members can import ideas about what the local congregation ought to be like that are not in line with leaders' interpretations of tradition. Members of Main Street Baptist are aware of this, and they articulate their concern about this particular form of diversity when they speak of the problems of integrating people without a Baptist background into their church.

More generally, members show themselves to be aware of the variations that are possible within their tradition in the specific form of other local congregations that have institutionalized a different model. At the Unitarian Universalist church in which I interviewed, members speak of another Unitarian congregation in the neighborhood as the one to go to if you want social action and leadership in the community; members of one Baptist church note that they leave leadership up to Main Street Baptist and are themselves more concerned with building up a close Christian community; members of an Episcopal parish define their own family model in contrast to the larger Episcopalian church down the street, which is a leader.

Congregations within the same denomination or tradition tend to specialize at the local level. They also use successful congregations from other traditions as exemplars and borrow from them explicitly. For example, many people in other congregations told me about the remarkable growth of the Lutheran congregation in the early 1980s and said that that success was something they were trying to emulate. The Lutheran church's focus on small fellowship groups, intimacy, and having open and inclusive decision processes all influenced other area congregations. Eiesland's (1998) study of churches in a Georgia town shows a similar kind of "niching" among the town's congregations.

Anecdotal evidence suggests that congregational history is important and that key events and leaders can push the congregation toward a different model. A negative experience with a pastor who was an activist in the Civil Rights movement in the 1960s and early 1970s pushed one Methodist church toward a house of worship model. Members of a small Disciples of Christ congregation report that a positive experience with a similar kind of pastor caused them to think of themselves and to act as a leader in issues of peace and justice for the intervening decades, despite their small size. They reaffirmed this commitment when they called their present pastor to serve primarily because of his qualifications in these areas. And social change in the congregation's community, be it demographic or economic, can be an important impetus for rearticulating and reworking the congregation's identity.[13]

Size and polity can also be thought of as resources, or perhaps as plausibility structures, for congregational models. It is undoubtedly easier to think of a small congregation as a family, but a small congregation can have another model in place, and several of the large mixed congregations have had a family model in place at one time. Hierarchical congregations are more likely to have a family or house of worship model, but this is not true in every case. It would also seem reasonable to think that, in a different community, one might find more of certain kinds of models.

How are the models reproduced once they are in place? Although congregations are places where beliefs are taken seriously and subject to discussion, it is rare to find one where members are quizzed in close detail about their beliefs before they are allowed to join. That is particularly true for the kinds of congregations in this community and for the kinds of beliefs that might affect the congregational model. Some congregations do, however, take some pains to communicate not only denominational heritage but also local culture in orienting new members. The pastor of the Lutheran church told me that he used to spend several new member classes on Lutheran history, but now he spends the time teaching people about the local congregation, including its goals and major programs, its mission approach, and its emphasis on community. In this he is more typical of the congregations in this sample than not.

Likewise, there is a certain amount of self-selection on an individual level, particularly in the area of commitment style. Norms of intimacy are both readily apparent and seem to be salient for people choosing to join congregations. Many of the people I interviewed, when asked what role the congregation played in their lives or what it meant to them, spoke without prompting of connections with other people and being comfortable with the way in which their current congregation provided opportunities for that. Others, like Carol, quoted in Chapter 3, spoke of how much they like it that such connections are optional and that there is no pressure to unwanted intimacy.

Intimacy norms also tend to be institutionalized within the Sunday morning (or Saturday) ritual life of the congregation, the time when newcomers are most likely to make their first contact with a congregation. In this way, they are "up front" and available for inspection early on. Before a potential member knows much else about a congregation besides its denominational affiliation, she knows how much of the public prayer revolves around individual needs; how many of the announcements include birthdays, anniversaries, and news of kids traveling home from college; how metaphors of family or community are invoked in sermons and songs; how many people will approach her to talk before, during, and after the service;

if someone will help her find her way through the prayerbook during the liturgy; if there is a coffee hour and if she is urged to stay for it. Programs are also an obvious and up-front way to communicate the dominant model to potential members; if a visitor is interested in social action and there is no committee for it, or interested in home visitation and is told that the staff takes care of that, she has some meaningful information about the congregation's priorities and expectations of involvement.[14]

During the course of my fieldwork, several congregations were going through a pastor search and several others had completed such a search within the last three or four years. Selecting a pastor is seen by many in lay leadership as an opportunity to symbolize the congregation as a whole, either solidifying current tendencies or starting off on a new trajectory. Most of the congregations were successful in selecting a pastor who reinforced the dominant model; in those that were not successful, the hiring of a new pastor became an opportunity for different groups to articulate preferences for different models. Managing the transition in pastoral leadership successfully is one way in which congregational models are reproduced. As the mixed congregations illustrate, this is difficult to accomplish, especially in denominations where pastors are centrally assigned or where the denomination plays a large role in matching congregations and pastors. Therefore, the transition in pastoral leadership can be a trigger for prolonged and serious conflict.

Dominant models are also reproduced by bracketing off or marginalizing groups or individuals who disagree. This is done differently in different kinds of congregations. In a house of worship, it can be done by inertia. Those who called for more commitment or more engagement with the community in the two house of worship congregations reported that they could certainly call a public meeting on women's roles, only to be met with poor attendance. They could make a "Sharing of Joys and Concerns" time part of the Sunday service, but they could not induce people to share intimate things. If part of the dominant model involves limited commitment, then change may be particularly hard to institute.

In other types of congregations, attempts to bring about change can be effectively reframed in the terms of the dominant model and so contained. In one family congregation, attempts by the pastor to put routine decision making onto a more businesslike footing were defined as a lack of personal trust and met with hurt feelings. In another, when a lay leader attempted to turn the vestry into a forum to discuss social and religious issues more broadly, he was at first ignored and then branded a troublemaker. Effectively, in these two congregations, attempts to change taken-for-granted routines were reframed as personal conflict. The effect of this was to substantially raise the cost of change to the point where it was prohibitive; people who proposed administrative changes found themselves in a situation where their personal relationships and goodwill were at stake. More generally, the congregational models tend to make taken-for-granted decision routines part of the moral order, infused with a sense of rightness for their own sake. Community congregations take this to an extreme, valuing process over outcome in some cases.

Each congregational model is prone to certain kinds of recurring organizational problems. There are two typical organizational problems that recur for houses of worship. The first is the tendency for "mission creep." Houses of worship are by far the least numerous congregation type in this community, and it is clear that many people who join them expect the congregation to take on other goals or tasks. Religious leaders (clergy) are trained to value outreach more than other kinds of congregational goals and may view houses of worship as parochial or indulgently self-centered.[15] This desire to "add on" functions might make a house of worship prone to schism. If the group of people wanting a community model had been larger and more vocal or if the pastor were more willing to push the issue, the UMC congregation discussed in Chapter 3 might have moved into the "mixed" category and seen a prolonged struggle over identity. The Catholic church with a house of worship model in fact has undergone a minor form of schism, with a group who wanted more intimacy splitting off several years ago into a Family Mass group. Also, houses of worship generally are prone to view growth favorably and to be large, which seems to be a factor that leads toward a danger of becoming a "mixed" congregation and subject to schism.

Another recurring organizational problem for houses of worship is the inability to mobilize members for broad-based participation in programs other than worship. While not a problem in times of prosperity, in times of membership decline or rapid demographic or economic change in the community it may be particularly hard for these churches to mobilize the resources to cope, be that in starting a new outreach program, changing the way the school is run, or instituting a new capital drive.[16] More generally, it is difficult to imagine a house of worship being mobilized for social action in its community; like family congregations, they will give money to programs that others run and staff, but they are not likely either to start outreach programs or to support community activism.

Family congregations have a recurring organizational problem with growth and self-reproduction. The small size of these family congregations makes them aware that growth is supposed to be a goal; certainly it is well institutionalized in the church-growth literature, and they receive some pressure from denominational officials to make an attempt to increase their membership. And yet when people talked about growth they exhibited reluctance and ambivalence. Incorporating newcomers is more difficult in communal groups than in those with more remote or segmented attachments.

Also, newcomers are prone to bring in new ideas, and family congregations are very resistant to changes in how things are done. More generally, family congregations would be expected to have trouble coping with rapid change in the community, not because of apathy, but because members are too wed to traditional ways of doing things to change easily. Family congregations are unlikely to be mobilized around issues unless they have a long-term, trusted pastor. Such a person may be the only one able, by using the power of the pulpit, to mobilize the congregation for social action or for important changes in policy or in ritual. The pastor at the one family congregation that reported "no conflict" described his success in changing the congregation's view on women's ordination, at least to the point where the congregation will tolerate sermons on the subject:

> I myself have always supported the ordination of women. At one point, I was on the muddy end of that fight, in the trenches. . . . The people in this church don't support the ordination of women, for the most part, except that they understand that it's an important issue to me. So they're willing to listen on this. Because they know me. Because they know me personally, because they've talked to me, because there isn't a family in this parish that I haven't been in their home, administering pastoral care in the face of some need. Because of that, they are willing to be tolerant on this issue. . . . A lot of clerical foibles are forgiven if you have that kind of relationship with the people in the parish.

He has successfully introduced a female deacon to this congregation, and she has spoken from the pulpit without overt conflict. Several lay leaders mentioned to me that this was unusual and would probably not have worked had it not been for the membership's respect for this pastor. There has even been some talk of inviting a female priest from a neighboring Episcopal parish to speak in this church.

Community congregations try to balance two core tasks – to be a caring community and to express members' values on social and religious issues. And this is the central contradiction that drives much of the conflict in the congregation and generates the central organizational problem. The expressive logic leads members to put issues on the agenda, and these churches and synagogues become arenas for debate on a huge variety of issues. Yet the communal logic means that issue-based debate must be carefully channeled, limited, and controlled, lest it escalate into ideological or political debate that excludes some members. Therefore, these churches tend to develop a wide range of decision-making spaces and processes that are designed to be inclusive and geared toward consensus. Rather than formal structures like boards, committees tend to be put together on an ad hoc basis to deal with issues as they arise, and committee membership is based as much on commitment to a particular issue or area as on formal position. Authority is broadly distributed, with wide congregational involvement in decision making, and leaders tend to be seen as facilitators of consensus more than anything else. Community congregations try to partially segregate out the communal from the expressive logics, fostering small groups that are primarily communal groups and that serve as "safe" spaces away from the broad issue debate that tends to go on in other forums. Community congregations face the same central problem that democracies face. The idea that values matter and should be debated clashes with the idea of communal identity. Diversity is both valued and feared, and keeping an identity that allows for both unity and debate is a huge challenge.

Community congregations are likely to cope well with rapid change in the environment, having a wide variety of energetic lay leaders who are likely to be informed about what is going on in the community and to care about it and who are likely to have the energy and ideas to mobilize rapidly if needed. Social activism does occur; the pastor and many members of one community congregation participated in a community march to show sympathy with the family of a victim of gang-related violence. But mobilization of this type tends to be around noncontroversial issues (everyone can agree that violence is damaging, for example) and issues not perceived as "political."

Leader congregations, like houses of worship, also have a problem with mission creep. The imperative to be a caring community is in demand; pastors of leader congregations note with some dismay that more and more people look to the congregation to meet a variety of personal needs and to provide experiences of closeness and intimacy that they (the pastors) find to be at best tangential to congregational mission priorities. Leaders of these congregations, both clergy and laity, are reluctant to divert resources to meet these needs. When they do, it takes the mode of forming small groups that are largely decoupled from the decision-making structure of the congregation.

Leader congregations may be prone to schism. They are more ideological, and there is less tempering of the debate that is provided by a communal logic. They tend to court controversy and involvement in the community, which may exhaust some members. On the other hand, those who join these congregations tend to be previously committed to a strong doctrinal or ideological stand, and this generates a kind of strong commitment that may bode well both for congregational adaptability and for a long-term ability to thrive.

Institutional Forms of Religious Community

The bundles of core tasks, local understandings, and habitual ways of doing things that comprise the four congregational models can help us to understand the constraints on the formation of congregational idiocultures. They also can give us a useful lens with which to analyze conflict and other group processes. Understanding the four models also helps us to understand larger questions about the institutional capacity of these local congregations to foster certain forms of religious community. These four types of congregations form distinct kinds of publics – public spaces or public arenas of action.

They do this by institutionalizing certain cultural logics of action in certain combinations, in some cases (family, for example) borrowed from other institutional fields. Foremost, these congregations all maintain the primacy of what Weber (1978) would call value-rational action, as opposed to instrumental-rational action. That is not to say that there are never decisions that are made with the primary goal of bringing in more members or increasing the chances of organizational survival. But it is the case that such goals remain, to a large extent, secondary in these congregations. Goals like surviving and growing always need to be framed in the public discourse in terms of other, more legitimate rhetorics, be that one of "saving souls" in the more conservative Protestant churches or of being a more vital presence or witness in the community in the more liberal congregations. In *every conflict* where some argument based on expediency or efficiency was posed against an argument based on moral reasoning, the expediency argument was soundly rejected. And ambivalence about growth for its own sake was expressed by everyone I interviewed in the family and community congregations.

This is not to say that these congregations do not function like businesses in some sense. But as arenas of public discourse, these congregations do not articulate or promote an instrumental-rational approach to action. Rather, in both their discourse and their repertoire of practices and programs, they serve as arenas in which other kinds of goods are preserved and articulated as goods in and of themselves. This argument also does not imply that individual action within congregations is always altruistic. It is of course likely that instrumental motives – a desire for power or status within the group – are part of what motivates individuals to engage in congregational conflicts.

Rather, my argument is that congregations serve as small, face-to-face moral arenas where noninstrumental discourses and bases for action are preserved both in public discourse and in decision-making routines and where instrumental rhetoric is illegitimate (cf. Jasper 1992). As Eliasoph (1996) notes, understanding the rules of moral discourse institutionalized in public spaces, from organizations to social movements to the national media, is a necessary step in understanding how participation is structured and how issues are defined as relevant for public consideration or designated as "private troubles" in various arenas of social action. The congregations in and around Oak Park provide different kinds of moral and religious communities, with different overall moral imperatives and moral styles. Table 11 outlines the moral imperatives and overall moral style that are not only spoken about in each congregation but practiced in daily interaction and decision making, institutionalized in valued programs, and reflected in the distribution of resources.

Primarily, a house of worship is instituted to preserve a ritual tradition. It does so by following the rules and formal procedures of the particular denomination or tradition of which it is a part, which Tipton (1982) has identified as a "regular" form of moral logic. This requires a limited amount of individual commitment on the part of lay members and a heavy reliance on the pastor and other paid staff who carry out minimal administrative duties and who are "experts" in the ritual tradition.

Table 11. *Cultural logics in each congregational model*

House of Worship	Family	Community	Leader
Overall Institutional Logic			
Rite/Transcendance	Family/ Particularism	Communal/ Personalism	Social Movement/ Activism
Moral Imperatives			
Preserve a ritual tradition	Preserve a ritual tradition	–	Preserve a doctrinal tradition
–	Care for individual needs	Care for individual needs	–
–	–	Express individuals' values	Express individuals' values
–	–	–	Change the world
–	–	–	–
Moral Style			
Regular (rule-oriented)	Conservative	–	–
–	Caring (patriarchal)	Caring	–
–	–	Expressive (democratic,	–
–	–	process-oriented)	Authoritative (orthodox, leader-oriented)

Family congregations are the most particularistic, concentrating not only on caring for individual members but on preserving the identity of the congregation as a particular caring group. Like a "real" family, particular members matter, and the joint history of the members together matters. Preserving standard ways of doing things and important corporate symbols like the building preserve this family history, which leads to what I call a conservative moral logic that values doing things as they have been habitually done as its own form of moral good, preserving the memory of a particular living community.

Community congregations balance the moral imperative to care for members as whole persons with the moral imperative to express members' value commitments. This leads to an overall moral style that can be called "personalism," the linking of public issues to private needs and the use of experience as a powerful basis of moral authority (cf. Lichterman 1996). It also leads to a valuing of inclusive, open processes, the seeking of consensus, and an eclectic approach to ritual.

Leader congregations are primarily expressive of values that are seen as emanating not from individual commitments or congregational life and history, but from traditions that transcend the local congregation. They do give some scope for individual expression, but the overall moral style is authoritative, with the pastor the final arbiter of the tradition's authoritative stand on any controversial issue. Less concerned about fostering community and intimate ties of caring, leaders also have a lot of issue-based debate but are more willing to rely on formal administrative procedures and the authority of formal offices to resolve disputes, which leads to shorter processes and fewer compromise solutions. In particular, the pastor's role as religious leader, and the ability of the pastor to translate that into a fair amount of administrative control, is bolstered here, and the strong pastorate is one way in which this model is institutionalized. These congregations also have less tension with their denominational officials than other congregations do, because their mission is more in line with denominationally approved goals of growth and outreach and because they also tend to be – but are not necessarily – large and prosperous.

Overall, each congregational model encompasses a distinct institutional logic – rite/family/democracy/movement. This logic is a combination of the moral imperatives and moral styles, the core religious-institutional tasks, and the particular bundle of programs and ways of doing things that go along with each model. In our society religion remains an institution through which members enact various forms of moral community, with different civic and political consequences. In doing so, they draw on the most widespread schema of or templates for community in our society (cf. Friedland and Alford 1991; Sewell 1992).

The bundle of programs and ways of doing things associated with each model can probably exhibit some range of variation according to time and place. That is to say, it is not possible to imagine a family congregation that does not focus on taking care of individual needs and does not have a conservative moral style that values the particulars of the congregation's own history over the demands of doctrine. But it is easy to imagine a family congregation where there is a great deal more conflict than there is in these six churches. Middle-class families may suppress conflict (Baumgartner 1988), but not all families do. This suggests that, while these basic models may be widespread in the American context, they may take somewhat different forms in different settings – just as real families, communities, and social movements do. Where these models come from and how widespread they may be is discussed in more detail in Chapter 9.

A Comparative Institutional Approach to the Study of Local Culture

I have argued that congregational models are a specific example of a more general phenomenon, the institutional model of the group or organization. But why do we need to understand institutional models? What does an approach that focuses on this level of analysis, this form of culture, add to traditional approaches that either see conflict and other group processes as dependent in some linear way on underlying variables (like size or formal organizational structure) or that analyze them through the lens of idioculture?

Institutional models are useful, I believe, because they serve as important mediating levels of analysis. As a form of public culture, they mediate between individual religiosity and larger religious institutions (denominations, faith traditions) at the level of organization at which most individuals encounter religion. The individuals here overwhelmingly exemplify an individualistic orientation to religious belief, and yet they organize themselves into local religious communities that vary in the amount and kind of commitment that they foster, that are more or less publicly engaged, and that locate religious authority in different persons (pastor versus laity) and anchor it in different bases (long-term membership versus expertise). So congregational models can be understood as different organizational forms that are compatible with and expressive of the individualism that has come to characterize much of American religion and that link this individualism to religious institutional repertoires for service, caring, and activism.

They are also mediating levels of analysis in understanding the relationship between culture and structure within organizations. The effects of size and polity on conflict and decision making are not directly expressed here but are channeled through these four models. Congregational models also mediate between larger religious traditions and local mission. The United Methodist Church may privilege activism, but the ability of any given UMC pastor to turn his congregation toward activism will be affected by the congregational model that is in place. At the local level, not only is there more than one way to be a UMC church, but the various ones in the same area consciously diversify their mission vis-à-vis one another, decreasing the likelihood that denominational mission priorities can have a uniform effect on local congregations in a single area. This insight draws on and extends the work of Fine (1984, 1996a) on negotiated orders by specifying the core institutional tasks that limit and shape the development of the idioculture in any particular organization.

The finding that there is stable variation in congregational models is contrary to some of the writings of the new institutionalists, who emphasize three distinct forms of institutional isomorphism in organizations within a given field (DiMaggio and Powell 1991). These are mimetic isomorphism (borrowing from peers), coercive isomorphism (state regulation), and normative isomorphism (the setting of standards by such entities as professional organizations). Religious organizations are shielded from the most intrusive forms of state regulation, reducing much of the effect of coercive isomorphism. The fact that local congregations tend to carve out their own distinct niches in relation to other congregations of the same denomination in their area, combined with high rates of member switching, reduce both mimetic isomorphism and normative isomorphism.[17] That is, what borrowing does go on does so across religious tradition and denominational heritage, increasing eclecticism and undermining the effects of a denomination's doctrinal or ritual distinctiveness on local congregations. This suggests that it may be well to supplement the study of the conditions that lead to isomorphism within a given institutional field with an analysis of the conditions that lead to a stable variation in models.

This may be particularly relevant for fields that are more "institutional," as opposed to those that are more task-centered (Orru et al. 1991). The family is a good example. It is commonplace to refer to the family as the institution where people are valued for their own individual sake, the institution that provides for emotional anchoring for adults and the nurturance of children (Friedland and Alford 1991). It might seem that isomorphism is the rule here. But families change over time; in the past, some have been at times more concerned with passing on property than with preserving emotional closeness. Skolnick (1991) argues that cultural and structural pluralism are becoming the norm in the family "field." Bellah et al. (1985) suggest that there are presently at least two models of the family in the United States, a therapeutic model and an authoritative or patriarchal model. But we do not really know much about the variation in family models in this field that has become increasingly pluralistic.

One person who does explore this is Arlie Hochschild. In *The Second Shift*, Hochschild (1997) develops a typology of family models that vary in both their ideology (beliefs about good and appropriate family forms) and in their habitual practices and ways of doing things (the household division of labor). *Traditionalists, egalitarians,* and *transitional families* stand in various relationships to the social changes that have transformed family life over the last forty years. These three bundles of family ideology and practice can be understood as mediating the effect of changes in the larger institutional environment, like the transformation of work, on the family (cf. Moen and Wethington 1992). They can also be understood as mediating the effects of individual-level changes on family life as well. Women's educational and occupational attainment has changed dramatically, but Hochschild makes a good argument that one must understand the variations in the working models of what it means to be a family that mediate the effects of these individual transformations on actual families.

Even the requirements of membership in the family change over time, and accompanying these are shifts in the moral obligations among members. For example, Stacey (1991) studies what she calls a new type of family, with members who are added and subtracted by divorce and remarriage, where good friends are accepted as part of the family circle, and where the traditional idea of family as blood relations radiating out from a nuclear family is rejected in favor of something more fluid. Would this new kind of family have a different pattern of conflict than a more traditional family of blood? Different, say, than the conflict-avoidance that Baumgartner (1988) found to be the dominant mode among more traditional middle-class suburban families? More importantly, if families are becoming more voluntaristic, more constructed by people on the basis of their individual history and preferences, might we want to begin exploring what families have in common with other small, voluntaristic groups in their styles of conflict and commitment?

Recently, conflicts over "family values" have been much in the news. How much of this can be understood as conflict over the content or implications of various contemporary models of the family? How much of this makes sense as a debate about what it means to be a traditional nuclear family in a society where most mothers of young children work outside the home? Or conflict over how to organize the extended, blended families created by divorce and remarriage that Stacey studied? And how much of the "culture war" in the arena of the family makes sense when understood as a conflict over which model should be normative within the field, waged by elites using their religious, ideological, and political resources to argue for one dominant model (cf. Dimaggio 1991)?

In short, families everywhere may be about intimate connections, but who belongs, the level of commitment, and the styles of moral obligations are different for different families. Scholars may strive for publication, but not every sociology department has the same expectations about how much to publish and in what venues. There may have been pressures in the institutional field that led to consolidation around one model of the art museum, but that may not be the case in all fields. Looking for stable variation in the institutional models for organizations, or groups, in a given field might be a fruitful way to begin understanding variations in decision making, conflict, commitment, and authority in various fields, not just religion.

A first step would be to determine whether it is the institutional nature of religion that leads to stable variation or its character as a voluntary institution. The former means that even core tasks are open to interpretation in the sense of not being structured by technical requirements. How does one really know when a soul is saved? Arguably, one does not, but it is possible to define a proxy – baptism or a conversion experience – that everyone agrees to accept. How can one know when a person is well educated? As with the saved soul, that would require a lot of time and intense interaction, and even then it might be difficult to know for certain. So members of a field agree on a proxy – the SAT score, a college degree. Such "institutional" fields may lend themselves to more variations in models. One sect accepts one kind of baptism, another accepts a different kind. Is a person well educated if she went to college? Or only to a certain kind of college?

On the other hand, it may be the voluntary nature of the religious field that pushes toward pluralism, or various models. Where people choose membership based on relatively unconstrained preference and where money and resources flow up from a broad member base rather than down from, say, corporate sponsors, pressures toward isomorphism are reduced.

There is some evidence that suggests that even fields that are more instrumental, task-oriented, or state-regulated might have variations in institutional models. Business people may seek profits, but Galaskiewicz (1985, 1991) demonstrates that they can do so within different frameworks that relate the pursuit of profit to other goals, like service or citizenship in the local community. Legal scholarship recognizes the existence of distinct "communities of law" that interpret and apply the law with considerable variation (LoPucki 1996). Baron et al. (1996) describe the emergence of different models of the employment relationship in Bay Area high-tech firms. Do these really function as distinct institutional models, with different core tasks, cultural logics, and bundle of practices?

These become important questions if we want to understand the capacity of a given institution to foster certain forms of community or certain forms of moral action. Sociologists of culture used to argue, following the work of anthropologists like Clifford Geertz, that culture influences action when it is deeply felt and deeply embedded – either in an individual's deepest and earliest habits and feelings or in the taken-for-granted "web of meanings" created through the repeated interaction of small intimate groups. This assumption is what led to the approach to idioculture that has dominated much of congregational studies and studies of organizational culture more generally. An alternative approach has been to focus on culture as effective in shaping action because it articulates ideologies that carry prescriptions for specific actions, produced by elites and institutions that have significant resources at their disposal. The entire literature on ideology is much too extensive to cover here, but this approach has shaped much of the way we think about culture and power.[18]

This study illustrates that culture can also shape action in two other ways. First, culture influences action because it constitutes a publicly available semiotic code, a set of rules that govern behavior whether or not any given individual can articulate them and whether or not they are deeply felt. This is similar to what Caplow argues in his discussion of the "rules" for Christmas gift-giving in Middletown or the rules of public discourse that Eliasoph discovered in different kinds of voluntary organizations.[19] Second, culture can influence action because it constitutes ways of doing things and habits of action that are themselves cultural – carriers of meaning, of schema – whether or not those carrying out institutional practices can articulate the full range and implication of their meaning.[20] This focus on culture as code and institutional practices is part of a new direction in cultural analysis that seeks to move away from culture as subjective, deeply felt beliefs and to understand public culture as a constraining ground and context of action.[21]

This new focus in the sociology of culture is highly compatible with an institutional analysis that sees institutions as composed of bundles of typical and legitimate ends (core tasks) and means of achieving those ends (ways of doing things) – bundles that are institutionalized in particular combinations in particular fields in specific times and places. This approach combines a serious consideration of the organizational and other resources that are necessary to perpetuate institutional forms with an understanding of the ultimately arbitrary – that is historical and cultural, not functional or logical – nature of social action. When applied with a sensitivity to the semiautonomous nature of different levels of institutions and organizations, this approach lends itself logically to a comparative analysis of institutional patterns of action as a first step toward understanding such things as collective decision making, conflict, and other group processes. In this study, such an analysis has yielded the discovery of institutional models that structure the idioculture of these congregations and that constitute the variation in their institutional capacity to form arenas of public moral discourse. The next chapter will consider how this causes us to reconsider the nature of moral community as it has developed in the field of American congregational religion.

Notes

1. See Abbot (1988, 1992, 1997) and Ragin and Becker (1992).
2. See Victor Turner (1974), May (1980), and Greenhouse (1986).
3. See Simmel (1955, 1971), Coser (1956), Hirschman (1970), Victor Turner (1974), Hall (1988), and Lawler (1996).
4. See Allahyari (1996), Eliasoph (1996), Lichterman (1996), and Eiesland (1998).
5. Abbott (1988, 1992, 1997) has developed this line of argument extensively in a series of theoretical pieces. The "new institutionalists" have also developed this argument, specifically calling for more research on organizational and institutional forms. See Friedland and Alford (1991), Nee (1998), and Mohr and Guerra-Pearson (forthcoming). Population ecologists have long studied the rise and fall of organizational forms; recently, these studies have incorporated an understanding of both organizational structures and organizational cultures, including mission (see Barron et al. 1996; Haveman 1997).
6. The work of John Mohr (1994), among others, would bear this out.
7. See Chapter 2 and Appendix A for reviews of this literature. For an example of an excellent study that also takes the difference between manifest and latent conflict seriously and that focuses on conflict events, see Kniss (1997).
8. Ammerman (1994, 1997a); cf. Roof and McKinney (1987), Wuthnow (1988), Hunter (1991), and Wedam (1997). For a good, up-to-date critical review of the "culture wars" thesis, see Williams (1997).
9. This is especially true for the Protestants and Jewish members I spoke to, who were more prone to self-identify as either liberal or conservative and who were aware of these as categories that had meaning in reference to the local church

or synagogue. For example, members of liberal Protestant congregations often told me that they had chosen the congregation because it was tolerant or because it was not fundamentalist or rigid, while members of conservative congregations would often say that they initially joined because the church was "doctrinal" or "biblical" or the pastor "preaches the Word" and doesn't take his sources from secular literature or everyday experience. Members of the Reform and Conservative synagogues tended to understand the liberal/conservative divide as having to do mainly with women's roles, intermarriage, and attitudes toward ritual (both in the Temple services and in the home). But even in the Catholic parishes, there was an awareness of local differentiation; for example, several members told me that they attended the parish that sits on the eastern edge of the village because of its reputation for being more liberal than other parishes nearby.

10. See Hadden (1969), Marty (1976), Roof (1978), Bellah et al. (1985), Ammerman (1987), Roof and McKinney (1987), Hammond (1988), Wuthnow (1988), and Hunter (1991).

11. This is not so surprising; see Coser (1956), Simmel (1971, 1995), and Kurtz (1986).

12. This insight owes something to Bass (1994) but also arises out of the fieldwork for this project. Congregations vary on other core tasks, but they all emphasize the value of worship and religious education to perpetuate a tradition.

13. Ammerman (1997a) provides the most extensive study of how social change impacts on congregational culture and programming in a study that compares twenty-three congregations from several cities in diverse regions of the country.

14. Fine (1987) notes that small groups sometimes hide elements of their idioculture until one is already becoming a committed member, but congregational models are not likely to be hidden. As the broad framework of the public culture, these models are likely to be displayed for potential members to consider in making their choice. Also, the models inform so many aspects of congregational life that it is easy for the visitor to pick up on their key dimensions. Pastors are usually very aware of the need to communicate congregational priorities upfront for potential members; my fieldnotes from one coffee hour conversation with an Episcopalian pastor read, "He told me, 'If you want a warm and caring church, this is for you, and we try to let people know that. But, if you want yoga classes, we suggest that you look elsewhere.'"

15. For a good discussion of this issue, see Marty (1986) and White (1990). For an example of this orientation on the part of religious leaders, see Gilkey (1994).

16. See Ammerman (1997a).
17. Population ecologists have studied the effects of this kind of niching on a variety of organizational fields. For example, see Barnett and Carroll (1987), Baum and Singh (1996), and Baum and Haveman (1997).
18. For short reviews see Swidler (1986) and Wuthnow (1989); see Thompson (1990) for a much longer discussion.
19. Cf. Caplow (1984), and Eliasoph (1996); this draws on a presentation given at Cornell University by Ann Swidler (April 4, 1997), titled, "How Culture Constrains: Codes, Contexts, and Institutions."
20. See Biernacki (1995) and Ortner (1996) for reviews of practice theory; see also Bourdieu (1978); cf. Sewell (1992).
21. See Wuthnow (1987), esp. Chapters 1 and 2, and Swidler (1986).

9

AMERICAN CONGREGATIONAL
RELIGION

Oak Park, River Forest, Forest Park

The understanding of American religion that motivates this study is that of an institutional field. A field is comprised of organizations with similar services or products (DiMaggio and Powell 1991:64). Eiesland (1998) shows that applying this concept to religious organizations within a specific locality is analytically useful in her study of how congregations reacted to social change in an exurban community outside of Atlanta.[1] I am arguing that it is useful to apply this concept more broadly, to encompass American religion as an organizational field. This is different than thinking of American religion as a set of faith traditions or as a market that aggregates believing individuals who have religious preferences into some structured relationship with a set of religious providers. It is useful to think of American religion as an institutional field because this draws attention to particular features of the American religious landscape that need more attention and a more refined understanding.

Highlighting the relative autonomy of levels of organization, the idea of a field helps us to examine the ways in which denominations do and do not influence local congregational belief and practice. Focusing on the pragmatic practices and ways of doing things that form much of organizational and small-group culture, it allows us to examine when and in what ways the *content* of beliefs (a liberal or a conservative view on gender roles, for example) influences group process and when group process is shaped more by *practices* and *ways of doing things* that are compatible with a range of explicitly articulated beliefs. It complements our focus on individual beliefs and elite discourse by documenting the range of local religious cultures in one setting.

In this case, a focus on American religion as an institutional field helps us to gain a better understanding of the nature of contemporary religious individualism and how a trend toward individual-expressive commitment has been channeled and shaped by institutions, including congregational models. It allows us to see how institutions shape the capacity of one set of local religious organizations to confer social capital on their members by fostering habits of tolerance, caring, and public engagement (Putnam 1995, 1996). In this community, as I will argue in this chapter, this institutional capacity is also shaped by the life experiences and the interests of the dominant group of mostly white managers and professionals who have, until very recently, retained power within the community's institutions despite residential integration.

This approach also shapes how to think about the kinds of implications this study has for our understanding of American religion as a whole, because it cautions us against thinking of this community as typical of American religion writ large. If the study of this community constitutes a case that might shed light on a larger phenomenon, it is not a typical case or a microcosm.

This is a particular place, and its importance as a case lies in its particularity. The most important feature of its particularity for this analysis is the recent history and achievement of stable racial integration. As noted before, it would be a mistake to think that residential integration led to an integration of the community's politics and civic institutions. That more complete integration is still in process. What happened in this community's civic institutions as a result of the racial integration was a transition in the dominant leadership group. The former rabbi of the conservative synagogue was the first one to tell me that the real change in his congregation's history was the fact that the group of white managers and businessmen who used to make all of the decisions, and write all of the checks, was replaced by a younger group of mostly white professional men and women. When the pastor of the Lutheran church said that he wanted to "reflect Oak Park," he meant that he wanted to attract this group of young, professional, and mostly white families. In every congregation, pastors and lay leaders were aware of this transition, each having reacted to it in diverse ways.

It is this specific characteristic of Oak Park and the surrounding villages that makes this community a useful case, in the sense of being an exemplar of a particular phenomenon of analytical interest.[2] These communities exemplify white, middle-class religiosity as it is institutionalized in the leadership and the dominant public culture of these congregations.

This middle-class religiosity exists here in two different generational styles – an earlier generation of mostly Republican managers and small-business people and a more politically diverse Baby Boom generation of managers and professionals.[3]

This observation does not disregard the fact that there is a large portion of nonwhite residents in Oak Park as well as a relatively large number of working-class and lower-middle-class residents. Rather, it acknowledges that the dominant leadership group in the community's civic life is not comprised of the nonwhite working-class people from the apartments along Harlem and Austin boulevards. It is comprised, instead, from the mostly white managers and professionals who live in the large houses on the leafy side streets. Only recently, with the development of a new local political party, have African American interests been forcefully put on the local political agenda in a way that is not filtered through a white middle-class community elite.

This set of observations is not meant to essentialize whiteness and "middle-classness." Instead, it does just the opposite; while a great deal has been written about American religion using data from white middle-class individuals and the communities and organizations dominated by them, much of this literature has universalized that set of experiences, using it as typical of American religion writ large. But white middle-class managers and professionals have specific and historically located sets of values and ways of doing things, and it is important to analyze this middle-classness and whiteness as such. In the United States, it is the source for a dominant set of values and ways of doing things, a cultural style that sets public expectations of behavior in public institutions such as work and civic institutions.[4] It is also important because recognizing whiteness and middle-classness as socially located sets of experiences and practices is the only thing that can keep us from treating them as normative.

The congregations in and around Oak Park provide an opportunity for understanding how this set of institutional models of congregational life are pervaded by white, middle-class culture and its assumptions, experiences, and habits. Likewise, analyzing how these congregational models are expressive of different styles of white, middle-class religiosity can help us to understand where these models might predominate and what other models might be found in other places.

These congregations place central importance on the values of individualism, tolerance, diversity, and consensus. This bundle of values characterizes a middle-class civic orientation, which gives play to a limited articulation of social and political issues while eschewing radicalism.[5] Some of the congregations weight diversity and tolerance more heavily (community, leader), while others emphasize consensus (family). The former are congregations whose lay leaders are predominately Baby Boom professionals, and the latter tend to be congregations whose lay leaders are an older generation of managers and small-business people. Some congregations (house of worship) are more individualistic than others.

Central to this overall value orientation, historically, has been a private/public dichotomy and the idea that personal concerns, intimate relationships, and emotional ties are at best orthogonal to political involvement or issue-based activism.[6] This dichotomy is reproduced in many of the congregations here. Most members of family congregations see politics or "issues" as threatening their intimacy and fellowship, while pastors of leader congregations worry about "needy people" sapping the congregation's energy, focusing the congregation inwardly, and undermining their outreach activities. Neither family nor leader congregations entertain the idea that "the personal is political," and both types foster the view that intimate fellowship and issue-based activism are two alternatives from which to choose, not things that can be easily integrated into one congregation's mission and identity.

Only community congregations do not reproduce this dichotomous understanding of a contradiction between issue-based activism and individual needs and experiences or between activism and fellowship. Community congregations forge a link between these two through personalism, an expressive style of moral reasoning that uses individual experience as a guide in interpreting and applying religious traditions within an ongoing community. The community congregations illustrate that personalism and an expressive or experiential mode of religious authority do not necessarily lead to an inward orientation that eschews involvement with political and social issues. While Tipton (1982) and Roof (1993) correctly note that personalism and an expressive moral style have been more common throughout our society since the 1960s, Hammond (1992) and Lichterman (1995a, 1995b, 1996) argue that it is most closely associated with middle-class individuals and organizations.

All twenty-three congregations are also influenced by a specifically *white* middle-class culture in their ability to speak, or rather not to speak, about race. While pastors of leader congregations do speak out on race in other forums, such as the village's newspapers and village meetings, there is very little public, internal dialogue about race in these congregations. Houses of worship are centers for multiracial worship, but not for a sustained public discussion of what that means; family congregations avoid the issue entirely. This is remarkable in a community where the transition from an all-white to a mixed-race community (stable residential integration) is by far the most significant recent historical event, one that has received major discussion in other public forums, such as community meetings and local newspapers, and one that was recently named one of the most important ongoing issues in village life in a community self-study.

Community congregations frame discussions of race in personal and interactional terms, understanding racial divisions as potential barriers to fellowship and community. Even this circumscribed discussion of race only receives attention in the most theologically liberal congregations, such as the Lutheran congregation (ELCA) and the Unitarian Universalist church, or in those with a very high percentage of African American members, like the independent Baptist church with over forty percent African American members. In no congregation is there a discourse that links an analysis of racism to a radical call for social justice, and there is no systematic critique of racism and its link to economic forms of injustice.[7]

How racial differences inform conflicts over liturgy, resources, or authority is also not discussed publicly in these congregations, although there is often backstage or private talk about this. Other controversial issues, such as women's roles in the church, homosexuality, adultery, and premarital sex, receive a fair amount of public debate in these congregations. There is a lack of comfort in speaking publicly about race that seems informed by the community's particular history and a desire to tell the story of residential integration as a success story, but that is also informed by a more general failure of middle-class, white America to develop a robust discourse about racial divisions. The presence of mostly middle-class blacks in these congregations has not prompted a different kind of dialogue about race.[8]

Other studies support the idea that some middle-class congregations with black members – even with all black members – may maintain a kind of silence on race that can be attributed to the existence of a previously institutionalized white, middle-class culture. A comparative ethnographic study of middle-class, black churches on Chicago's southwest side indicates that those in a white church tradition (for example, the United Methodist Church) are very unreceptive to the introduction of explicit discourse about race into sermons and other public forums (Daniels 1996). Congregations from the Black Church traditions, however, are consciously and corporately confronting changing meanings and implications of race and racism, for example, in their incorporation of Afrocentric discourse, rituals, and daily practices. However, even in these churches, while compassionate ministries to help the poor are the norm, a kind of middle-class individualism pervades the discourse, and the link between racial and economic justice is not explicitly made; rather, "none of them corporately addresses the structural or systemic issues of the economy or acts to change economic structures" (Daniels 1996:219).

Individual-Expressive Religion

One of the most important ways in which these congregations are exemplars of a white, middle-class religiosity does not have to do with the values that they promote or the discourses for which they provide a venue. Rather, it is in the style of attachment or affiliation that individual members have. These churches all exemplify what Hammond (1988, 1992) has called an individual-expressive style of religious attachment. This style of affiliation is the paradigmatic mode of religious commitment for white, middle-class Americans.

It is important to understand this style of affiliation because it has become the dominant one in a large portion of the religious field. Moreover, if Wuthnow (1988) and others who write about the effects of ongoing modernization on American religion are correct, there is reason to believe that this style of affiliation is becoming more common outside of white, middle-class America and in the future will characterize more of the religious field. I argue that the implications of this style of affiliation have been to some extent misunderstood even as a characterization of white, middle-class religiosity; developing a better understanding of these implications will be doubly important as we attempt to understand the effects of increasing individualism and voluntarism on American religion as a whole.

In his influential 1988 book, *The Restructuring of American Religion*, Wuthnow argued that the effects of ongoing modernization have been reconfiguring the American religious landscape at all levels since the 1960s. Increasing levels of education fostered a cultural revolution that led to more egalitarianism and the questioning of traditional sexual morality. The effects on American religion included the decline of denominational loyalty and authority, the rising importance of the congregation as the unit of religious attachment, and new forms of organization (parachurch or special-purpose groups). It also included a new cultural division, the con-solidation of a liberal/conservative divide based in part on education, running through religious organizations.[9] Wuthnow posed the term "restructuring" in part to try to combat the underlying teleology of reli-gious decline in earlier accounts of religious change.

In *Religion and Personal Autonomy,* Philip Hammond (1992) argues that these changes, plus the rapid rise in residential and employment mobility in the post-1960s economy, add up to a qualitatively different orientation toward religious affiliation. They foster the rapid growth of an individual-expressive style of religious attachment, an attachment that is achieved and voluntary, not ascribed. Put another way, individual-expressive religion is expressive of secondary, chosen, voluntary ties rather than of primary, ascriptive ties. It is not an expression of overlapping and rein-forcing connections of neighborhood, kinship, and ethnicity. Hammond argues that individual-expressive religion is gradually replacing a communal-expressive form of religious attachment, where membership in the religion overlaps and expresses membership in family and community, and where the members of one's church or synagogue are also part of one's network of everyday family and work connections (cf. Warner 1994).

Hammond's thesis is that individual-expressive religion is becoming increasingly common in the United States because of two interrelated sets of changes that have taken place since the 1960s. The first is the cultural change that Wuthnow and others have noted – the emergence of what Hammond calls "the new morality," a questioning of traditional values in many institutional spheres but particularly in the arenas of family and sex-uality.[10] The second is a set of changes in geographical and occupational mobility that have resulted in a decreased capacity to maintain local ties. More and more middle-class people are what Hammond calls "cos-mopolitans," people who live and work in various areas over the course of their lives and whose ties of friendship and group membership are not rooted in one neighborhood but are geographically dispersed. Cosmopoli-tans, Hammond shows, either drop out of organized religion entirely or use it to constitute connections that they do not find in their residential neighborhoods.[11]

Hammond believes that the conditions that foster parochialism more generally and communal-expressive religious affiliation in particular are eroding, and that individual-expressive religious affiliation is on the rise in all parts of American society. However, he finds that an individual-expressive form of attachment is more likely to be found among people who are white, who have more education, and who hold professional or managerial occupations – persons like the ones in leadership in Oak Park congregations.

While virtually everyone agrees that this broad set of social changes has occurred and that they have an impact on religious organizations, there is disagreement over exactly what the effects are. Wuthnow is careful to argue that the changes that he documents do not necessarily lead to an ongoing decline in religiosity, in membership, or in attendance.[12] The term "restructuring" was meant to replace terms like "secularization" and "decline," with their underlying teleology of religion's eventual disappearance.[13] Others are not so sanguine on this point. Bellah et al. (1985, 1991) wonder if the rationale for religious belonging is not being undermined, and Hammond (1992) shares the same concern. The most memorable evocation of this in the sociological literature remains the description of Sheila in *Habits of the Heart* (Bellah et al. 1985). Sheila rejects clerics, organizations, and doctrines as her source of religious authority and instead is guided by her own "inner voice." The authors fear that it is a short step from relying on the "inner voice" to the erosion of the entire basis for belonging to organized religion.

The particular argument in *Habits of the Heart* has been contested,[14] but most scholars of contemporary American religion do agree that there have been serious postwar changes in American religion that can be understood broadly as the effects of increasing individualism and ongoing modernization (Bruce 1996; cf. Glenn 1987). One change has been the decline of denominational authority and attachment and the rise of congregationalism, evidenced by such trends as the increased numbers of members switching among congregations of different denominations and increasing eclecticism in worship and ritual life.[15] The religious "seeking" behavior of Baby Boomers is paradigmatic of this (Roof 1993). Congregationalism also describes a shift in religious authority from denominations and religious officials to the individual or, at most, the small, face-to-face community of the congregation or the prayer group, as discussed by Warner (1994) and Wuthnow (1994a).

These are all trends in individual religiosity that affect religious organizations directly. However, much of this research is based on aggregated individual-level data from surveys and interviews, although there are beginning to be more comparative studies of religious groups and organizations as well. Middle-class, white professionals may be paradigmatic of these changes in life-style and religiosity, but most analyses imply that other parts of the field may soon follow suit. Scholars feel that these changes are, to use Wuthnow's term, "restructuring" the entire field of American religion; education levels are rising in all groups, and residential and employment mobility are affecting increasing portions of American society across traditional class and occupational boundaries (Livezey 1996).

These individual-level changes can be summed up as increasing *voluntarism* in religious affiliation (cf. Roof and McKinney 1987). Of course, in one important sense, voluntarism has characterized the religious field from the beginning of our history due to the absence of a state-endorsed religion (Hatch 1989; Warner 1993). And yet, as recently as the 1920s, church attendance was directly linked to social class and was an expression of status and respectability that limited the voluntary nature of belonging (Caplow et al. 1983; cf. Bruce 1996). As recently as 1960, Herberg (1960) could still talk about Protestant, Catholic, or Jew as religiously based ascriptive identities (cf. Hirschman 1970). Increasingly, not only has membership in religious organizations come to be voluntary in law, but also, in fact, as membership has become less directly linked to status, respectability, and ethnic identity for most Americans.[16]

Scholars care about increasing voluntarism because it is thought to have very specific extra-individual effects on religious organizations and institutions. The first is the fear that Sheila aroused in the authors of *Habits of the Heart* – that there is an erosion of the basis for belonging to organized civic and religious groups in our society. Robert Putnam[17] would call this the decline of the social capital necessary for a vital civic life, and he thinks that it is affecting the majority of voluntary organizations in the United States to a general effect of a decline in civic vitality.

The second effect is a related solidification of a liberal/conservative divide as people react to the cultural changes and the "new morality." This division is seen as decreasing tolerance, increasing polarization, and impoverishing public debate on a variety of important social issues. The argument is that, at the local level, people with different orientations isolate themselves more and more among the like-minded, while activists and other elites engage in more and more polarized debate in national policy and media arenas. Both cause the undermining of tolerance and consensus.[18]

The third consequence of increasing voluntarism is thought to be increasing *privatization*, or a decline in public religion.[19] This distinction is developed most explicitly by Martin Marty (1976, 1986, 1994) to explain a historic division between Protestant groups, but most see it as

a division that pervades the whole religious field. Private religion emphasizes "individual salvation out of the world, personal moral life congruent
with the ideals of the saved, and fulfillment or its absence in the rewards
and punishments in another world in a life to come," while public religion is more "exposed to the social order and the social destinies of men"
(Marty 1986:179). Even Wuthnow (1994a, 1994b), who does not think
that individualism leads inevitably to religious decline, does worry that it
leads to a domestication of religion, a concern with personal piety and spirituality, emotion and private matters of family life, over a public prophetic
engagement. Warner (1994) echoes this theme. He writes that denominations are often the champions of universal, egalitarian, and publicly
engaged values in the face of congregational attachment to ascriptive
values and narrow concerns; increasing individualism creates a situation
where these local concerns are reinforced. To his credit, Warner treats this
as an open, empirical question rather than a logical outgrowth of an underlying teleology.[20]

In short, people who study American religion care about increasing
individualism and voluntarism because they think that these are not just
trends in individual styles of affiliation, but because of what Hammond
has called the "qualitative difference" in the meaning of affiliation that
arises when people treat religion as a voluntary expression of individual
preferences. They care because they think that these individual-level
changes lead to a change in the moral order of religious life and broader
changes in the institutional capacity of American religion. The erosion of
the basis for belonging, increasing liberal/conservative polarization, and
the decline of publicly engaged religion are seen as impoverishing religious and civic life. These concerns are expressed in a metanarrative that
has the particular form of a lament for lost community and lost public
influence in the face of religious decline (Demerath and Williams 1985,
1987). While this decline is supposed to have begun among white,
middle-class, mainstream Protestants, it is thought to be spreading and
coming to characterize the whole field of American religion.

If any community ought to have experienced these corrosive effects of
ongoing modernization, it is the tri-village area of Oak Park, River Forest,
and Forest Park. Individual-expressive commitment is the norm here, and
it characterizes the mode of affiliation in all twenty-three of these congregations. Moreover, the people who live in this community and provide the
lay leadership of these congregations are those who are supposed to have
been affected the most by these changes. So if the standard narrative about

215

the effects of increasing voluntarism does not hold here, and if the resultant religious landscape does not look the way that that narrative predicts it would, then we need to rethink our standard account.

This study does in fact suggest that our standard narrative needs to be reworked. This comparative study of local congregations makes it clear that voluntarism does *not* lead to one single pattern of local participation and decision making, to one reaction to religious authority and tradition, or to one norm of member commitment. It does not lead to one dominant congregational model but to four different ones. Voluntarism leads to pluralism – even within the part of the religious landscape that is supposed to be exhibiting the uniform effects described above. The effect of voluntarism on local congregations is the freedom to negotiate and implement a *limited range of local institutional cultures*, to figure out together, in an ongoing way, different sets of answers to the fundamental questions of identity and mission – "Who are we?" and "How do we do things here?" These different answers have different implications for the cultural cleavages that structure local religious institutions, for the nature of member commitment, and for the structure of religious authority.

For example, the "private religion/public religion" divide is present in this community, but with some surprising twists. On the one hand, the private/public dichotomy is reproduced in the split between the family and house of worship models on the one hand and the leader and community models on the other. The former are privatized models that focus on the nurturing of individual members through worship and fellowship and reject a focus on social issues, while the latter are more publicly engaged. Leader congregations not only adopt internal policies on social issues, they also conduct active, issue-based outreach in the local community. For a community where we would expect the decline of public religion to have proceeded apace, it is somewhat instructive to note that there are more congregations with a public model than a private one.

Most interesting are the community congregations that reject the public/private dichotomy. They incorporate an emphasis on individual spiritual nurture, religious education, and providing a caring and intimate set of ties among members, but they combine that with the idea that the local church is indeed the place where stands on issues ranging from race to gender roles to sexuality and civil rights are to be debated and institutionalized. Further, doing so – embodying the congregation's values on social issues – is seen as part of the congregation's witness to the local community (cf. Becker et al. 1993).

Privatization is linked to secularization. If secularization is defined as the declining scope of religious authority, a private-religion orientation can be understood as one aspect or process of secularization (Casanova 1994). Privatized religion reproduces at the individual and organizational levels the differentiation of institutional spheres that is characteristic of modernity at the societal level, by rejecting the idea that one's religious beliefs have implications for public problems and issues. A privatized model of religion draws small the circle around what is "religious." Some sociologists have used particular organizational forms as a proxy for this kind of decline in authority. Chaves (1993) argues that the weakening or disappearance of formal religious authority structures indicates this kind of secularization and the privatization of religious authority at the level of the religious organization.

Using this kind of proxy, we would expect that a church with a congregational polity would be more "secularized" than one with a hierarchical polity, because the authority and influence of the pastor, the formal religious leader, is less. However, as Table 4 in Chapter 2 shows, churches with a community or leader model are also more likely to have a congregational polity, and churches with a family or house of worship model are more likely to be hierarchical. That is, the congregations that have the most publicly engaged religious cultures also have the most "privatized" form of formal authority.

There are several possible interpretations of this. One interpretation is that, at the local level, members of hierarchical congregations are more willing to think of public religion as something for which someone else is responsible. That is, they are likely to delegate the taking of stands on social issues to religious professionals and, perhaps more importantly, to other levels or kinds of organizations. This was true of some Oak Park congregations. For example, some members of one family congregation, an Episcopalian parish, sympathize with the idea of granting more legal protections to homosexuals, but they told me that they do not see the local church as the appropriate place for that kind of issue-based activism. Members of some community and leader congregations are concerned about social issues and *do* think that the local congregation is the place to talk about them.

Another possible explanation is that these congregational models function not only as institutional models of the congregation, but as institutional models of religion more generally. Again, for some congregations this seemed to be the case. For example, the members of the Presbyterian church that has a family model are divided on political issues like abortion and the legal rights of homosexuals. But they see their religion as having little to do with these issues, and they are annoyed when their denomination takes a stand on such an issue. They tend to think that that is not what religion in general is about. This is not the same thing as delegating stands on social issues to another level of the organization; rather, it is rejecting the idea of "public-religion" more broadly.

It is hard to get an accurate count of how many of the family and house of worship congregations fit into the former category (delegating public religion to some other level of organization) and how many fit into the latter (rejecting public religion). It is clear that members of community and leader congregations all share a public-religion orientation that is applicable both to religion as an institution and to religion as it is instituted at the local level – in congregations. A congregational polity fosters this public-religion orientation. In contrast, a hierarchical polity may foster a truly privatized view of religion, or it may simply foster a willingness at the local level to let someone else worry about social issues.

Ironically, congregational polity, the polity type with the least formal religious authority and the most "secularized" by a formalist definition, is the most likely to lead to congregations that embrace a public-religion view and are therefore less secular along another dimension. The very congregations that reproduce more of a public-religion view, that reject the neat separation of spheres that allows members to think of religion as something that concerns only their own relationship to God or each other, and that are in this sense the least secularized are the most secularized on another dimension – that of formal polity. This stands on its head the conventional wisdom that congregationalism leads to parochialism and to a situation where religious leaders and elites are the only ones concerned with social issues and social action.[21]

It also suggests that using formal organizational structures as proxies for differences in authority and commitment is not sufficient; these need to be supplemented by an understanding of the cultural models of mission that may or may not vary in expected ways with formal polity. In our list of organizational forms that we need to understand to examine religious authority, we need to include institutional models as well as formal organizational features like the structure of the pastorate.

If the private/public dichotomy does not play out as expected in this community, it is also the case that a liberal/conservative division is not the only cultural cleavage found here. This study supports the idea that "liberal" and "conservative" are relevant to the study of local congregations, but it also supports Ammerman's (1994, 1997b) idea that this set of categories is not determining of many aspects of local congregational life. Most of the congregations here are identifiable by the outsider and would self-identify as being either in a "liberal" or a "conservative" camp, even though some reject using those labels and do not like to emphasize ideology. However, as in most other groups and organizations, the explicit ideology has only an indirect relationship to group process and decision making (see Swidler 1986; Rhys Williams 1996). Knowing whether the congregation is liberal or conservative tells us some important things about it, but it does not tell us everything that we need to know about how decisions are made and where religious authority resides (cf. Wedam 1997).

The effect of liberal and conservative ideologies on organizational process and on religious authority is dampened in these congregations by several factors. First, there is a pragmatic ethic of compassionate outreach and service that informs congregational practices more than explicit ideology does, what Ammerman has called "Golden Rule Christianity."[22] Second, ideas about mission, core tasks, and identity seem to be determined by religious-institutional imperatives that are common among religious organizations and that cut across, rather than reinforce, a liberal/conservative divide. Third, some congregations, in avoiding issue-based debate entirely, limit the polarizing effects of different ideologies on their practices. Fourth, those congregations that do engage in issue based debate find that the relevant cultural division or cleavage they have to grapple with is not a liberal/conservative divide, but a question of how much to emphasize an ethic of caring and how much to emphasize an ethic of authoritative judgment or how to balance their expressive and their caring moral logics (Becker 1997a).

Rethinking Restructuring

To suggest that this study can help us to generate a better understanding of how American religion has been restructured in the postwar era is not to claim that these four congregational models structure the entire religious field. History shows us that the core tasks of worship, fellowship, and witness are widespread features of the field that are found across religious traditions throughout much of our history. Yet history also shows us that, in different historical times, congregations privilege some of the core tasks over others and that different bundles of programs and ways of doing things can exist in combination with the basic tasks of congregational life (Holifield 1994). The question, then, is where might we find models that are similar to the ones found in this community and where might we find different ones?

These four models are probably widespread in white, middle-class America and have been since at least the 1960s. In particular, the community model may well be a new form, one that was not found before the kinds of cultural changes about which Tipton (1982) and Hammond (1992) write. This form draws on the history of democratic local control of congregations that is characteristically American, but it extends it in ways that grow out of the post-1960s cultural change toward more experiential forms of religious authority (cf. Dolan 1994). It draws on the metaphor of congregation-as-community that is as old as the colonial era in our history (Holifield 1994) and that was found in Oak Park in other forms as early as the turn of this century (Bundy 1991), but it reconfigures this as an individual-expressive community of values, not a community of residence or ethnicity.

Holifield (1994) suggests that the family model, or something very like it, may have been around since colonial times. The house of worship model seems to fit the ideal type of "suburban religion" in its heyday in the 1950s, and it also fits with the memories of some of the older respondents who remember Oak Park in that decade. Those who lament the decline of public religion assume that the leader model was once much more common than it is now; while this may or may not be true among mainline Protestants, it almost certainly is not true for evangelical and fundamentalist Protestants or Catholics, both of whom have seen more public involvement at all levels since World War II.[23] More generally, because there are few comparative studies of congregations over time and because the dominant narrative of decline has tended toward nostalgia and an overgeneralization from the liberal mainline Protestant experience, it is difficult to tell with any certainty how common these forms were in the past.

It may be that some locations call for different mixes in models. The distribution of lay leadership in these congregations suggests that locations with more managers and small-business people may have more family congregations than those with large populations of professionals who value autonomy and an expressive moral style. Urban areas, with their history of religious activist and reform movements, may select against family models and houses of worship; the pilot study for this one, conducted in the community around Hyde Park and the University of

Chicago, found by far more community and leader churches than family or house of worship congregations. Conversely, rural areas may be home to more family congregations and fewer community and leader congregations; but this remains a matter for empirical investigation.

Similar models that are not the same in all particulars may also be found outside of white, middle-class communities. For example, it is easy to imagine that there would be congregations that are like the family model in their core tasks – worship, education, and providing a caring atmosphere of fellowship – but that would nevertheless carry out these core tasks quite differently. Some families no doubt fight more than the polite middle-class ones here; suppression of most conflict is a feature of middle-class families, not all families (see Baumgartner 1988). Models are metaphors, not blueprints, and can be interpreted and applied with some variation across contexts (cf. Clemens 1997:53ff).

Likewise, the idea that the congregation mirrors and exists in relation to the nuclear family, instead of a more extended and fluid family, may be a particularly white, middle-class notion (Stacey 1991). Daniels (1996) writes of a middle-class, black congregation on Chicago's southwest side that holds as its primary tasks religious reproduction and care-taking of members. However, instead of a family model, he identifies a "village" model here, where the care-taking is more spread out and specifically designed to provide a more flexible support system in an area where nuclear families may not be the norm.

Just as there is more than one form of family, there are different forms of community, and one can easily imagine forms of the community model where the values that are being expressed are essentially those of a subculture. Daniels's (1996) comparative study of black, middle-class congregations in a Chicago neighborhood makes it clear that they serve as forums for debate about such concerns as the meaning and practice of Afrocentricity in African American life. Davidman's (1991) study of orthodox Jews shows a similar phenomenon; one of the things that individuals can choose to re-create, once ethnic and racial ties themselves become less ascriptively binding, are communities that voluntarily affirm an ethnic or racial subcultural identity (cf. Hammond 1988).

It is extremely important, however, not to romanticize the urban scene or nonwhite ethnic and racial groups as the last bastions of "pure" community, religious or otherwise (see Lincoln and Mamiya 1990). The middle class, black churches that Daniels studies are engaged in voluntary affirmations and explorations of identity, just as are their white, middle-class "neighbors" to the northwest, in Oak Park. Tim Nelson's (1997) study of a very poor, black AME congregation in Charlotte provides a good cautionary tale against assuming that we, as a scholarly community, know more than we really do about the contemporary forms that nonwhite religious communities take. In particular, he argues that our image of poor, black urban congregations as close-knit networks for self-help, social support, and caring relations may not be accurate. His description of Eastside Chapel reveals a community ravaged by drugs and crime, where the conditions that foster social trust and caring are so eroded that there is no way to sustain a family or community model of congregational life. Eastside Chapel, despite its strong Black Church heritage, functions as a house of worship, a support for individual beliefs and spiritual sustenance, but where a more communal and care-taking orientation cannot be maintained. Against all of our stereotypes, this poor, black congregation functions in the most individualistic way because of specific environmental conditions that make trust impossible to maintain.

More generally, urban areas are not untouched by the same social changes that have influenced other portions of the American religious landscape. Livezey (1996) notes that the urban scene is marked by a high level of mobility and long commutes. He finds that many congregations in the urban Chicago area are not themselves heavily rooted in neighborhoods, but instead are selected by those who commute from across the urban area for individual-expressive reasons, forcing people to become "cosmopolitans" whether they want to or not. This feature of urban life, he writes, leads to increasing voluntarism in religious attachment across all city neighborhoods and across class, ethnic, and racial boundaries. The city is no better a home for "natural community" than are the suburbs.

If there are similar models in some areas, it is also likely that there exist entirely different congregational models than the four found in this community. First, as Hammond points out, communal-expressive religion is declining but not disappearing. In some places, for example in ethnically homogeneous rural areas with low rates of mobility, congregations may yet be expressive of ascribed identity and overlap with ties of family, friends, and place. Warner suggests that the congregations of new ethnic and immigrant groups that his team of researchers studied in Chicago may be places where membership overlaps and reinforces not only ties of ethnicity but also of extended family, friendship, and business associations.[24] Even here, though, in urban areas, new ethnic groups are not always organized into tight-knit residential enclaves, and commuter congregations develop (Numrich 1996). How this influences their ability to function in a communal-expressive manner, and how the meaning of that term itself changes as residential community comes to anchor other forms of community less, is a matter for empirical examination.

Some new congregational models have arisen precisely in response to changes in the relationship between "community" and "place." The megachurch is one model that may be suited to a particular exurban locale. Megachurches seem to offer multiple modes of attachment (Thumma 1996). In the megachurch that Eiesland (1998) describes, one can find fellowship and intimacy through myriad small groups or one can be more loosely bound and treat the congregation more as a house of worship. Megachurches often have the resources to be leaders in local politics and community affairs, and yet it is not clear that they actually adopt this role. The implications here need to be explored further. Do megachurches foster an extralocal orientation that undermines public engagement? Or do their vast resources offer a new potential for constructive engagement with civic life?

Finally, Wuthnow (1994a, 1995) takes the lead in pointing out that one of the changes in the religious field is that congregations and denominations are no longer the only common organizational forms. The rise of special-purpose political action groups and the coevolution of small fellowship groups seem to reproduce the public/private dichotomy that some congregations are questioning and to exacerbate liberal/conservative cleavages in political action while fostering a "domestication" of religion in its daily manifestation. How they will eventually reconfigure the institutional field remains to be seen, but they add a new feature to the landscape that we need to take into account in any discussions of the shape and the future of American religion.

The Field of American Congregational Religion

Religious restructuring has been a real result of the social changes in the United States since World War II. Individual-expressive religion has become the dominant mode of religious attachment for white, middle-class persons, especially professionals and those in urban areas. And to the extent to which economic and educational changes foster mobility and the questioning of traditional values and institutions in other segments of society as well, there is likely to be increased religious voluntarism.

But how do we understand the effects of increasing voluntarism on religious organizations and institutions? On local congregations? Using this community as a kind of paradigmatic case or exemplar, a place where individualism and voluntarism should have had their strongest effects, can help us to assess how this restructuring has played out in that part of the religious field that has been most affected by it.

One effect has been an increasing congregationalism. Of course, Americans have always channeled their religious activity largely through local congregations, and congregations have historically fostered a certain amount of democratic, local, and lay control of decision making (Hatch 1989; Bass 1994; Dolan 1994). But it is also true that postwar social changes have fostered more "de facto congregationalism" across the board and an accompanying relocation of religious authority away from denominational leaders and formal doctrines and toward individuals and congregations as interpretive communities that are eclectic and particular in their faith expressions. Only in the leader congregations did I find a strong pastorate and a consensus that the role of the pastor is to lead the congregation in interpreting and applying religious ideas, symbols, and doctrines. Family and house of worship congregations tend to view the pastor more as a provider of religious services (sermons, liturgy), and community congregations see the pastor as the facilitator of a congregation-wide discussion of religious and other important matters.

But it is not so clear that congregationalism leads to an increase in "private religion" at the expense of the kind of public-religion orientation that Marty (1994) writes about. First, to conclude that something has increased is first to demonstrate that there was less of it before. There has always been a strong emphasis on pietism, fellowship, and the rituals of family life in local congregations in the United States. While religious authority has shifted toward congregations and individuals, there is little evidence that the nature or the importance of piety and fellowship in congregational life has changed; comparative historical studies are rare, but those available, like Caplow's study of "Middletown," do not support this idea.[25]

More importantly, while denominations may have been the institutional locations for public religion in America's recent past, this analysis suggests that public religion can find an institutional home within local congregations, even among individualistic, cosmopolitan professionals. Community and leader models both embody and perpetuate public religion. Personalism and an experiential mode of religious authority, the specific products of the cultural revolution of the 1960s that were supposed to be most corrosive to public religion, can also lead to community congregations where the private and the public are reintegrated in a new rationale for public engagement.

One is perhaps more likely to find these rationales at the organizational or group level than in individual discourse. Lichterman (1996) found the same kind of personalistic rationale for commitment in his study of middle-class, white environmental groups. Allahyari (1996) and Eliasoph (1996), in their studies of volunteer organizations, also point out the necessity of moving away from analysis of individual attitudes and beliefs to a comparative organizational study to discover in situ how institutions perpetuate a variety of modes of commitment, caring, and moral community, filtering and channeling the effects of social change on individuals through providing repertoires of moral rhetoric and committed practice.

Of course, Eliasoph (1996) is right in emphasizing that there is often quite a distance between the public rhetoric and the private, backstage talk in groups and organizations. Some of the people I interviewed mentioned that gap between the public and private discourse surrounding conflict in these congregations (cf. Fine 1987). But it is also true that publicly institutionalized rhetorics of discourse and practice mediate individual responses to social change and provide a repertoire into which people are socialized and from which they draw in conceptualizing and enacting their own styles of commitment. They also affect group-level actions, like which policies to put in place, which programs to which to direct resources, and which educational and ritual materials to use (cf. Barthel 1997). Individuals can bring their own style of commitment in line with one of these congregational models, or they can reject or negotiate with them, or they can search for a more compatible model, but the models provide an important frame of reference within which individuals act, speak, and choose (cf. LoPucki 1996).

Ammerman's (1997a) *Congregation and Community* uses a comparative organizational study design to discover how congregations react to social change in their local communities and finds that strong denominational leadership is not as much of a precondition for congregations' community involvement as are the presence of active, committed lay leaders who feel ownership of the congregation's programs and who are able, through a congregational approach to decision making, to take responsibility for outreach and activism. Even a strong pastorate is not enough if it is not coupled with a strong lay leadership. This is one consequence of individualism and congregationalism that does not get enough attention. Feelings of ownership and egalitarian decision-making processes can increase commitment for some members (cf. Dolan 1994; Lawler 1996). Ammerman also found that the caring that is inherent within a focus on pietism and fellowship can mobilize congregations for new outreach and public involvement when social changes reduce the health and well-being of congregation members and the rest of the community.

As for the other major fear, of religious decline, it is difficult to tell anything from a cross-sectional study except in the most anecdotal way. But the anecdotal evidence here is instructive. The congregations that themselves have a story of decline in this community are mainline Protestant congregations – Baptist, Methodist, Presbyterian, and Episcopalian. A few of these congregations also have "resurrection tales" of newfound prosperity, a development of the last twenty years. But the other congregations – the fundamentalist churches, the synagogues, and the Catholic parishes – for the most part tell stories of growth or stability since the 1950s.

This suggests that the lament for lost public influence that pervades many accounts of American religion may have less to do with the place of American religion as a whole in civic and political life than it does with the experiences of one particular segment of the Protestant elite, who find their authority displaced to local churches and their voices joined in the public sphere by religious leaders whose politics and theology seem foreign.[26] Holifield (1994) argues convincingly that the stories about decline – decline of religion, decline of community – are often less objective statements about the overall effects of social change than they are expressions of the concerns of elites who are disproportionately disadvantaged by particular changes (cf. Lichterman 1996). Hammond's (1992) work suggests that the lament for lost community may be a generalization of the particular experience of displaced cosmopolitans, many of whom eschew congregations and other venues for community-building and who then wonder if everyone else will not abandon them as well.

Much of this metanarrative of decline has been generated by sociologists and those in the field of religious studies. Some historians have taken a different view, one that is often not integrated into sociological accounts. For example, Hatch's (1989) historical account of American Christianity suggests a different kind of narrative structure within which to make sense of the most recent increase in religious voluntarism in the United States. His work would suggest that this is not a new development, but rather a reassertion of the fundamentally democratic, voluntaristic impulse that has been the defining characteristic of American Christianity and that has affected other religious traditions in the United States as well. Rather than decline, this return to congregationalism might be better understood as one instance of a recurring populist theme throughout American religious history, one that has generally been accompanied by religious renewal (cf. Finke and Stark 1992; Warner 1993, 1994).

In other words, the disestablishment of a liberal/centrist and largely Protestant elite is a real consequence of postwar social changes (Baltzell 1976), but it is not the same thing as a decline in religion per se or even in public religion. To state this explicitly also makes sense of the heatedness of the contemporary "culture war." It is possible that a public debate between a declining liberal Protestant elite, which has tended to champion egalitarianism and the other cultural changes associated with modernity, and a conservative elite, which decries them, has provided much of the "war" that Hunter (1991, 1994) writes about (cf. Warner 1994). But in privileging two levels of analysis – individual attitudes as reported in surveys and the political and social discourse of elites – we tend to reify the categories of liberal and conservative. It is easy to overlook the fact that local-level religious practices and institutional structures have as much to do with a pragmatic religious ethic as they do with doctrine and ideology – and sometimes more (cf. Becker 1997a, 1998c).

Using this community as an exemplar was useful because the standard story did not play out here as expected; and because this is the part of the field where it should have had the best fit, it suggests that we need to rethink our analysis of the field as a whole. Of course, the skeptic might say that it is only a matter of time; individualism and voluntarism may eventually lead to decline, parochialism, and isolated pockets of liberals and conservatives eyeing one another with mutual suspicion, even if they have not done so as yet. But for the moment let us assume that forty to fifty years is ample time for the worst to have come about if it were going to, and let us take seriously the vitality of public religion even among the people who were supposed to have rejected it and see what that might suggest about how to approach the study of American religion as an institutional field.

First, it suggests that we need a new set of questions. There is little point in asking if individualism has increased. Clearly, individualism has changed how people relate to a host of traditional institutions, organizations, and movements, including work, family, and religion. But we need to sort out more carefully the effects that these changes have on different parts of any given institutional field. Features such as class, ethnicity, and geographic location matter because they shape how people previously related to these institutions and therefore the specific set of institutional interrelationships through which social changes are filtered.

Also, social change may not have uniform and aggregative effects. The cultural changes that lead to a questioning of traditional authority and the increasing mobility that affects most parts of our society may have complex and contradictory effects on local congregations. Some congregations clearly become locations for re-creating parochialism and localism, while others are locations for constituting new, "cosmopolitan" forms of community. In addition to liberal and conservative orientations, there are new cultural cleavages emerging as voluntarism fosters pluralism along multiple dimensions and within categories that we previously have thought of as unitary (mainline Protestantism, the Black Church). The culture war may be real, but it is not located evenly at all levels of religious organization or among all religious institutions.

We also need to pay much more attention to the different levels of analysis at which social change can have an effect. Changes in individual beliefs and styles of affiliation are important, but they clearly do not have a straightforward and uniform effect on local religious organizations or on the relationship between congregations, historic denominations, and new structures like the small groups movement and parachurch organizations. Institutions, and the practices and organizational forms that they legitimate, are slow to change. They are "sticky," as Douglas (1986) points out, and they can absorb, filter, and redirect a high degree of individual-level change (cf. Mohr and Guerra-Pearson, forthcoming).

Finally, we need to rethink our analysis of voluntarism. Voluntarism has been the fundamental and defining feature of American religion from the early colonial period. But over time, voluntarism has led to very different forms of local religious organization. In the colonial period, voluntarism meant the right of community elites to control membership in their congregations through the restriction of membership to "the elect." In the early period of our national history, it meant the explosion of more populist, democratic, and individualist denominations, as Methodist and Baptist preachers bypassed the then-traditional elites and took their messages of salvation directly to the people. Black Church leaders organized their own churches in protest to the racism of white churches, and voluntarism fostered the development of this kind of alternative and parallel institution. In the nineteenth century, voluntarism meant the construction of Catholic parishes as alternative civic spheres, where immigrants could band together for mutual help and service while affirming their ethnic identity and learning skills needed to survive in their new society. In the post–World War II era, voluntarism has meant that religious institutions have provided resources and a relevant repertoire of beliefs and practices that men and women have used to reconstruct new forms of community that are more appropriate for a more educated, mobile, and modern population.

We should bring a different rhetoric and narrative structure to bear on understanding these and other changes in the formation of religious community. Questions like "Is religion declining?" or "Is meaningful religious community declining?" provide a subtext, if not an explicit thesis, for much of our current scholarship. But these are extremely difficult to answer with any kind of objectivity. What is "meaningful" is judged too often by a nostalgia that values the older forms simply because they are older and familiar. Decline is also difficult to sort out from a lament for lost influence by a very specific Protestant elite, from a sociological predisposition to see religion as an outdated relic that has no place in a modern and enlightened society, from the nostalgia of cosmopolitans for their own more parochial roots and from the reaction of some conservatives to feminist critiques of older constructions of "the public." This is true not only for our analysis of American religion but also for our understanding of the broader changes in American community and civic life since World War II.

Those who bring a rational choice perspective to bear on the study of religion are to be credited with forcing discussion on this important issue. They contend that increasing modernization, voluntarism, and pluralism lead to religious vitality because they release pent-up religious demand that had been suppressed by older monopolies, thus creating the preconditions for a better and more diverse supply of religious commodities. Rational choice approaches have generated a great deal of controversy; some disagree with their assumptions about rationality or about the universality of religious "demand," while others feel that many of the important and interesting things about religion cannot be explained with this approach.

Nevertheless, these scholars have generated the first serious reconsideration of the meaning and implication of voluntarism to occur in decades.

Lawrence Young's (1997) *Rational Choice Theory and Religion* contains a good summary and debate of these arguments. I tend to agree with the positions that Ammerman and Warner take in this volume; pluralism and voluntarism are features of the American religious institutional field that lead to great adaptability and flexibility and therefore to ongoing vitality. One does not need to agree with the other assumptions of a rational choice framework to analyze voluntarism or even individual religious preference and choice. But recognizing that voluntarism and pluralism can lead to religious and civic vitality is important.

A better set of questions would have to include ones about the changes in the nature of voluntarism in American religion and how they are linked to very specific historical changes in religious organizations and institutions. Changes in individual modes of attachment and affiliation are of course important and real. But they are not linked uniformly to decline in public religion or a reduced capacity for the habits of caring and connection that make for a robust civic life. They do necessarily lead to the elimination of all forms of communal-expressive religion.

Of course, not all is happy vitality and pluralism, and some real things may be lost, as well as gained, through the historical changes taking place. That is, one may legitimately argue that, while not everything is lost with increasing voluntarism, some important things might be. Congregations are not for the most part locations for discourses that examine the persistence of systemic economic inequality. And while personalism may link the private and the public in new ways, it has its limits. For example, Lichterman (1996) shows, and this work supports the idea, that it may limit the formation of multicultural alliances.

Another effect of increased voluntarism may be the emergence of a relatively stable group of nonjoiners. That is, there may be an increasing social division between those who are choosing to join local congregations and those who choose not to join. We may want to start asking questions about the people who are not joining at all and those who are dropping out. If neighborhood ties are eroding and family ties are becoming thinner, the choice not to join an organized church, synagogue, or other civic group may indeed signal a choice not to participate in one of the few forms of connection now available. If Wuthnow (1988) is correct, the nonjoiners are now a larger and more stable group in our society than before. The meaning and impact of a solidifying division between those who join voluntary organizations and those who do not is one of the largely understudied phenomena of the postwar period; Hammond's work suggests that

this may overlap somewhat with another largely understudied phenomenon – the emerging political and cultural division between parochials and
cosmopolitans.

Apart from these concerns, I would indeed assert, in the best contrar-
ian academic tradition, that there is a place for the cheery voice raised
against the ongoing lament. Ammerman's (1997a) work confirms that congregations can be vital players in civic life and in helping individuals deal
with some of the corrosive effects of rapid social change. Warner's study
of new ethnic and immigrant groups shows that, for this group, congregations continue to play the vital role in adjustment and integration into
civic life that they always have, in addition to providing much-needed networks of support in our individualistic society (Warner and Wittner 1997).
Demerath and Williams (1992) confirm that religion is still an important
source of moral critique in our political arena, whether we academics
always like the content of the critique or not. Individualism and voluntarism also are the bases for these patterns.

These two sets of insights need to be integrated, just as Putnam's (1995,
1996) work on declining social capital needs to be integrated with the
findings of his critics who point out that, while there is a great deal of
change, the evidence for a net loss – in community, in social capital, in
civic vitality – is far less clear-cut (cf. Roof 1996). Our study of these questions now needs to turn to a less pejorative and less linear set of analyses
to understand the ongoing restructuring of religious and civic life in the
United States. This analysis must take the creation of new forms of community as seriously as the loss of old ones. In particular, it must seek to
understand the nature of modern institutions, including religious ones, on
their own terms. It must understand that the relocation of religious
authority and the reformation of religious commitment are not the same
as their disappearance. And it must not tell the story of white, middle-
class Protestant elites as though it were the only story.

This study suggests that the story, at the level of local religious life, is
a story of religious communities that worship together, provide help and
support in times of crisis, and link family and domestic life to a larger
group of neighbors and friends and to a larger religious tradition. It is a
story of eclecticism and change in religious traditions, but it is also a story
of traditions that are reproduced and carried on in new ways. It is a story
of compassionate outreach to those in need, of the bonds that Putnam
describes as "social capital." It is a story of moral discourses that link individualism to family, community, history, and politics in a variety of ways,

and moral practices like outreach and worship. And if we want to under-stand the effects of individualism on American religious life, we need to tell this story of local believing communities, not just the stories of indi-viduals who are their members, because communities are more than just the sum of their individual parts.

Notes

1. This is a common approach for population ecologists. Baum and Haveman (1997) do the same for the Manhattan hotel industry, and Baum and Singh (1996) examine the dynamics of competition on day care centers in Toronto. McPherson (1983) takes a similar approach to studying populations of vol-untary organizations in local communities. Usually, this approach is applied to explain rates of organizational founding or demise, rather than to under-stand internal organizational processes, like decisions about mission, pro-gramming, or distribution of resources. See Eiesland (1998) for an exception.
2. For two excellent discussions of the various purposes of and ways to conduct case study and comparative case study research, see Feagin et al. (1991) and Ragin and Becker (1992). In Ragin and Becker, see especially the introduc-tion (Ragin), which has an excellent discussion of using cases as exemplars of various kinds of action, and the chapter by Abbott (which includes a discus-sion of cases as exemplars). In Feagin et al., see especially the chapter by Snow and Anderson on "Researching the Homeless."
3. Recent sociological accounts emphasize the existence of distinct middle-class groups and experiences that are based in large part on occupational and eco-nomic differences, but also note that there can be an identifiable "middle-class" influence on the character of public institutions and public culture in a given time and place (see Archer and Blau 1993 for a review).
4. See Lamont (1992), Chapter 1, for a longer discussion of this argument. Bellah et al. (1985: viiiff) probably have the most famous discussion of "middle-class" religious values; compare with Hammond et al. (1991) for a discussion that places more emphasis on the *variety* of middle-class, religious styles (cf. Roof 1993). Kanter (1977) also discusses the relationship of this middle-class public culture to masculinity and trust among corporate managers; Daniels (1996) discusses it in relation to racial identity in middle-class, black con-gregations. All of these authors make it clear that such "public culture" can be effective in shaping behavior and belief regardless of the presence of people for whom it is a poor fit, or even people who do not agree with it (cf. Caplow 1984; Becker 1998b).
5. Gans (1988) discusses the more conservative end of the spectrum of these

values among "middle-Americans," while Jenkins and Wallace (1996) discuss the more liberal end.

6. Much of our social-scientific literature takes this dichotomy for granted and sees it as logical and natural, not as a product of social and historical circumstances. Lichterman discusses how this dichotomy undergirds traditional scholarly approaches to community and public life. He critiques how these approaches privilege a gender dichotomy in which "the public" is constructed as a mostly male arena, where male concerns and styles of interaction become the norm. He also reviews feminist scholarship that has critiqued these traditional approaches. See Lichterman (1996:18ff); cf. Allahyari (1996). Bellah et al. (1985) is a good example of the naturalization of a private/public dichotomy in social analysis; cf. Coser (1956) and Gans (1988). Feminist scholars have developed an extensive critique of this view, arguing that public and private are not natural or logical oppositions but historical and institutional distinctions or categories that vary across time and space. See Epstein (1988), Lopata (1994), and Becker (1998b). Marty (1994) shows that a Protestant elite historically has been at the vanguard of conceptualizing the distinctions between private and public religion in the United States.

7. For a longer discussion, see Becker (1997a).

8. Although that may have changed; I have not been in these congregations since the O. J. Simpson trial and the Million Man March, both of which have prompted renewed discussions of race in other forums (such as the national news media).

9. Roof and McKinney (1987) argue that this divide runs between families of denominations, not through individual denominations, but schisms in organizations such as the one between moderates and conservatives in the Southern Baptist Convention indicate that some denominations were affected as well (see Ammerman 1990). Roof and McKinney are probably correct in their characterization of most denominations as being largely on one side of the divide or another in terms of theology, political outlook, and social policy, and Wuthnow (1988) is no doubt right in pointing out that individuals within each denomination may be far more varied in their views and that some denominations are themselves split on this dimension.

10. See Tipton (1982) for an excellent discussion of this cultural change and its effects on religious traditions and moral discourse in American society; cf. Glock (1993), who puts the timing of this cultural revolution a little earlier.

11. Livezey (1996) finds that this cosmopolitan form of attachment is on the increase in urban neighborhoods, due in part to increasing job-related commutes that take people out of their residential neighborhoods for most of their waking hours; this is evidenced in the increasing number of "commuter congregations" that draw members from widely dispersed parts of the urban

region. There is also the mobility related to a long "establishment" phase for professional careers, something that was brought home to me quite forcefully in my fieldwork in interviews with professionals in their late twenties to early thirties. These individuals regularly told me about the loneliness that comes from moving from place to place every few years, establishing their careers. For many, their congregation was where they could "plug into the community," make friends, and become involved. This life-course effect may intervene in the formation of religious connections because it tends to occur at the same point when many people who have been inactive return to active religious participation as they start to raise children.

12. He does note that the 1960s saw a decrease in attendance and membership over the 1950s, but he also notes that this trend leveled out at the end of the 1960s and that attendance in the 1950s was exceptionally high. See Wuthnow (1988:159, 164–5).

13. Riesebrodt argues that sociologists tend to reproduce narratives of religious decline and eventual disappearance because of the historical relationship between sociology and modernity. He writes: "Representative of the new secular academic elites, sociologists consider themselves agents of enlightenment, committed to a rational implementation of progress that they often equate with secularization. . . . Religion is regarded as the relic of a past epoch, destined either to disappear entirely or to be forced into the private sphere" (1993:3).

14. For an explicit argument against it, see Wuthnow (1991).

15. See Caplow et al. (1983), Carroll and Roof (1993), and Warner (1994).

16. With some notable exceptions, one of which is the link between ethnicity and identity for new ethnic and immigrant groups; see Warner and Wittner (1997). Voluntarism is also an ideology, a set of ideas about how one ought to be related to a variety of organizations and institutions. But I am referring not to the ideology but to the mode of individual attachment to religious organizations and institutions.

17. Putnam, in the Winter 1996 issue of *American Prospect;* the following issue is devoted to a series of rebuttals of Putnam's thesis by, among others, Theda Skocpol and Michael Schudson; see also Putnam (1995).

18. See Wuthnow (1988), Bellah et al. (1991), and Hunter (1991, 1994).

19. "Privatization" is a word that is used in several ways in the sociological literature on religion. It is used in the sense that I use it here, to denote a difference in cultural orientation toward public engagement. This kind of privatization may be a property of individual belief, but it is also a property of the public culture of an institution or organization; by using the term in this way, the question, "Is the Catholic Church more privatized now?" is a sensible one, and one would answer it by finding out such things as whether the church has reduced its willingness to take official, public stands on social

and political issues. But privatization is also used as a term that describes the kind of individualism and decline of denominational authority discussed above. In this sense, individualism equals privatization, and there is not much use in debating if the American religious field, and the individuals within it, are privatized; the rise of the kind of individual-expressive commitment style that Hammond identifies is de facto evidence that it is. Finally, some people use the term "privatization" to denote the condition of differentiation of institutions that is a condition of modernity – the separation of politics and religion, for example, or the growing autonomy of the market. Under this definition, religion in a modern society (like the United States), where there is no established church, is "privatized" by definition. See Bruce (1996) for an excellent discussion of the latter position. I use the term in the way I do because it lets me address a particular debate about whether increasing voluntarism leads to a difference in the way that religious individuals (and the institutions they comprise) conceptualize the boundaries between their religion and other institutions and the kinds of action they engage in to cross those boundaries.

20. This concern that "public religion" is declining while a liberal/conservative polarization is increasing is not as ironic or as contradictory as it seems. Ammerman (1994) has noted that the culture wars thesis of increasing division between liberals and conservatives is due to a concentration on denominational officials and other religious leaders and that this divide is not so enduring a feature of local religious life. Those who decry a decline in public religion most often concentrate on increasing personalism and an inward focus in local religious life, so it is quite possible to notice an increasing culture war between religious officials while noting increasing parochialism among laity. Also, some authors, like Wuthnow, emphasize the effects of a liberal/conservative "divide," not because it leads to inflammatory political rhetoric and political mobilization directly, but because those with opposing views do not fellowship together in local churches.

21. See Roozen et al. (1984), Gilkey (1994), Marty (1994), and Warner (1994) for various statements of this argument.

22. See Ammerman (1997a, 1997b). Her work indicates that this pragmatic religious ethic and set of practices cross-cuts a liberal/conservative divide at the level of individual values and practices, as well as among congregations. Cf. Swidler (1986) on how practices and ethics may be more robustly linked to action in times of social change than are articulated and explicit ideologies.

23. See Wuthnow (1988) and Glock (1993).

24. As reported in the panel on the New Ethnic and Immigrant Congregations Project at the 1996 Society for the Scientific Study of Religion Annual Meeting in Nashville. See Warner and Wittner (1997) for a more complete account.

25. See Caplow et al. (1983), Holifield (1994), and Warner (1994). Wuthnow (1994a, 1994b) argues that it is primarily in the small groups movement that there is an increase in pietism and a "domestic" orientation toward religion.
26. For longer discussions see Baltzell (1976), Demerath and Williams (1985, 1987), Johnson (1985), and Marty (1994).

APPENDIX A
DATA AND METHODS

Beginning in the fall of 1990, I began a community profile of all three suburbs. I subscribed to two local newspapers and read them weekly. I read histories of the communities in the public library and local historical society offices. I talked to community leaders in politics, business, and the local press, and I gathered census data. By the time I had completed fieldwork in the winter of 1993, I was able to put together a fairly detailed and rich picture of the tri-village area, as residents call it.

Access – Interviewing and Participant Observation

In each congregation I interviewed the pastor, the head of the lay administrative council, the liturgical/worship director (or equivalent), and the director of religious education (or equivalent). I then interviewed lay members who were reported to be involved in specific conflicts, making sure that I covered all "sides."

Issues of access are always important in any fieldwork-based study. Access is in part physical, and Oak Park was within commuting distance of my own home. Access is also in part social, and my education, race, and socioeconomic status are similar to those of the majority of the people I interviewed, particularly of the pastors and lay leaders who served as important gatekeepers in providing background information on the congregations, directing me to other members and encouraging members to cooperate with me. My own history of religious involvement in United Methodist churches also made access easier, particularly with members of more conservative Protestant churches.

In the course of fieldwork, this similarity seemed to outweigh the racial differences I encountered. All of the African Americans I interviewed are used to interacting with white professionals on a regular basis. Race did not appear to affect people's willingness to talk to me. It is impossible to answer for sure the more basic question of whether racial differences influenced the kinds of things that people told me in interviews. On the other hand, racial similarity no doubt had the same influence, and that is generally not considered a problem. I can say that people, both white and black, exhibited a great deal of frankness in interviews on the subjects of race and racism. African Americans would tell me about the fears involved in being the first black family on a block, and more than one white person told me about the mixed feelings of guilt and apprehension when walking through a group of black young men clustered outside the movie theater at night.

Something that proved to be more salient in my fieldwork was the liberal/conservative dimension. Some members of four of the more conservative congregations – two fundamentalist Baptist, one Plymouth Brethren, and one Assemblies of God – did express some concern that I might myself be "too liberal" or "too feminist" to listen with an open mind to their views, particularly on such issues as abortion, homosexuality, or the roles of women in the church. Men in these churches were especially concerned not to be judged as either sexist or uncaring, as indicated in the "bracketing remarks" they would make. For example, I heard "You'll probably think we're really sexist, but" or "You will probably think that we're really terrible, but" at the start of these interviews.

For the most part, an openness to talk with them about their concerns, a revelation that I had grown up in and around evangelical Methodist congregations in Ohio and am familiar with evangelical beliefs, and an assurance that I was not there to convert anyone to my views, won at least enough confidence to begin the interview process. During the interview, maintaining a high level of professionalism and respectfulness seemed to give more assurance that I was there to take them seriously and learn about their point of view. Without exception, interviews with people in these four churches, including those who initially expressed some hesitation, were lengthy and informative.

In addition to interviews, I also engaged in participant-observation of services and meetings. I also engaged in extensive document review in each congregation, analyzing mission statements, annual reports, constitutions, promotional brochures, written histories, and sermons. I was also able to choose two congregations as "focus" congregations and did more in-depth fieldwork in them, as a kind of check on the information gathered from less extensive interviews and fieldwork in other congregations. One is a fundamentalist Baptist congregation and the other a liberal (ELCA) Lutheran congregation. This included visiting each congregation fourteen to sixteen times over the course of six months, observing Sunday services, home Bible studies, fellowship groups for women, and committee meetings. I got transcripts and tapes of sermons and engaged in more extensive interviewing, talking to more than twenty people in each congregation singly or in focus groups. This was made possible through my work as a research assistant on the Congregations in Changing Communities Project, directed by Nancy Ammerman. That study is now available in the book *Congregation and Community*, by Nancy Ammerman (1997a). That book also contains a brief description of Oak Park and extensive summaries of the work on these two focus congregations, with particular attention to how they have reacted to the racial and other changes that have taken place in Oak Park since the late 1970s.

When engaged in participant-observation of services and meetings, maintaining access meant being sensitive and nonintrusive. When I attended the main Saturday or Sunday service at each congregation for the first time, I did so anonymously and told people, if asked, that I was a visitor who was "checking out" several congregations in the area. Although I tape-recorded all of my interviews, I did not feel comfortable bringing a tape recorder into a service, so instead I would keep one in the car. I would take notes in a small notebook or, more often, on my bulletin or program. Then, in the car afterward, I would drive to some quiet place and record my impressions on tape and then would type up more detailed fieldnotes when I returned home. Later, after I had identified myself as a researcher and was invited to visit some other congregational activities, I followed the same note-taking procedure for small group meetings like Bible studies or committee meetings.

Choosing the Congregations

Some studies indicate that some types of congregations might have more conflict, or different kinds of conflict, than others. The size of the congregation and the polity type may affect the amount of conflict. The support for this ranges from case studies to comparative case studies to statistical analyses of schism to theoretical accounts: Moberg (1962), Takayama (1975), Roof (1978), Liebman et al. (1988), Ammerman (1990), Rothauge (1990), Becker et al. (1993); cf. Collins (1975).

Roof (1978) writes that liberal congregations may be more conflict-prone because they are more democratic. Conversely, conservative churches have better maintained their religious authority in matters ranging from politics to personal morality and may be better at binding congregants into close-knit and supportive communities, which might reduce conflict. The differences between liberals and conservatives, in general, is a subject that has received a great deal of attention in scholarship on American religion in the last twenty years or so. To see only those that specifically link differences to conflict, look at Hadden (1969), Marty (1976), Bellah et al. (1985), Ammerman (1987), Roof and McKinney (1987), Hammond (1988), Wuthnow (1988), and Hunter (1991). For more general, theoretical accounts of the relationship between commitment and conflict, see Hirschman (1970) and Simmel (1971).

The twenty-three congregations in this study were chosen to vary on the three factors that previous studies suggest might cause one congregation to have more conflict, or a different style of conflict, than another congregation: size, polity type, and a liberal or conservative cultural orientation (see also Becker 1997a). The congregations were chosen to fit in the cells of Table 2 (see p. 36). I had planned to choose three congregations for each cell, but I was able to find only two congregations in the tri-community area (Oak Park, River Forest, Forest Park) that were "large, conservative, and hierarchical."

Congregations were labeled as liberal or conservative by how the head clergyperson and a majority of lay respondents categorized the congregation's religious orientation. In fact, in no case in this study was there any discernible disagreement about whether a congregation fit into a "liberal" or "conservative" classification. Polity type is divided into hierarchical and congregational. Hierarchical congregations include both presbyterian and episcopal types as described by Moberg (1962). The episcopal type emphasizes the role of bishops and the church hierarchy, with the pastor as the representative of this hierarchy, while the presbyterian type is more "connectional," with control of the church in the hands of a regional presbytery or equivalent body of clergy (Moberg 1962:61,62).

"Small" congregations correspond to Rothauge's (1990) family and pastoral categories, defined as congregations where the administrative structure revolves around the pastor and a small group of lay leaders. "Large" congregations include what Rothauge terms "program" and "corporation churches," roughly churches with more than 150 regular Sunday attendees, in which the administration is more formally divided into boards and committees. So in this case, "size" captures a distinction in organizational structure.

A short telephone survey administered to all seventy-seven congregations in the three-community area indicates that these twenty-three are well representative of the area in size, membership, and programs.

Following is a list of the congregations that were chosen to fit into each cell in Table 2, p. 36. Names are excluded, but other information, including size and denomination, is included for each congregation. The numbers given for membership and attendance were current as of the end of the field period in 1993. Unless otherwise stated, churches have a fairly even distribution of members throughout all age groups. Most of the congregations report that about fifty-five percent of their members are women and forty-five percent are men, which is supported by my observations in most cases.

Cell 1: Small, Liberal, Congregational Polity

1) Disciples of Christ

They have about 130 baptized members.

Average attendance is reported as 70–80.

I observed 60–65 people there on Sunday.

They are 60–65% white and at least 30% African American. Some African Americans and Asian Americans attend.

The members mostly come from Oak Park and from Austin (Chicago). The dominant group is middle-class professionals, but members cover a fairly broad range of occupation and income.

Model: **Leader**

Conflict: – over whether to install elevator

– over the last pastor's mission activity

– over baptism/communion rituals

2) United Church of Christ

They have 130 baptized members.

They report an average attendance of 55–60.

I observed 60+ members there on a Sunday.

They have older members, a gap in the age range of 45–60, and a growing younger generation.

Over 95% white, they have a few African American members.

They used to be residential; now one-half live in Oak Park and one-half drive in from other suburbs.

Most have a college education; most of the younger members are professionals; the older members are professionals and business people, and some are in service/administrative work.

Model: **Family**
Conflict: – over the pastor

3) United Church of Christ

Identifies as "congregational."

They have 200 baptized adults.

They report an average of 120 in Sunday attendance.

I observed 110–120 there on a Sunday.

The largest group is young professional families, aged 25–45.

They are about 90% white, although perhaps as many as 30% of the children are African American. (They have many multiracial families.) Most live in Oak Park.

Model: **Community**
Conflict: – inclusive language
    – policy of affirming lesbians and gay men

Cell 2: Large, Liberal, Congregational

4) Unitarian

They have 310 adult members.

They report an average attendance of 175.

When I attended, I observed 130 people there.

Over 95% white.

Mostly middle- to upper-middle-class, many professionals and some in business.

Model: **Mixed**
Conflict: – over turning the parsonage into an education center
    – over the restoration board
    – over the pastor

5) Presbyterian Church, USA/United Church of Christ

Identified as congregational because they have a council, from the UCC tradition, not a Presbyterian session. The pastor identifies their governance as "congregational."

They have a membership of 1175.

They report an average attendance of 360 at their main service, which conforms to my observations.

About two-thirds of their members are women.

Most live in Oak Park.

They are 90% white.

Most members are college-educated; many professionals and administrators.

Model: **Leader**
Conflict: – inclusive language
    – policy affirming lesbians and gay men
    – hymnals (which to choose)

6) Reform Jewish

They have 750+ members.

Attendance at Saturday service varies, up to 100.

Members are predominantly white, middle-class professionals.

Many live in Oak Park, but up to 30% come in from Chicago or from other suburbs.

Model: **Leader**

Conflict: − budget

  − participate in homeless shelter? conflict over approval procedure

  − fire the cantor?

  − role of intermarried couples (spouse)

Cell 3: Small, Liberal, Hierarchical Polity

7) United Methodist

They have a membership of over 400.

They report an average attendance of about 140.

When I attended, I observed between 100 and 110.

Largely residents of Oak Park. Mostly middle-class professionals.

80–85% white, rest African American or Asian; some mixed-race couples.

Model: **House of Worship**

Conflicts: − over whether to raise pastor's salary

  − over staff, replacing secretary, firing custodian

  − over how to stem decline, several years ago

8) Episcopalian

They have a membership of over 250.

They have 80 pledging units.

They report an average combined attendance of 120 on Sunday at all three services; I observed 65 at main eleven o'clock service.

Mostly middle-class professionals who reside in Oak Park.

Core leadership provided by a group of young professionals with children, in their 30s and 40s.

90% white, rest African American.

Model: **Family**

Conflicts: − over style of man on vestry, mode of decision making

  − one family has interpersonal conflict with pastor and lay leaders, leaves

  − over last pastor

  − whether to sell rectory

9) United Methodist

56 members.

Attendance reported to average 40–50.

I observed 45–50 people there on a Sunday.

Most are residents of Forest Park and Oak Park. There is a gap in the 45–65 age range. Maybe 45% have a college education, but that is the growing group.

Over 90% white, rest Hispanic or Asian.

Model: **Family**

Conflicts: – whether to sell parsonage

– what to do after fire (rent/buy/merge with another congregation?)

Cell 4: Large, Liberal, Hierarchical Polity

10) Episcopalian

They have about 450 members, 192 giving units.

They reported an average attendance of 215 in 1991, but that dropped to about 100 in early 1992.

80% white, 15% African American, 5% other nonwhite.

Mostly residents of Oak Park.

Mostly middle-class and professional.

Model: **Mixed**

Conflict: – over pastor

– over former pastor

– over how to minister to two members with AIDS

– over woman priest who was guest speaker

11) Catholic

600+ active parishioners.

In mid-1993 I observed just over 300 people at main Sunday Mass, and people reported to me that attendance was down over 200.

60% white, 40% African American.

Members come from Oak Park and Austin and cover a wide range of income and occupation, although most of the leadership are professionals, business people, or administrators.

Model: **Mixed**

Conflict: – over Sister speaking from the pulpit

12) Lutheran Church in America

They have 400 baptized members, 150 giving units.

Average attendance reported at 185, which conforms to my observations.

About 95% white, rest African American.

Dominant group is middle-class professionals with young families.

Most are resident in Oak Park.

Model: **Community**

Conflict: – renovations to building

Cell 5: Small, Conservative, Congregational Polity

13) Assemblies of God

Average attendance reported at 140–150.

I observed 85–90 there on a Sunday.

About 50% are white, 15–20% Hispanic, 10% Asian, and 15% African American.

About one-third are from Oak Park; the rest are from Austin and Galewood (another Chicago neighborhood).

Great diversity in education, occupation, and income, from the well-off to the unemployed.

Model: **Community**

Conflict: – over youth pastor

    – two over premarital sex

    – choosing new pastor

    – changing church name

    – song style

14) Nondenominational (Plymouth Brethren heritage)

They have 100+ active adults and around 50 children.

They have 50+ attendance on Sunday mornings, confirmed by my observations.

They are a young congregation, with the dominant group 25–35 years old. More than one-half live in Oak Park.

They have about 70% white, 15% African American, 5% Asian, and some Latinos.

Model: **Community**

Conflict: – two over premarital/extramarital sex

    – over whether to move to new building

    – over hiring Bible teacher

    – over whether to institute new programs to bring in more people

15) Independent Baptist

They have 255 members.

They report an average of 155 on Sunday, which is correct according to my counts.

They are 60–65% white, 35–40% African American.

Residential, Oak Park and Austin.

There is a core group of black and white professionals from Oak Park that provides much of the leadership, although there is great economic and educational diversity in the congregation as a whole.

There is a gap in the 35–55 age group.

Model: **Community**

Conflict: – over funding a missionary

    – over worship style (music)

    – over fund-raising

Cell 6: Large, Conservative, Congregational Polity

16) Missouri Synod Lutheran

They have 1600 baptized members and 1300 communicants; 600–700 are active.

Average Sunday attendance, reported and observed, 550–600 members.

They are 95% white.

One-half are from Forest Park, the rest from surrounding suburbs.

Model: **Mixed**

Conflict: – over hiring a business manager

– school budget

– pastor asked to marry a couple currently living together (pastor refuses)

– over structure of administrative boards

– guest speaker

17) Independent Baptist

1500 on mailing list; 700 members.

Sunday attendance averages 700, confirmed by observation.

They are over 95% white.

Lots of young families, but also many active singles.

They are middle- to upper-middle-class.

One-half from Oak Park and one-half from other suburbs.

Model: **Leader**

Conflict: – fire assistant pastor

– women on board/ordination

– fund-raising

– music style

18) Conservative Jewish

They have just under 400 family units.

They have 80–100 people at Saturday service.

They are mostly white professionals and business people.

About one-half are resident, and one-half come from other western suburbs.

Model: **Community**

Conflict: – timing of school classes

– hire new rabbi

– role of women (Sisterhood)

– participate in village rotating homeless shelter

Cell 7: Small, Conservative, Hierarchical Polity

19) Episcopalian

Membership 180.

Sunday attendance ranges from 50 to 85, depending on season. I observed 60–65 there in winter.

Over 95% white, middle- to upper-middle-class, largely residents of River Forest and Oak Park.

Model: **Family**

Conflict: – None

20) Nazarene

90 members.

Average attendance reported at 45–50, confirmed in my observations.

Over 95% white.

Mostly not residential; most commute from other suburbs.

Older congregation, with gap in 25–40 range.

Model: **Family**

Conflict: – pastor

21) Presbyterian Church, USA

86 adult members.

50–75 reported as average attendance, depending on season. In winter, I observed around 60.

75–80% white, rest African American.

Older congregation, most over 50, some younger families with children coming in.

Model: **Family**

Conflict: – rent building

– treasurer (record-keeping)

Cell 8: Large, Conservative, Hierarchical Polity

22) Catholic

2100 households.

Five Sunday Masses; total attendance 1800–2000.

The membership is 95% white.

Resident, split between Oak Park and Chicago.

Mostly professionals, with a working-class contingent from Chicago

Model: **House of Worship**

Conflict: – None

23) Presbyterian Church, USA

859 members.

Average attendance reported at 263, confirmed 250–260 through observation.

99% white, 1% Asian.

Mostly residential, River Forest and Oak Park.

Most are college-educated, professional or business people.

Model: **Leader**

Conflict: – Boy Scout troop use of facilities
        – fire choir director
        – small group of charismatics
        – budget/missions

APPENDIX B
THE INTERVIEW QUESTIONS

The following questions provided a guide for a structured interview. In almost every case, each question was asked of each person interviewed. In some cases, additional follow-up questions were asked. Some members and clergy were also asked background questions about their communities – Forest Park, Oak Park, and River Forest.

In each interview, there was an opening/introduction time, when I explained the project and answered questions. Interviews for clergy skipped section A, below, and instead contained a series of questions about the membership, attendance, weekly activities, officers/lay leadership, and organizational structure, followed by a request for access to written materials and referrals to congregation members. I also asked clergy respondents about their education, age, family situation, and tenure with the congregation.

After the end of the questions on conflict in section C, I would thank the respondent for his or her time. I would also ask if there might be any written records, like policies that were adopted or minutes of meetings, and whom I would have to contact to get access to those records.

A. Background of the Member

1) How long have you been a member of this congregation?
2) Were you raised in this denomination/tradition?
   (Prompt: "Tell me how you came to decide on this church/synagogue.")
3) What offices do you hold in the congregation?
   What offices have you held in the last five years or so?
4) Would you describe yourself as liberal or conservative?
   What do those words mean to you?
5) How old are you?
6) What is your level of education?

7) Where do you work, and what is your job?

8) Are you married or single? Do you have children?

9) How many of your friends are from this congregation?
(Prompt: "More than one-half, or less?" If less, "More than one-quarter, or less?")

10) In a typical week, how many times would you be either at the church/synagogue or involved in some related activity?

11) What has being a member of this congregation meant for you?
(Prompt: "What role does it play in your life?")

B. Background of the Congregation

1) Is this congregation liberal or conservative? What do those words mean for this church/synagogue?

2) What percentage of the people who are active and attending today would have been involved five years ago? ten years ago?

3) What percentage of the members would say that the congregation is the center of their social lives?

4) In this congregation, are matters of life-style open to individual interpretation?
(Prompts: "Would there be consensus in this congregation about homosexuality? About women's roles in the congregation? About abortion?")

5) What is the role of the laity in interpreting doctrine or congregational policy?

6) What brings this church together?
(Prompt: "What are the activities and events in which there is the greatest fellowship or harmony?")

7) What does this church/synagogue do particularly well?
(Prompt: "Finish this sentence, 'We're really good at . . .'")

8) What does this church/synagogue not do quite so well?
(Prompt: "What would you improve if you could?")

9) Does your church/synagogue have a strong sense of history? Tell me about the history.

10) What pressing issues are facing the congregation right now?

11) What are the congregation's goals in the short term — say, in the next five years or so?

C. Conflict

1) In the past five years, have there been issues or events in the life of the congregation that you would describe as conflicts?

After they list conflicts, take the first one and ask:

2) Who was involved in that?
3) What were the issues?
4) How did this start?
5) What happened? What was the outcome?
6) Who else would know about this?

Repeat for each conflict listed.

If no conflict, ask:

a) Have there been any issues or events that have been a challenge for the congregation?
b) Have there been any painful or difficult things that the congregation has had to deal with?
c) During the last five years, what events or issues in the congregation have been the subject of disagreement?
d) Have there been any events or issues that have resulted in prolonged or heated debate? Over which people have left the church? Which have caused hurt feelings or other problems?

REFERENCES

Abbott, Andrew. 1988. "Transcending General Linear Reality." *Sociological Theory*, 6:169–186.

Abbott, Andrew. 1992. "What Do Cases Do?" Pp. 53–82 in *What Is a Case? Exploring the Foundations of Social Inquiry*. Eds. Charles Ragin and Howard Becker. Cambridge, England: Cambridge University Press.

Abbott, Andrew. 1997. "On the Concept of Turning Point." *Comparative Social Research*, 16:85–105.

Abu-Lughod, Lila. 1986. *Veiled Sentiments*. Berkeley: University of California Press.

Alexander, Victoria. 1996. "Pictures at an Exhibition: Conflicting Pressures in Museums and the Display of Art." *American Journal of Sociology*, 101(4):797–839.

Allahyari, Rebecca Anne. 1996. "'Ambassadors of God' and 'the Sinking Classes': Visions of Charity and Moral Selving." *International Journal of Sociology and Social Policy*, 16(1/2):35–69.

Ammerman, Nancy Tatom. 1987. *Bible Believers: Fundamentalists in the Modern World*. New Brunswick, NJ: Rutgers University Press.

Ammerman, Nancy Tatom. 1990. *Baptist Battles*. New Brunswick, NJ: Rutgers University Press.

Ammerman, Nancy Tatom. 1994. "Telling Congregational Stories." *Review of Religious Research*, 35(4):289–301.

Ammerman, Nancy Tatom. 1997a. *Congregation and Communitiy*. New Brunswick, NJ: Rutgers University Press.

Ammerman, Nancy Tatom. 1997b. "Golden Rule Christianity." Pp. 196–216 in *Lived Religion in America*. Ed. David Hall. Princeton, NJ: Princeton University Press.

Anderson, Benedict. 1991. *Imagined Communities*. New York and London: Verso.

Apter, Andrew. 1992. *Black Critics and Kings*. Chicago: University of Chicago Press.

Archer, Melanie and Judith Blau. 1993. "Class Formation in Nineteenth-Century

References

America: The Case of the Middle Class." *Annual Review of Sociology*, 19:17–41.

Baltzell, Digby. 1976. "The Protestant Establishment Revisited." *American Scholar*, 45(4):499–518.

Barley, Stephen R. 1986. "Technology as an Occasion for Structuring." *Administrative Science Quarterly*, 31:78–108.

Barnett, William P. and Glenn R. Carroll. 1987. "Competition and Mutualism Among Early Telephone Companies." *Administrative Science Quarterly*, 32:400–421.

Baron, James N., M. Diane Burton, and Michael T. Hannan. 1996. "The Road Taken: Origins and Evolution of Employment Systems in Emerging Companies." *Industrial and Corporate Change*, 5(3):239–275.

Barthel, Diane. 1997. "The Role of 'Fictions' in the Redefinition of Mission." *Nonprofit and Voluntary Sector Quarterly*, 26(4):399–420.

Bass, Dorothy. 1994. "Congregations and the Bearing of Traditions." Pp. 169–191 in *American Congregations, Vol. 2*. Eds. James Wind and James Lewis. Chicago: University of Chicago Press.

Baum, Joel and Heather Haveman. 1997. "Love Thy Neighbor? Differentation and Agglomeration in the Manhattan Hotel Industry, 1898–1990." *Administrative Science Quarterly*, 42(2):304–338.

Baum, Joel and Jitendra Singh. 1996. "Dynamics of Organizational Responses to Competition." *Social Forces*, 74(4):1261–1297.

Baumgartner, M. P. 1988. *The Moral Order of a Suburb*. New York: Oxford University Press.

Becker, Penny Edgell. 1997a. "'What Is Right' and 'What Is Caring': Identifying a Religious Logic in Local Congregations." Pp. 121–146 in *Contemporary American Religion: An Ethnographic Reader*. Eds. Penny Edgell Becker and Nancy Eiesland. Newbury Park, CA: Alta Mira Press/Sage.

Becker, Penny Edgell. 1997b. "Understanding Local Mission." Pp. 267–285 in *Connectionalism: Ecclesiology, Mission, and Identity*. Report on the United Methodism and American Culture Project, Duke University. Eds. Dennis Campbell, William Lawrence, and Russel Richey. Nashville, TN: Abingdon Press.

Becker, Penny Edgell. 1998a. "Congregational Models and Conflict: A Study of How Institutions Shape Organizational Process." Pp. 231–255 in *Sacred Companies: Organized Aspects of Religion and Religious Aspects of Organization*. Eds. Jay Demerath, Peter Dobkin Hall, Terry Schmitt, and Rhys H. Williams. New York: Oxford University Press.

Becker, Penny Edgell. 1998b. "Rational Amusement and Sound Instruction: Constructing the True Catholic Woman in the *Ave Maria*." *Religion and American Culture*, 8(1): 55–90.

Becker, Penny Edgell. 1998c. "Making Inclusive Communities: Congregations and the 'Problem' of Race." *Social Problems*, 45(4): 451–472.

Becker, Penny Edgell, Stephen J. Ellingson, Richard W. Flory, Wendy Griswold, Fred Kniss, and Timothy Nelson. 1993. "Straining at the Tie that Binds: Congregational Conflict in the 1980s." *Review of Religious Research*, 34(3):193–209.

Bell, Michael M. 1994. *Childerley: Nature and Morality in a Country Village*. Chicago: University of Chicago Press.

Bellah, Robert N., Richard Madsen, William Sullivan, Ann Swidler, and Steven Tipton. 1985. *Habits of the Heart*. Berkeley: University of California Press.

Bellah, Robert N., Richard Madsen, William Sullivan, Ann Swidler, and Steven Tipton. 1991. *The Good Society*. New York: Knopf.

Biernacki, Richard. 1995. *The Fabrication of Labor*. Berkeley: University of California Press.

Blau, Joseph L. 1976. *Judaism in America: From Curiosity to Third Faith* (Chicago History of American Religion Series). Chicago: University of Chicago Press.

Bourdieu, Pierre. 1978. *Outline of a Theory of Practice*. Cambridge, England: Cambridge University Press.

Brint, Stephen and Jerome Karabel. 1991. "Institutional Origins and Transformation." Pp. 337–360 in *The New Institutionalism in Organizational Analysis*. Eds. Walter W. Powell and Paul J. DiMaggio. Chicago: University of Chicago Press.

Brinton, Mary C. and Victor Nee, eds. 1998. *The New Institutionalism in Sociology*. New York: Russell Sage Foundation.

Bruce, Steve. 1996. *Religion in the Modern World: From Cathedrals to Cults*. New York: Oxford University Press.

Bundy, James. 1991. *Fall from Grace: Religion and the Communal Ideal in Two Suburban Villages, 1870–1917*. Brooklyn, NY: Carlson Publishing Company.

Burawoy, Michael, et al. 1991. *Ethnography Unbound*. Berkeley: University of California Press.

Campbell, Dennis, William Lawrence, and Russell Richey. Eds. 1997. *Connectionalism: Ecclesiology, Mission, and Identity*. Report on the United Methodism and American Culture Project, Duke University. Eds. Dennis Campbell, William Lawrence, and Russel Richey. Nashville, TN: Abingdon Press.

Cantrell, Randolph, James F. Krile, and George A. Donohue. 1983. "Parish Autonomy: Measuring Denominational Differences." *Journal for the Scientific Study of Religion*, 22(3):276–287.

Caplow, Theodore. 1984. "Rule Enforcement without Visible Means." *American Journal of Sociology*, 89(6):1306–1323.

Caplow, Theodore, Howard M. Bahr, and Bruce A. Chadwick. 1983. *All Faithful People: Change and Continuity in Middletown's Religion*. Minneapolis: University of Minnesota Press.

Carroll, Jackson and Wade Clark Roof. 1993. *Beyond Establishment*. Louisville, KY: Westminster/John Knox Press.

References

Casanova, Jose. 1994. *Public Religions in the Modern World.* Chicago: University of Chicago Press.

Chaves, Mark. 1993. "Intraorganizational Power and Internal Secularization in Protestant Denominations." *American Journal of Sociology,* 99(1):1–48.

Clemens, Elizabeth. 1997. *The People's Lobby.* Chicago: University of Chicago Press.

Collins, Randall. 1975. "A Conflict Theory of Organization." Pp. 268–347 in *Conflict Sociology.* Ed. Randall Collins. New York: Academic Press.

Coser, Lewis. 1956. *The Functions of Social Conflict.* New York: The Free Press.

Daniels, David D. 1996. "Chatham and Greater Grand Crossing: The Dominance of Religion and Race." Pp. 204–220 in *Religious Reorganization and Structural Change in Metropolitan Chicago: The Research Report of the Religion and Urban America Program.* Chicago: Office of Social Science Research, University of Illinois at Chicago.

Davidman, Lynn. 1991. *Tradition in a Rootless World.* Berkeley: University of California Press.

Demerath, N. J. III and Rhys H. Williams. 1985. "Civil Religion in an Uncivil Society." *The Annals of the American Academy of Political and Social Science,* 480:154–166.

Demerath, N. J. III and Rhys H. Williams. 1987. "Separation of Church and State? A Mythical Past, an Uncertain Future." Pp. 139–153 in *Church–State Relations: Tensions and Transitions.* Eds. Thomas Robbins and Roland Robertson. New Brunswick, NJ: Transaction Press.

Demerath, N. J. III and Rhys H. Williams. 1992. *A Bridging of Faiths.* Princeton, NJ: Princeton University Press.

DiMaggio, Paul J. 1991. "Constructing an Organizational Field as a Professional Project: U.S. Art Museums, 1920–1940." Pp. 267–292 in *The New Institutionalism in Organizational Analysis.* Eds. Walter W. Powell and Paul J. DiMaggio. Chicago: University of Chicago Press.

DiMaggio, Paul J. and Walter W. Powell. 1991. "Introduction." Pp. 1–40 in *The New Institutionalism in Organizational Analysis.* Eds. Walter W. Powell and Paul J. DiMaggio. Chicago: University of Chicago Press.

Dolan, Jay. 1994. "Patterns of Leadership in the Congregation." Pp. 225–256 in *American Congregations, Vol. 2.* Eds. James Wind and James Lewis. Chicago: University of Chicago Press.

Douglas, Mary. 1986. *How Institutions Think.* Syracuse, NY: Syracuse University Press.

Dudley, Carl, ed. 1983. *Building Effective Ministry.* San Francisco: Harper and Row.

Dudley, Carl. 1988. "Using Church Images for Commitment, Conflict. End Renewal." Pp. 89–113 in *Congregations, Their Power to Form and Transform.* Ed. C. Ellis Nelson. Atlanta, GA: John Knox Press.

Dudley, Carl and Sally A. Johnson. 1993. *Energizing the Congregation*. Louisville, KY: Westminster/John Knox Press.

Eiesland, Nancy. 1998. *A Particular Place: Exurbanization and Religious Response*. New Brunswick, NJ: Rutgers University Press.

Eliasoph, Nina. 1996. "Making a Fragile Public: A Talk-Centered Study of Citizenship and Power." *Sociological Theory*, 14(3):262–289.

Emirbayer, Mustafa and Ann Mische. 1998. "What Is Agency?" *American Journal of Sociology*, 103(4):962–1023.

Feagin, Joe R., Anthony M. Orum, and Gideon Sjoberg. 1991. *A Case for the Case Study*. Chapel Hill: University of North Carolina Press.

Fine, Gary Alan. 1984. "Negotiated Orders and Organizational Cultures." *Annual Review of Sociology*, 10:239–262.

Fine, Gary Alan. 1987. *With the Boys*. Chicago: University of Chicago Press.

Fine, Gary Alan. 1996a. *Kitchens: The Culture of Restaurant Work*. Berkeley: University of California Press.

Fine, Gary Alan. 1996b. "Justifying Work: Occupational Rhetorics as Resources in Restaurant Kitchens." *Administrative Science Quarterly*, 41(1):90–115.

Finke, Roger and Rodney Stark. 1992. *The Churching of America, 1775–1990*. New Brunswick, NJ: Rutgers University Press.

Fligstein, Neil. 1990. *The Transformation of Corporate Control*. Cambridge, MA: Harvard University Press.

Flynt, Wayne. 1994. "'A Special Feeling of Closeness': Mt. Hebron Baptist Church, Leeds, Alabama." Pp. 103–158 in *American Congregations, Vol. 1*. Eds. James Wind and James Lewis. Chicago: University of Chicago Press.

Friedland, Roger and Robert Alford. 1991. "Bringing Society Back In: Symbols, Practices, and Institutional Contradictions." Pp. 232–266 in *The New Institutionalism in Organizational Analysis*. Eds. Walter W. Powell and Paul J. DiMaggio. Chicago: University of Chicago Press.

Furman, Frida Kerner. 1987. *Beyond Yiddishkeit: A Struggle for Jewish Identity in a Reform Synagogue*. Albany, NY: SUNY Press.

Galaskiewicz, Joseph. 1985. *Social Organization of an Urban Grants Economy*. Orlando, FL: Academic Press.

Galaskiewicz, Joseph. 1991. "Making Corporate Actors Accountable." Pp. 293–310 in *The New Institutionalism in Organizational Analysis*. Eds. Walter W. Powell and Paul J. DiMaggio. Chicago: University of Chicago Press.

Gans, Herbert. 1988. *Middle American Individualism: The Future of Democracy*. New York: Free Press.

Geertz, Clifford. 1973. *The Interpretation of Cultures*. New York: Basic Books.

Giddens, Anthony. 1984. *The Constitution of Society: Outline of the Theory of Structuration*. Cambridge, England: Polity Press.

Gilkey, Langdon. 1994. "The Christian Congregation as Religious Community."

Pp. 100–132 in *American Congregations, Vol. 2*. Eds. James Wind and James Lewis. Chicago: University of Chicago Press.

Glaser, Barney and Anselm Strauss. 1967. *The Discovery of Grounded Theory*. New York: Aldine de Gruyter.

Glenn, Norval. 1987. "Social Trends in the United States: Evidence from Sample Surveys." *Public Opinion Quarterly*, 51:S109–S126.

Glock, Charles. 1993. "The Churches and Social Change in Twentieth-Century America." *The Annals of the American Academy of Political and Social Science*, 527:67–83.

Goffman, Erving. 1974. *Frame Analysis*. New York: Harper and Row.

Goodwin, Carole. 1979. *The Oak Park Strategy*. Chicago: University of Chicago Press.

Greenhouse, Carol J. 1986. *Praying for Justice*. Ithaca, NY: Cornell University Press.

Greenwood, Royston and C. R. Hinings. 1988. "Organization Design Types, Tracks and the Dynamics of Strategic Change." *Organizational Studies*, 9(3):293–316.

Gremillion, Joseph and Jim Castelli. 1987. *The Emerging Parish: The Notre Dame Study of Catholic Parish Life Since Vatican II*. San Francisco: Harper and Row.

Griswold, Wendy. 1987. "A Methodological Framework for the Sociology of Culture." Pp. 1–35 in *Sociological Methodology*. Ed. Clifford Clogg. Washington, DC: American Sociological Association.

Griswold, Wendy. 1992. "The Writing on the Mud Wall: Nigerian Novels and the Imaginary Village." *American Sociological Review*, 57(6):709–724.

Hadaway, C. Kirk, Penny Long Marler, and Mark Chaves. 1993. "What the Polls Don't Show: A Closer Look at U.S. Church Attendance. *American Sociological Review*, 58(6):741–752.

Hadden, Jeffrey. 1969. *The Gathering Storm in the Churches*. New York: Doubleday.

Hall, John R. 1988. "Social Organization and the Pathways of Commitment." *American Sociological Review*, 53(5):679–692.

Hammond, Phillip. 1988. "Religion and the Persistence of Identity." *Journal for the Scientific Study of Religion*, 27(1):1–11.

Hammond, Phillip. 1992. *Religion and Personal Autonomy: The Third Disestablishment in America*. Columbia: University of South Carolina Press.

Hannan, M. T., M. D. Burton, and J. N. Baron. 1996. "Inertia and Change in the Early Years: Employment Relations in Young, High-Technology Firms." *Industrial and Corporate Change*, 5(2):503–534.

Hatch, Nathan. 1989. *The Democratization of American Christianity*. New Haven, CT: Yale University Press.

Haveman, Heather. 1997. "Structuring a Theory of Moral Sentiments: Institutional and Organizational Coevolution in the Early Thrift Industry." *American Journal of Sociology,* 102(6):1606–1651.

Hawley, Amos H. 1950. *Human Ecology.* New York: Ronald Press.

Herberg, Will. 1960. *Protestant, Catholic, Jew.* Garden City, NY: Anchor Books.

Hirschman, Albert O. 1970. *Exit, Voice and Loyalty.* Cambridge, MA: Harvard University Press.

Hochschild, Arlie, with Anne Machung. 1997. *The Second Shift.* New York: Avon Books.

Hoge, Dean. 1976. *Division in the Protestant House.* Philadelphia: Westminster.

Holifield, E. Brooks. 1994. "Toward a History of American Congregations." Pp. 23–53 in *American Congregations, Vol. 2.* Eds. James Wind and James Lewis. Chicago: University of Chicago Press.

Hopewell, James F. 1987. *Congregation: Stories and Structures.* Philadelphia: Fortress Press.

Hummon, David. 1990. *Commonplaces: Community, Ideology and Identity in American Culture.* Albany, NY: SUNY Press.

Hunter, James Davison. 1991. *Culture Wars.* New York: Basic Books.

Hunter, James Davison. 1994. *Before the Shooting Begins.* New York: Free Press.

Jackall, Robert. 1988. *Moral Mazes.* New York: Oxford University Press.

Jasper, James M. 1992. "The Politics of Abstractions: Instrumental and Moralist Rhetorics in Public Debate." *Social Research*, 59(2):315–344.

Jehn, Karen. 1997. "A Qualitative Analysis of Conflict Types and Dimensions in Organizational Groups." *Administrative Science Quarterly,* 42(3):530–557.

Jenkins, Craig and Michael Wallace. 1996. "The Generalized Action Potential of Protest Movements: The New Class, Social Trends, and Political Exclusion Explanations." *Sociological Forum*, 11(2):183–207.

Jepperson, Ronald L. 1991. "Institutions, Institutional Effects, and Institutionalism." Pp. 143–163 in *The New Institutionalism in Organizational Analysis.* Eds. Walter W. Powell and Paul J. DiMaggio. Chicago: University of Chicago Press.

Johnson, Benton. 1985. "Religion and Polities in America: The Last Twenty Years." Pp. 301–316 in *The Sacred in a Secular Age.* Ed. Phillip E. Hammond. Berkeley: University of California Press.

Kanter, Rosabeth Moss. 1977. *Men and Women of the Corporation.* New York: Basic Books.

Kniss, Fred. 1997. *Disquiet in the Land: Cultural Conflict in American Mennonite Communities.* New Brunswick, NJ: Rutgers University Press.

Kosmin, Barry A. and Seymour Lachman. 1993. *One Nation Under God: Religion in Contemporary American Society.* New York: Harmony Books (Crown).

Kriesberg, Louis. 1973. *The Sociology of Social Conflicts.* Englewood Cliffs, NJ: Prentice-Hall.

Kunda, Gideon. 1992. *Engineering Culture.* Philadelphia: Temple University Press.

Kurtz, Lester. 1986. *The Politics of Heresy*. Berkeley: University of California Press.

Laitin, David. 1986. *Hegemony and Culture*. Chicago: University of Chicago Press.

Lamont, Michele. 1992. *Money, Morals, and Manners: The Culture of the French and the Ameircan Upper-Middle Class*. Chicago: University of Chicago Press.

Lawler, Ed. 1996. "Commitment in Exchange Relations: Test of a Theory of Relational Cohesion." *American Sociological Review*, 61(1):89–108.

Leas, Speed. 1992. *Leadership and Conflict*. Nashville, TN: Abingdon Press.

Leas, Speed and Paul Kittlaus. 1973. *Church Fights: Managing Conflict in the Local Church*. Philadelphia: Westminster Press.

LeFevre, Perry, ed. 1975. *Conflict in a Voluntary Association*. Chicago: Exploration Press.

Levine, Donald. 1971. "Introduction." In *Georg Simmel on Individuality and Social Forms*, ed. Donald Levine. Chicago: University of Chicago Press.

Lichterman, Paul. 1995a. "Piccing Together Multicultural Community: Cultural Differences in Community-Building Among Grass-Roots Environmentalists." *Social Problems*, 42(2):513–534.

Lichterman, Paul. 1995b. "Beyond the Seesaw Model: Public Commitment in a Culture of Self-Fulfillment." *Sociological Theory*, 13(3):275–300.

Lichterman, Paul. 1996. *The Search for Political Community*. New York: Cambridge University Press.

Liebman, Robert C., John R. Sutton, and Robert Wuthnow. 1988. "Exploring the Social Sources of Denominationalism: Schisms in American Protestant Denominations, 1890–1980." *American Sociological Review*, 53:343–352.

Lighthall, Frederick. 1989. *Local Realities, Local Adaptations*. New York and Philadelphia: Falmer Press.

Lincoln, C. Eric and Lawrence H. Mamiya. 1990. *The Black Church in the African-American Experience*. Durham, NC: Duke University Press.

Livezey, Lowell W., ed. 1996. *Religious Organizations and Structural Change in Metropolitan Chicago: The Research Report of the Religion in Urban America Program*. Chicago: Office of Social Science Research, University of Illinois at Chicago.

Lofland, John and Lyn H. Lofland. 1995. *Analyzing Social Settings*. New York and Boston: Wadsworth Publishing Co.

Lopata, Helena Znanieka. 1994. *Circles and Settings: Role Changes of American Women*. Albany, NY: SUNY Press.

LoPucki, Lynn M. 1996. "Legal Culture, Legal Strategy, and the Law in Lawyers' Heads." *Northwestern University Law Review*, 90(4):1498ff.

Martin, Joanne. 1992. *Cultures in Organizations*. New York: Oxford University Press.

Marty, Martin. 1976. *A Nation of Behaviors*. Chicago: University of Chicago Press.

Marty, Martin. 1986. *Protestantism in the United States*. New York: Scribners.

Marty, Martin. 1994. "Public and Private: Congregation as Meeting Place." Pp.

133–168 in *American Congregations, Vol. 2*. Eds. James Wind and James Lewis. Chicago: University of Chicago Press.

May, Elaine Tyler. 1980. *Great Expectations*. Chicago: University of Chicago Press.

McDannell, Colleen. 1995. *Material Christianity*. New Haven, CT: Yale University Press.

McKinney, William and Daniel Olson. 1989. "Protestant Church Leaders: A Preliminary Overview." Unpublished manuscript, cited by permission.

McPherson, Miller. 1983. "An Ecology of Affiliation." *American Sociological Review*. 48(4):519–532.

Meyer, John W. and Brian Rowan. 1991. "The Iron Cage Revisited." Pp. 41–62 in *The New Institutionalism in Organizational Analysis*. Eds. Walter W. Powell and Paul J. DiMaggio. Chicago: University of Chicago Press.

Meyer, John W., W. Richard Scott, and Terence Deal. 1983. "Institutional and Technical Sources of Organizational Structure." Pp. 45–67 in *Organizational Environments: Ritual and Rationality*. Eds. John W. Meyer and W. Richard Scott. Beverly Hills, CA: Sage.

Meyer, John W., W. Richard Scott, and David Strang. 1987. "Centralization, Fragmentation, and School District Complexity." *Administrative Science Quarterly*, 32:186–201.

Moberg, David. 1962. *The Church as a Social Institution*. Englewood Cliffs, NJ: Prentice-Hall.

Mock, Alan. 1992. "Congregation Religious Styles and Orientations to Society." *Review of Religious Research*, 34(1):20–33.

Moen, Phyllis and Elaine Wethington. 1992. "The Concept of Family Adaptive Strategies." *Annual Review of Sociology*, 18:233–251.

Mohr, John. 1994. "Soldiers, Mothers, Tramps, and Others: Discourse Roles in the 1907 New York City Charity Directory." *Poetics*, 22(4):327–357.

Morrill, Calvin. 1995. *The Executive Way*. Chicago: University of Chicago Press.

Nee, Victor. 1998. "Sources of the New Institutionalism." Pp. 1–16 in *The New Institutionalism in Sociology*. Eds. Mary C. Brinton and Victor Nee. New York: Russell Sage Foundation.

Nee, Victor and Paul Ingram. 1998. "Embeddedness and Beyond: Institutions, Exchange, and Social Structure." Pp. 19–45 in *The New Institutionalism in Sociology*. Eds. Mary C. Brinton and Victor Nee. New York: Russell Sage Foundation.

Neitz, Mary Jo. 1987. *Charisma and Community: A Study of Religious Commitment within the Charismatic Renewal*. New Brunswick, NJ: Transaction Books.

Nelsen, Hart M. and Mary Ann Maguire. 1980. "The Two Worlds of Clergy and Congregation: Dilemma for Mainline Denominations." *Sociological Analysis*, 41:74–80.

Nelson, Tim. 1997. "The Church and the Street: Race, Class, and Congregation." Pp. 169–190 in *Contemporary American Religion: An Ethnographic Reader*. Eds.

References

Penny Edgell Becker and Nancy Eiesland. Newbury Park, CA: Alta Mira Press/Sage.

Numrich, Paul D. 1996. "Some Recent and Different Immigrant Religions of Chicago." Pp. 223–246 in *Religious Organizations and Structural Change in Metropolitan Chicago: The Research Report of the Religion in Urban America Program.* Chicago: Office of Social Science Research, University of Illinois at Chicago.

Olson, Daniel. 1989. "Church Friendships: Boon or Barrier to Church Growth?" *Journal for the Scientific Study of Religion,* 28(4):432–447.

Orru, Marco, Nicole Woosley Biggart, and Gary G. Hamilton. 1991. "Organizational Isomorphism in East Asia." Pp. 361–389 in *The New Institutionalism in Organizational Analysis.* Eds. Walter W. Powell and Paul J. DiMaggio. Chicago: University of Chicago Press.

Orsi, Robert. 1985. *The Madonna of 115th Street.* New Haven, CT: Yale University Press.

Ortner, Sherry. 1996. *Making Gender: The Politics and Erotics of Culture.* Boston: Beacon Press.

Park, Robert E. and Ernest W. Burgess. 1924. *Introduction to the Science of Sociology.* Chicago: University of Chicago Press.

Pfeffer, Jeffrey. 1981. *Power in Organizations.* Marshfield, MA: Pitman Publishing Co.

Powell, Walter W. 1991. "Expanding the Scope of Institutional Analysis." Pp. 183–203 in *The New Institutionalism in Organizational Analysis.* Eds. Walter W. Powell and Paul J. DiMaggio. Chicago: University of Chicago Press.

Powell, Walter W. and Paul J. DiMaggio. Eds. 1991. *The New Institutionalism in Organizational Analysis.* Chicago: University of Chicago Press.

Prell, Riv-Ellen. 1989. *Prayer and Community.* Detroit, MI: Wayne State University Press.

Putnam, Robert. 1995. "Bowling Alone: America's Declining Social Capital." *Current,* 373:3–9.

Putnam, Robert. 1996. "The Strange Disappearance of Civic America." *American Prospect,* no. 24, Winter (http://epn.org/prospect/24/24putn.html).

Ragin, Charles. 1987. *The Comparative Method.* Berkeley: University of California Press.

Ragin, Charles and Howard Becker. Eds. 1992. *What Is a Case? Exploring the Foundations of Social Inquiry.* New York: Cambridge University Press.

Raymond, Roberta L. 1972. *The Challenge to Oak Park.* Master's thesis, Sociology Department, Roosevelt University, Chicago, Illinois.

Riesebrodt, Martin. 1993. *Pious Passion.* Berkeley: University of California Press.

Roof, Wade Clark. 1978. *Community and Commitment.* New York: Elsevier.

Roof, Wade Clark. 1993. *A Generation of Seekers.* San Francisco: Harper.

Roof, Wade Clark. 1996. "God Is in the Details: Reflections on Religion's Public

Presence in the United States in the Mid-1990s." *Sociology of Religion*, 57(2):149–162.

Roof, Wade Clark and William McKinney. 1987. *American Mainline Religion*. New Brunswick, NJ: Rutgers University Press.

Roozen, David A., William McKinney, and Jackson W. Carroll. 1984. *Varieties of Religious Presence: Mission in Public Life*. New York: Pilgrim Press.

Rothauge, Arlin J. 1990. *Sizing Up a Congregation for New Member Ministry*. Washington, DC: Alban Institute, On Demand Publications.

Sahlins, Marshall. 1985. *Islands of History*. Chicago: University of Chicago Press.

Scott, W. Richard and John W. Meyer. 1991. "The Organization of Societal Sectors." Pp. 108–140 in *The New Institutionalism in Organizational Analysis*. Eds. Walter W. Powell and Paul J. DiMaggio. Chicago: University of Chicago Press.

Searing, Donald. 1991. "Roles, Rules and Rationality in the New Institutionalism." *American Political Science Review*, 85(4):1239–1260.

Seidler, John and Katherine Meyer. 1989. *Conflict and Change in the Catholic Church*. New Brunswick, NJ: Rutgers University Press.

Selznick, Philip. 1949. *TVA and the Grassroots*. Berkeley: University of California Press.

Sewell, William H. Jr. 1992. "A Theory of Structure: Duality, Agency, and Transformation." *American Journal of Sociology*, 98(1):1–29.

Simmel, Georg. 1955. *Conflict and the Web of Group Affiliations*. Trans. Kurt H. Wolff and Reinhard Bendix. Glencoe, IL: Free Press.

Simmel, Georg. 1971. "Conflict." Pp. 70–95 in *On Individuality and Social Forms*, ed. Donald Levine (Series: The Heritage of Sociology). Chicago: University of Chicago Press.

Skolnick, Arlene. 1991. *Embattled Paradise: The American Family in an Age of Uncertainty*. New York: Basic Books.

Snow, David A. and Leon Anderson. 1991. "Researching the Homeless: The Characteristic Features and Virtues of the Case Study." Pp. 148–173 in *The Case for the Case Study*. Eds. Joe R. Feagin, Anthony M. Orum, and Gideon Sjoberg. Chapel Hill: University of North Carolina Press.

Stacey, Judith. 1991. *Brave New Families*. New York: Basic Books.

Starke, Frederick A. and Bruno Dyck. 1996. "Upheavals in Congregations: The Causes and Outcomes of Splits." *Review of Religious Research*, 38(2):159–174.

Strang, David. 1994. "Institutional Accounts of Organizations as a Form of Structural Analysis." *Current Perspectives in Social Theory* (supplement), 1:151–174.

Strauss, Anselm. 1995. *Qualitative Analysis for Social Scientists*. New York: Cambridge University Press.

Swatos, William. 1981. "Beyond Denominationalism." *Journal for the Scientific Study of Religion*, 20:217–227.

References

Swidler, Ann. 1986. "Culture in Action: 'Symbols and Strategies.'" *American Sociological Review*, 51:273–286.

Takayama, K. Peter. 1975. "Formal Polity and Change of Structure." *Sociological Analysis*, 36:17–28.

Takayama, K. Peter. 1980. "Strains, Conflicts, and Schisms in Protestant Denominations." Pp. 298–329 in *American Denominational Organization: A Sociological View*. Ed. Ross Scherer. Pasadena, CA: William Carey Library.

Taves, Ann. 1986. *Household of Faith*. South Bend, IN: University of Notre Dame.

Thompson, John. B. 1990. *Ideology and Modern Culture*. Stanford, CA: Stanford University Press.

Thumma, Scott. 1996. *The Kingdom, the Power, and the Glory: The Megachurch in Modern American Society*. Doctoral dissertation, Emory University, Atlanta, GA.

Tipton, Steve. 1982. *Getting Saved from the Sixties*. Berkeley: University of California Press.

Tolbert, Pamela S. and Lynne G. Zucker. 1983. "Institutional Sources of Change in the Formal Structure of Organizations." *Administrative Science Quarterly*, 28:22–39.

Turner, Joyce Olson. 1981. *Impact of Change on an Older Suburban Community: Oak Park, Illinois*. Master's thesis, Department of Geography, University of Chicago, Chicago, Illinois.

Turner, Victor. 1974. *Dramas, Fields, and Metaphors*. Ithaca, NY: Cornell University Press.

Warner, R. Stephen. 1988. *New Wine in Old Wineskins: Evangelicals and Liberals in a Small-Town Church*. Berkeley: University of California Press.

Warner, R. Stephen. 1993. "Toward a New Paradigm for the Sociological Study of Religion in the United States." *American Journal of Sociology*, 98(5):1044–1093.

Warner, R. Stephen. 1994. "The Place of the Congregation in the American Religious Configuration." Pp. 54–99 in *American Congregations*, Vol. 2. Eds. James Wind and James Lewis. Chicago: University of Chicago Press.

Warner, R. Stephen and Judith G. Wittner. 1997. *Congregations as Cultural Spaces: Immigration, Ethnicity, and Religion in the United States*. Philadelphia: Temple University Press.

Watt, David Harrington. 1991. "United States: Cultural Challenges to the Voluntary Sector." Pp. 243–287 in *Between States and Markets: The Voluntary Sector in Comparative Perspective*. Ed. Robert Wuthnow. Princeton, NJ: Princeton University Press.

Waugh, Earle H. 1994. "Reducing the Distance: A Muslim Congregation in the Canadian North." Pp. 572–611 in *American Congregations*, Vol. 1. Eds. James Wind and James Lewis. Chicago: University of Chicago Press.

Weber, Max. 1947(1921). *The Theory of Social and Economic Organization*. Trans. A.

M. Henderson and Talcott Parsons. New York: Oxford University Press.

Weber, Max. 1978. *Economy and Society*, Vol. *1*. Eds. Guenther Roth and Claus Wittich. Berkeley: University of California Press.

Wertheimer, Jack, ed. 1987. *The American Synagogue: A Sanctuary Transformed*. New York: Cambridge University Press.

White, Harrison C. 1981. "Where Do Markets Come From?" *American Journal of Sociology*, 87:517–547.

White, Warner. 1990. "The Breakdown in Our System of Pastoral Relations." Report submitted to the Diocese of Western Michigan, Commission on Management of the Episcopal Church. Spring 1990.

Williams, Peter W. and Phillip Hammond. 1991. "The Third Disestablishment: A Symposium." *Journal for the Scientific Study of Religion*, 30(4):516–547.

Williams, Rhys. 1996. "Introduction." *Sociology of Religion*, 57(1), Spring.

Williams, Rhys, ed. 1997. *Culture Wars in American Politics: Critical Reviews of a Popular Myth*. New York: Aldine de Gruyter.

Wind, James and James Lewis. 1994. *American Congregations*, Vols. *1 and 2*. Chicago: University of Chicago Press.

Wolfe, Alan. 1998. *One Nation After All*. New York: Viking.

Wood, James R. 1981. *Leadership in Voluntary Organizations: The Controversy over Social Action in Protestant Churches*. New Brunswick, NJ: Rutgers University Press.

Wuthnow, Robert. 1987. *Meaning and Moral Order*. Berkeley: University of California Press.

Wuthnow, Robert. 1988. *The Restructuring of American Religion*. Princeton, NJ: Princeton University Press.

Wuthnow, Robert. 1989. *Communities of Discourse*. Cambridge, MA: Harvard University Press.

Wuthnow, Robert. 1991. *Acts of Compassion*. Princeton, NJ: Princeton University Press.

Wuthnow, Robert, ed. 1992. *Vocabularies of Public Life*. New York: Routledge.

Wuthnow, Robert. 1994a. *Sharing the Journey*. New York: Free Press.

Wuthnow, Robert, ed. 1994b. *I Come Away Stronger*. Grand Rapids, MI: Eerdmans.

Wuthnow, Robert. 1995. *Learning to Care*. New York: Oxford University Press.

Young, Lawrence A., ed. 1997. *Rational Choice Theory and Religion*. New York: Routledge.

Zald, Mayer N. and Roberta Ash. 1966. "Social Movement Organizations." *Social Forces*, 44(3):327–341.

Zucker, Lynne, ed. 1988. *Institutional Patterns and Organizations*. Cambridge, MA: Ballinger.

INDEX